Cosmos and Society in Oceania

EXPLORATIONS IN ANTHROPOLOGY
A University College London Series

Series Editors: Barbara Bender, John Gledhill and Bruce Kapferer

Joan Bestard-Camps, *What's in a Relative? Household and Family in Formentera*

Henk Driessen, *On the Spanish-Moroccan Frontier: A Study in Ritual, Power and Ethnicity*

Alfred Gell, *The Anthropology of Time: Cultural Construction of Temporal Maps and Images*

Tim Ingold, David Riches and James Woodburn (eds), *Hunters and Gatherers*

  Volume 1. *History, Evolution and Social Change*
  Volume 2. *Property, Power and Ideology*

Bruce Kapferer, *A Celebration of Demons* (2nd edn.)

Guy Lanoue, *Brothers: The Politics of Violence among the Sekani of Northern British Columbia*

Jadran Mimica, *Intimations of Infinity: The Mythopoeia of the Iqwaye Counting System and Number*

Barry Morris, *Domesticating Resistance: The Dhan-Gadi Aborigines and the Australian State*

Thomas C. Paterson, *The Inca Empire: The Formation and Disintegration of a Pre-Capitalist State*

Max and Eleanor Rimoldi, *Hahalis and the Labour of Love: A Social Movement on Buka Island*

Pnina Werbner, *The Migration Process: Capital, Gifts and Offerings among Pakistanis in Britain*

Joel S. Kahn, *Constituting the Minangkabau: Peasants, Culture, and Modernity in Colonial Indonesia*

Gisli Pálsson, *Beyond Boundaries: Understanding, Translation and Anthropological Discourse*

Stephen Nugent, *Amazonian Caboclo Society*

Barbara Bender, *Landscape: Politics and Perspectives*

Christopher Tilley (ed.), *Interpretative Archaeology*

Ernest S. Burch Jr and Linda J. Ellanna (eds), *Key Issues in Hunter-Gatherer Research*

Daniel Miller, *Modernity – An Ethnographic Approach: Dualism and Mass Consumption in Trinidad*

Robert Pool, *Dialogue and the Interpretation of Illness: Conversations in a Cameroon Village*

Cécile Barraud, Daniel de Coppet, André Iteanu and Raymond Jamous (eds), *Of Relations and the Dead: Four Societies Viewed from the Angle of their Exchanges*

Christopher Tilley, *A Phenomenology of Landscape: Places, Paths and Monuments*

Victoria Goddard, Josep Llobera and Cris Shore (eds), *The Anthropology of Europe: Identity and Boundaries in Conflict*

Pat Caplan, *Understanding Disputes: The Politics of Argument*

Daniel de Coppet and André Iteanu (ed.), *Society and Cosmos: Their Interrelations or Their Coalescence in Melanesia*

Alisdair Rogers and Steven Vertovec (eds), *The Urban Context: Ethnicity, Social Networks and situational Analysis*

Saskia Kersenboom, *Word, Sound, Image: The Life of the Tamil Text*

Cosmos and Society in Oceania

Edited by
Daniel de Coppet and André Iteanu

BERG

Oxford • Washington, D.C.

First published in 1995 by
Berg Publishers Limited
Editorial offices:
150 Cowley Road, Oxford, OX4 1JJ, UK
13950 Park Center Road, Herndon, VA 22071, USA

Library of Congress Cataloging-in-Publication Data

A catalogue record for this book is available from the Library of
Congress.

British Library Cataloguing-in-Publication Data

A catalogue record for this book is available from the British
Library.

ISBN 1 85973 037 X (Cloth)
      1 85973 042 6 (Paper)

Printed in the United Kingdom by WBC Bookbinders, Bridgend,
Mid Glamorgan.

Contents

Introduction

Daniel de Coppet and André Iteanu[1]

Ever since Marcel Mauss, in his *Essai sur le Don* (1974: 76), substantiated the idea of a 'total social fact', anthropologists, and Oceanists especially among them, have learned to be wary about the alleged universality of Western distinctions like that between economics, politics and religion. This collection of essays is faithful to that concern, since it questions the validity of another distinction highly favoured in the West, that between society and cosmos. The contributors to this volume have centred their study of several Pacific societies around the examination of the following two questions: Do Pacific societies, as our societies, distinguish society from cosmos? And if not, what are the forms and social consequences of this partial or total 'non-distinction'?

This volume thus questions the problematic projection on to Pacific societies of the Western distinction between society and cosmos. The analysis must therefore be placed in a comparative framework embracing both Pacific and Western societies.

For long centuries, and even today, European societies have opposed two qualitatively distinct domains. One, attributed lesser value, is governed by relative human laws: we call it society. It is dominated by a wider realm, understood as an intrinsic universal order, and represented variously, at different times and places, by the figures of God, Nature or the Individual (Dumont 1986: 25–33). This larger domain fits perfectly into the dictionary's definition of the term cosmos, as 'an orderly harmonious systematic universe, a complex orderly self-inclusive system'.[2] Since the primary characteristic of a cosmos is its claim to wholeness, no higher values than those which characterize it may exist.

Throughout Western history the definition of these two domains has changed, as the relation which linked them has evolved. In simplified form, one might say that, since the rise of

Christianity, they have either occasionally concluded a truce, illustrated by Christ's famous reply: 'Render unto Caesar the things which are Caesar's, and unto God things that are God's' (Matthew 22, v. 21), or stood in a relation of open conflict, in which the dominant realm repeatedly attempted to negate the legitimacy and even sometimes the existence of subdued society. This alternative clearly illustrates the opposition between holistic and individualistic tendencies which have marked our history. Holism, as contained for example in Pope Gelasius' propositions, orders contradictory values in a hierarchy, allowing for their coexistence, and even for inversion of superiority at a subordinate level, that of 'mundane matters that regard the public order'. Individualism, on the other hand, does not overcome contradiction (the excluded party). From its point of view, therefore, the two domains are irreparably in conflict and one of them must subdue the other (Dumont 1986: 45–52).

The dichotomy was thus at times blurred, while at other moments it became quite sharp. However, the highest values which order the cosmos – whether considered as deriving from a divine order, from a natural one, or from the supremacy of the individual – have at all times, invariably, been credited with universal validity, and have been consequently more highly valued than any particular human social order. Thus, analysing Melanesia and the West in comparative perspective, Kenneth Read (1955: 250–1) has written:

> The most widespread concept of Christian ethics is that it consists in a belief in the brotherhood of man. It would be a mistake, however, to interpret our traditional teaching simply as a claim for the common humanity of all mankind. It implies much more than this. To the Christian, the spiritual component which in all men constitutes them persons also confers on them an incomparable value which man is required to recognise and to espouse above all others. This worth is inalienable: it is also intrinsic, belonging to all men irrespective of status or individual accomplishments or what they do or may have done in the usual moral sense. Thus, the absolute value of the human person is prior to all other created values. It cuts across all other moral categories, and it is the reason why we are enjoined to love all men, even our enemies, for, quite apart from their actions, they possess a worth which cannot be measured by the standards of society.

Following Read, one understands how the universality of Christian values has progressively led to the negation of society. In this respect, the advent of modernity followed the same line. The transition from tradition to modernity – which consisted, above all, in the gradual replacement of the Christian cosmos and hierarchies by an ideology centred on autonomous individuals dwelling in a political world – has occurred, one could argue, without ever contesting the universality of the superior value and the legitimacy of the distinction between society, a relative realm, and cosmos, an absolute one. It is thus that in 1793, in Notre-Dame Cathedral, the French revolutionaries attempted to substitute the cult of Reason for the Christian faith.

A configuration constructed on the supremacy of an indisputably universal set of values over the subordinate social realm has thus consistently characterized Western ideology. In Europe, the assumption of successive cosmoses, which all claimed universality, appears as directly responsible for the degradation of the idea of society. It may account, therefore, for our past and present difficulties in recognising cultural diversity. Whether from the point of view of Christian theology, from that of universal sovereignty (Maine 1887) developed by the Holy Roman Empire, or from that of French revolutionary individualism, the existence and the extension of society seem grounded only on secondary values, if at all.

Early European anthropologists, influenced by this deeply rooted ideology, have often aimed at universals considering cultural diversity a subordinate level of reality. Even traditional societies were viewed by them as dominated by a universal religious cosmos where mythological heroes held the stage. Closer to us, even Marxist materialism seems founded on the same pattern, since it encapsulates social specificity in the universality of natural individual needs. The same difficulty has re-emerged in the numerous recent studies devoted to determining the existence or the absence of a notion of society in traditional cultures. Yet the relation between society and cosmos has never been investigated systematically, and only partial appraisals of this relation have been attempted.

The contributions to this volume all deal, in one way or another, with the global order inherent in the societies they study. This global order always distinguishes different domains, which sometimes stand in a hierarchical relation to one another. In no case, however, does this distinction resembles the Western division between society and cosmos. Consequently, an understanding of these societies, which requires transposing them into our own terms, cannot be achieved by literal translation.

In his contribution, **Alfred Gell** directly confronts this problem. He offers a comparative study of the cosmologies of certain Central–Eastern Polynesian cultures. His main argument is that 'Polynesian cosmology is correlated with the religious concept of immanence' (p. 50).

The Polynesian cosmos was originally one, until the God separated it into a 'bi-cameral world', thus creating the possibility for action. The successive separations introduced thereafter took the form of a series of encompassments. In this world, the God is immanent because 'what the God does is to articulate, or differentiate, the world into its distinct components and qualities, but the substance of the newly-articulated cosmos remains what it always was, nothing other than the God himself' (p. 23). Thus the same God who permitted separation is also the principle of unity. Distinction is considered unstable, and the demon of re-unification is a permanent threat. Ritual action is the countervailing force which repeatedly succeeds in postponing the dreaded reunion.

Polynesian rituals, like the Greek sacrifice of the ox by Prometheus (Detienne and Vernant 1979), are aimed at 'the opening of a space between the subject and the sacred domain from whence he [the subject] originated' (p. 25). The central correlative of such a cosmological construct is that: 'Polynesian ritual operated in precisely the inverse sense to Christian communion [. . .] There were no rituals through which persons (e.g. Kings) were consecrated, because they were already all-too-sacred [. . .] Instead of being sanctified, Polynesians of high intrinsic [. . .] rank had to be elaborately de-sanctified' (pp. 25–6). A tightly reasoned analysis of both Polynesian art objets and tattoos is further developed to support the argument.

Although 'differentiation' is the principle of the Polynesian cosmological process, the realms thus separated do not parallel our 'distinction' between society and cosmos, since both are made up of the same material, the God. At one level, the God is unity beyond any distinction; at another, once he has introduced 'differentiation', he is more closely associated with universality, for he has managed to secure for humans a world of light and life *ao*, different from the world of night and death *po*. That is why ritual repetition strives to maintain the gap opened between the realm of the living and that of the dead. In Polynesian cosmology, separation and hierarchy both create action and permit the return of life from beyond death. If one attempts to order the two stages of the Polynesian world in value terms, the unified state of origin appears as having lesser value than the state of differentiation which has opened for human social achievement. For the Christian, on the contrary, society is situated on the side of the Fall.

The same contrast can be recognized in the way gender differentiation is organized. In the case of Adam and Eve as analysed by Louis Dumont (1970: 239–45), Adam's twofold identity manifests two levels of value: when first created, he is the universal human being, principle of all humanity, as opposed to God; when later opposed to Eve, he is a male as distinct from a female. At this second subordinate level, his former identity is only recalled in the superiority of status it gives him over her. In Polynesian cosmology, on the contrary, man comes into the world out of the woman's shell. The stage of gender differentiation is superior in value to the original and undifferentiated woman's shell. Here again, for Polynesians, the realm of social relations is attributed higher value, while for the Christians, it is subordinate.

Christina Toren's contribution, like Gell's, revolves around a major distinction which organizes kinship, marriage and religious representations in Fiji. Here, however, the society's ideology does not elaborate a unified discourse constructed around a series of encompassments, but is predicated on two simultaneously contradictory and complementary notions, 'mutual compassion' and 'mutual desire'. 'Mutual compassion' is a relation in which the partners' systematic and permanent differentiation of status is stressed. In contrast, 'mutual desire' – which characterizes exchange and sexual relations between cross-cousins – does not emphasize status differences, but, rather, other dimensions which give it an egalitarian overtone. Most interestingly, the author observes a permanent tension between these two types of relations, whereby 'in each domain, relations

which are either hierarchical or equal are the very grounds of the
possibility of the opposing form' (p. 76). This implies that the
relative status of each individual varies in time, since 'the
relations between chiefs or between chiefs and people were never
fixed, for they were *always and inherently* open to [. . .] challenge'
(p. 70). However, the principles which order this competition
obey a general fixed cosmogonic form. 'Attendance on a God or
a chief is what actually empowers him' (p. 69). The author
analyses a major cosmogonic myth, offering an understanding of
the outline of this ideological construct. Two men willingly
submit themselves to a God in order to obtain *mana* from him. To
mark their submission, the God asks one of them to allow himself
to be cooked like food in an oven dug in the earth, a fate which is
equivalent to sexual consumption. When, afterwards, the man
rises unharmed from the oven, he has acquired the God's
powers. In this most characteristic manifestation of his power, the
God combines the two contrasted dimensions of relations:
compassion (hierarchical submission) and desire (egalitarian
food exchange or sexual relations). This intimate intermingling of
two otherwise distinguished forms of relation seems to be the
exclusive attribute of *mana* holders (the God and chiefs) and to
constitute a necessary step in the process of power transmission
to followers. At the end of the myth, the composite nature of this
power is shown to produce a clear hierarchy in the two types of
relations, when the former wives of the two men finally agree
properly to fulfil their *subordinated* position. In conclusion, the
author shows that Fijians have understood the Christian God
according to the same general framework.

In Fiji, just as in Central–Eastern Polynesia, cosmos and
society are not distinguished, but together form a hierarchical
continuum ordered along the line of *mana*. The principle of this
hierarchy, equated with the God's power, is characterized by the
intimate combination of the two contrasted dominant forms of
relation. From a subordinated, partial point of view, the relative
status position of each individual living person is open to
competition within the framework of the cross-cousin relation,
that of 'desire'. Curiously enough, competition seems here to be
a 'sub-district' of hierarchy, rather than of power, as it appears to
be in the West. This paradox may well be susceptible to
generalization to other societies of Oceania.

In both preceding examples, two distinct levels can be

distinguished. At one of them, both cosmos and society are crosscut by a series of distinctions; at the other, these distinctions are blended within an encompassing term: in Polynesia, the original world was undifferentiated, in Fiji all those who hold a relatively superior *mana* combine the two major types of social relations.

One way to explore the levels of reality where all categories mingle is to analyse major 'clusters of meaning' which manifest themselves in central ritual events. **Nancy Munn**, in her contribution, undertakes this task by exploring the remembering process in the well-known Gisalo ceremony of the Kaluli of Papua New Guinea. She insists: ' [. . .] I have not considered remembering simply as a subjective process triggered by an objective mnemonic medium; or as a particular activity going on *within* a *given* spaciotemporal field. Instead, I have argued that in any given instance remembering is a particular 'configuring' of this field, and that its form consists of the relations of the field that are being produced' (p. 95).

During the Gisalo ceremony, the hosts invite dancers from another village to perform in their long house. The dancers sing songs about the hosts' landscape, thus eliciting memories which make the hosts cry. In grief, the latter stand up and burn the dancers' backs. The songs performed in Gisalo indirectly call forth 'biographical memories of past co-presence with absent others – sometimes a currently absent person, but prototypically, the dead [. . .]' (p. 85). As such, the songs are not themselves biographical memories, but 'memory worlds' which entice these memories into being. To elicit them, they depend on two major devices, place names and evocations of relations. The former recall co-presence with the now gone, which constitute the principles of the hearer's identity and therefore differentiate the latter from the singers who come from afar. 'In sum, place names in songs occupy a special position [. . .] because they encode a self-related or "centred" space – a space not merely particularized but also "possessed"' (p. 91). In contrast, relations are not denoted by the names of the people they link, but by kinship terms or by pronouns. They therefore refer directly to what is lost: 'a co-presence once enjoyed, which is no longer' (p. 92). However, death does not totally separate the living from the dead, since the latter are transformed into birds that make their presence felt only through their songs. Although songs are the sign of the absence of the once present, in Gisalo they render present their absence. 'In sum, the mode of spatial co-presence which characterizes the dead, and defines their absence, pervades the spatiotemporal field of the present' (p. 94). This contradictory manifestation 'characterizes the symbolic field of the present in Gisalo remembering' (p. 95). Therefore, Gisalo ritual creates 'detachable or portable landscapes [. . .] to put their displaced dead back in place and re-identify with them by remembering them *where they used to be*' (pp. 98–9).

Nancy Munn shows how, in Gisalo memory construction, social relations and 'natural' elements (like place names, but also bird songs, the outside and the inside, the dead and the living) are indissolubly mingled in the construction of the 'memory world'. Polynesian rituals keep away the pervasive invisible presence and even expel it, as far as possible, from the present. In Fiji, one has to submit to the gods to partake in the universal force of *mana* which governs the cosmos. Among the Kaluli, 'displacing' the ever-present absent implies a ritual procedure which completes the present as it is lived. In all three cases, there is a a an interplay of presence and absence, in the constitutive relation between the living, the supernatural, and the cosmos to which they belong.

Denis Monnerie's contribution focuses on the specific combination of human and supernatural beings which characterizes the Mono-Alu society of the North Western Solomons. His 'general argument is that the relations between the living and the notions corresponding to these different forms of "ancestors" account not only for much of the social life of the Mono-Alu people but also for [. . .] the way they conceptualize the universe' (p. 106). Two types of 'ancestral figures', 'grandfathers' and 'grandmothers', are associated with each matrilineal descent group. These figures are also called upon in most rituals, and especially in funerals, where each category is offered a different component of the deceased. 'Thus [. . .] belonging to a *latu* [descent group] does not merely imply matrilineal transmission, or even the common reference to the 'grandfather' and 'grandmothers' of one's *latu*. For the nobles it also implied, after death, [. . .] the ingestion of the remains of the body by a subaquatic 'grandmother' related to the *latu* (p. 111). But this is not all, since 'grandmothers' and 'grandfathers' are associated respectively with the world below and the world above, while the surface is for the living. 'Spatially, [. . .] the world above and the world below are contiguous with the surface, and this corresponds to a characteristic emphasis on interactions between the living and various aspects of the notions of "grandfather" and "grandmother". [. . . These three domains] are elements of society *and* of the universe, which is conceived in the same terms and organized in a structured socio-cosmic system' (pp. 115–6). There also exists a different set of oppositions, concerning supernatural beings, between the *nitu* of the recent dead (ghosts that were once men) and the original *nitu* (spirits that were never men). Although, in everyday life, the former *nitu* are honoured more highly and worshipped, the latter encompass them (see p. 125). This specific hierarchic feature may be explained by the tight relation between 'original' *nitu* and the notion of 'grandmother', which in turn clearly prevails over the notion of 'grandfather'. In virtue of their mutual relation, each of these two notions affords a different type of superiority over the notion to which it is directly opposed.

In Mono-Alu, no clear-cut distinction between sacred and profane may be drawn, but the whole cosmos is infused with both natural and supernatural. Although supernatural beings seem to be of various types (Codrington's spirits that were or never were men), they are all ordered in an overall hierarchical structure. Curiously enough, this hierarchy grants the highest status to beings that in every day life seem to play a minor role.

André Iteanu's contribution explores a similar issue in the Orokaiva society of the Oro Province of Papua New Guinea. His overall conclusion is that he is 'forced to abandon the idea that Orokaiva supernatural beings are all powerful Universal beings and [is] led to consider that, like the living and objects, they are subordinated to a superior local value, manifested in rituals' (p. 138). Two different kinds of supernatural beings are known here: the ghosts and the ritual characters that perform in initiation. The ghosts, like the living, possess no ontological identity, but are rather gradually shaped by the rituals. 'Three forms of the Orokaiva person, *hamo*, *ahihi* and *onderi*, alternate in the unfolding of the rituals that punctuate the cycle of life and death. They should not, consequently, be understood as heterogeneous entities, but as different stages in a continuous process driven by the rituals' (p. 144). These stages are differentiated by the relations with which they are associated: the living *hamo* are conceived of in terms of relations between persons; the first transformation of the dead, *ahihi*, is conceived of in terms of relations to things; and *onderi* is not conceived of in terms of relations at all. Within this continuum, the ghosts, as opposed to the living, appear weak and ill-defined. A hierarchy of status is thus manifested, whereby the former are subordinated to the latter. On the contrary, the ritual characters that perform in initiation are powerful and clearly individualized. Their performance presents a twofold image of society as a whole. At the higher level of value, society is constructed as a hierarchy of initiation classes, ordered by the value of familiarity with initiation. At the lower one, it is seen as a collection of distinct family groups defined in an esoteric form. Two levels of value are thus distinguished. At the superior one, a ritual hierarchy is dominant and the distinction between ghost and living is absent. At the subordinated one, a relational conception of identity prevails and the second form, ghost, stands for a devalued form of the ritual characters. This specific configuration of values implies that 'in Orokaiva society [. . .] the distinction between the living and supernatural beings does not parallel a distinction of realm like that between society and cosmos or between profane and sacred. On the contrary both categories appear to be full members of the same hierarchically ordered cosmos and to participate in each of its levels' (p. 160). And it seems, more generally, in a comparative framework, that 'in such a cosmomorphic society, where ritual is accorded a dominant value position, deities and ancestors may merely be devalued representations of the ritual characters that stand for the whole of society and even of the cosmos' (p. 161).

At the higher level of value, the Orokaiva cosmos, undistinguished from society, is thus seen as an ordered whole that does not discriminate between natural and supernatural beings. At a lower level, encompassed by the former, however, the distinction between the living and the dead or between natural and supernatural beings prevails, and the strictly hierarchical initiation order is replaced by a rather less marked relational conception of identities. It is on this subordinated level that witchcraft, sickness, its cure, and death are dealt with.

Gilbert Lewis, in his contribution, examines illness among the Gnau people of the West Sepik of Papua New Guinea. He attempts to sharpen our perception of the notion of belief prevalent at this less studied, subordinated level. He closely analyses every phase of illness and of its cure, never losing sight of comparison with our Western medical setiology and with everyday medical conceptions. His central argument is that 'in different situations, the relevance and intensity of different beliefs vary. Single unswerving commitment to only one set of beliefs is characteristic of monotheist religious expectations, the idea that truth is single and exclusive; local patterns did not seem to me at all like that' (p. 183). Illness and the beliefs relative to it, thus appear to be complex polymorphous phenomena possessing numerous different facets. 'The Gnau considered the events of illness in a matter of fact way first, trying to deduce what might be the likely cause' (p. 170). Among these, some are relative to the visible realm of living persons and some to the non-visible world of spirits, which resembles 'fields of force which may be more or less powerful at different times, more or less concentrated. These forces can affect people who move into their field, or may follow them in their movements, and the forces may vary in response to human actions' (p. 170). Visible and invisible agencies do not threaten all people equally, and the system of food taboos clearly demonstrates these individual variations. 'We speak of food taboos and may imagine a rigid system of rules. It is not like that. People keep some of their customs strictly; but the rules and prescriptions are not all equally sharply defined. There is room for interpretation, the curious, the sceptical' (p. 174). Sickness and treatment, which are not here exclusively oriented towards efficiency, may at first sight appear to counterbalance these variations by constructing an authorized version of belief, since 'the actions make the diagnosis public, they present what has been agreed about the nature of the illness. They conform to theory and cultural expectations. The agent of illness – the cause or the illness itself – is embodied or objectified. The imagery may both inform and reinforce; it may confirm suspicions or provide material evidence in support of an idea; it may show to the young what the older people think'

(p. 184). However, in the course of action, all the questions implying belief are not resolved unequivocally, since 'theories of illness implied by the actions do not have to be made precise. The sense in which an image is the spirit, or only a representation of it, is open to different interpretations and does not have to be the same for all participants' (p. 185). Thus individual variations of belief are at the heart of the Gnau system, and, for example, account for the fact that the Gnau, if necessary, resort to diverse successive and, for us, incompatible forms of treatment of sickness (traditional, Christian, medical . . .). But whatever their centrality, these variations are embedded in a system which compels them to remain only individual, since 'doubts did not mount up to outweigh and topple the authority of consensus in established belief: they bred no attitude of general scepticism' (p. 177).

Gilbert Lewis' contribution considers a level of reality which was partially concealed in the previous papers. While the Gnau generally adhere to a common ideology, each individual simultaneously enters a negotiation with that ideology. Sickness, as a symptom, emerges at the cross-section of these two levels and seems, at least partially, to manifest an individual divergence with regard to the social.

A similar question is raised by **Lisette Josephides**, but from a different vantage point. She deals with the ideological diversities which distinguish whole groups of people and not only individuals. Her theoretical position, which departs from the phenomenological perspective adopted by most approaches so far proposed here, is based on the study of the Kewa of the Southern Highland Province of Papua New Guinea. Her central argument is that 'cultural markers that separate domains of social action such as ritual, politics, marriage relations and those of everyday life [. . .] denote the formal and implicit distinctions locally made, [. . .] so that analytic attempts to remove them currently reduce cultural creativity to the recreation of its most spectacularly "visible" aspects, its privileged representations' (p. 189). In myth, in courting songs and in marriage, two apparently contradictory discourses confront each other, that of women and that of men. The author equates this opposition to 'a tension between "cosmology" and "practice"' (p. 193). In myth, women's stories are ontologically self-empowered, while men's gain value only in reference to forefathers. In courting songs, men use magical powers that they have bought, while women enhance the desirability of their own bodies. In pig-killing activities, 'the message is that the agnatic group of males manages these matters and the affective, emotional matters of the kin group and domestic unit have no room here. [. . .] Men use the past to empower their claims, [. . . while] women expect their perform-ance and their charms, to draw men. Therefore their powers are their own and innate' (pp. 203–4). Two contrasting values are therefore invoked. For men, 'it is the past that is important rather than divinities and supernatural beings. What gives the past its power is the fact that it has already happened, it has been externalized in the culture (or at least it is claimed to be so) and is therefore validated by a present, for which it is seen to provide a basis' (p. 193). On the contrary, in the case of women, 'present practice [. . .] follows on a direct line from past practice, so that the songs that the women sing to construct their male partners were previously sung by their mothers. But this past legitimacy is not invoked by the women, who consider their songs to be powerful enough in the present, in their performance, and by the empowerment that their own bodies give them' (pp. 193–4).

Obviously, this radically contrasted view sometimes threatens the stability of marriages, and violent disputes between husbands and wives seem to be common. Yet, at the same time, the stories of these disputes demonstrate that women are not totally foreign to their husbands' concerns, just as men sometimes appreciate woman's arguments. How indeed could it be otherwise? Would any woman marry a man who neglects pig-killing? And would any man marry a unattractive woman? Both values are therefore to some degree shared by men and women alike, but their ordering seems to be reversed. The confrontation of this reversed hierarchy of values even has a role in sexual arousal, as the content of courting songs demonstrates. It is quite remarkable that, just as the offering of pig to allies during the pig killing festival takes the form of a fight (see pp. 202–3), the constitution and preservation of the relation between a man and a woman assumes an aggressive mode.

Josephides rightly reminds us that, in societies like those of Oceania, different and sometimes contradictory voices partake in the construction of a common social reality. Therefore, the anthropologist should not simplify that reality, but rather try to understand how ostensibly paradoxical combinations of conflicting ideas and actions may constitute the coherent reality of the people under consideration. Just as war between men is not a purely negative phenomenon, but holds a place in the social structure, aggressive behaviour between men and women must also be accorded a social status.

Eric Hirsch, addresses the coalescence of society and cosmos 'in trying to understand the central importance the Fuyuge [of Papua New Guinea] ascribed to their ritual' (p. 213). He distinguishes 'two alternative ways of thinking, talking and acting'. One of them, 'the way of an ancestral, creator force called *tidibe'*, implies that the Fuyuge 'had no personal agency in these actions, but . . . act out a socio-cosmic plan which has its origins in the ancestral past' (p. 213). The other, on the contrary, shows that 'the agency of the person [is] prominent [in making] actions and events happen, so that others would be able to witness their efficacy' (p. 214). Of these two contrasted modes of description of the cosmos, the former focuses on a 'transcendent process initiated by the ancestral creator force', the second on 'the realization of specific social relations and [personal] achievements' (p. 214). The author, therefore, conceives of the Fuyuge as constructing 'the coalescence of the ancestral and of achievement' (p. 214) in a manner which parallels two current anthropological models: the socio-cosmic one developed by D. de Coppet 'with its emphasis on an encompassing image of the social whole', and M. Strathern's model of sociality 'with its emphasis on the revelatory nature of social practices' (pp. 214–5).

In accordance with *tidibe* life-force, the Fuyuge perform in different places of their lowlands a series of celebrations called *gab* which renews 'social relationality in a *tidibe*-like lifeworld'. Thus 'men and women see themselves as constituted by a series of *gab.*' (p. 219) From one *gab* to the other, there are paths to be followed, along which different feasts must be held. These various directionalities of persons and things, lead to the *gab* central plaza, where 'betelnut, foods, pigs, dancers and valued objects' (p. 220) are aligned in the newly achieved unity. This unity appears to be the result of successive preparatory events which culminate in the *gab* performance itself.

These interlinked rituals, which recompose unity in the ultimate *gab* performance, 'emphasize on both timeless transcendence and on [personal] achievement, each implying and completing the other' (pp. 228–9). In the same way the two anthropological models mentioned above, that of socio-cosmic encompassment and that which builds on the revelatory nature of social practices, show how 'recurrent contingency ultimately points towards "cosmological" encompassment' (p. 229).

Eric Hirsch concludes by stating that 'the aim of ritual process is to make revelation lead to encompassment' (p. 229). Therefore, beyond complementarity, the author seems to recognize here a form of hierarchical relation between two domains: the subordinate achievement and the encompassing ancestrality. So that, cosmos and society may be ordered in their coalescence.

Prolonged observation of 'Are'are society of Big and Small Malaita and North-Eastern Guadalcanal, in the Solomon Islands, has led **Daniel de Coppet** to focus his contribution on two main issues: the intricate relation between society and cosmos and the place of bigmanship in 'Are'are social structure. He argues that the overall system of 'Are'are rituals, organized in a remarkably coherent series of ceremonial feasts, manifests the unity of society and cosmos: 'All the main activities of the society – marriage and funerals, flirtation and murder, together with all the different feasts – constitute an overall movement which *animates* different kinds of beings such as cultivated plants, domesticated pigs, men and women, and especially shell money. This movement can be [. . .] understood only if we [. . .] accept that [. . .] these different beings [. . .] are living combinations of three kinds of socio-cosmic relations which [may be called] "external form relations", "breath relations" and "representation relations" (p. 237). These three kinds of relations are kept flowing in "streams [. . .] sometimes separated from each other, as in funerals, and sometimes reunited in a single current of socio-cosmic relations, as in each individual during his lifetime" (p. 241). Daniel de Coppet then shows that the series of different feasts 'are [. . .] concerned not simply with the fate of individual subjects but with the three fundamental streams' (p. 248).

Moreover, the series of feasts is divided into two different sets. The first one deals with marriages, funerals and blood money, and organizes the correct flow of the three streams of socio-cosmic relations following each of these particular events. The second one deals with the two categories of deceased – those

who fell victim to their ancestors and those who were murdered
– and manages to return to the living the former socio-cosmic
relations of all the dead. It therefore protects society and cosmos
from any loss or entropy due to the flow of generations and time.
Within this movement even the socio-cosmic relations of the
murder-victims are reintegrated into the 'Are'are dynamic of the
universal socio-cosmic streams.

Bigmanship appears, in 'Are'are, as a hierarchical construct
whereby the killer is subordinate in value-terms to the peace-
master, who stands for the whole of the 'Are'are society. But the
interdependence between the two figures of bigmanship means
also that neither can rule without the other. Together they
constitute a vivid example of the hierarchic whole that seems to
inform all the particular deeds of the 'Are'are as well as their
capacity to ensure the permanence of an 'Are'are coalescence
between society and cosmos.

Annette Weiner's contribution is an ambitious attempt to
'reconfigure' the concepts of reciprocity in exchange theory.
Criticizing Lévi-Strauss's normative position as well as Marshall
Sahlins's empirical one, she demonstrates that reciprocity is but
a secondary effect of 'keeping-while-giving'. This process, which
is central to any society, establishes differences between
participants and generates a 'cultural reproduction and the
development of hierarchy'(p. 275).

The ideal social locus for her demonstration is the opposed-
sex sibling relationship between what our languages call 'sisters
and brothers'. Annette Weiner strongly contests the view that the
sibling incest taboo entails an unavoidable 'exchange of women'
between brothers-in-law. She argues that in the Trobriands, in
Samoa and in ancient Hawaii, before, during and after their
(sometimes serial) marriages, sisters are the key figures of
'cultural reproduction', and not simply biological operators of
human procreation. Instead of a strict sibling incest taboo,
'sibling intimacy', with its different modes of expression, gives
sisters a fundamental role in extending *mana*, rank and political
control. In that sense, it appears that women as sisters are in fact
'kept-while-given' and consequently do not only take part in the
reproduction of society but in that of the cosmos as well, society
and cosmos constituting two inseparable realms.

'Keeping-while-giving', when applied to cloth and inalienable possessions, also sheds light on the particularities of the political systems in these same three societies. In Hawaii, 'women and men rulers guarded their most prized cloaks as inalienable possessions' (p. 297). In Samoa, women and men, who during ceremonial events are sisters and brothers, exchange sacred fine mats. But the most precious mats had only limited circulation, and were kept by their owner because of the many dangers and powers these mats embodied. In the Trobriands, cloth wealth (bundles and skirts) is necessary at death ceremonies, as it symbolizes 'the "purity" of matrilineal identity reproduced through the ancestral and political union of brother and sister' (p. 304). In all these instances, 'inalienable possessions are the markers of the difference between one ranking person or group in the face of the flux of exchange that repays debts and obligations to all those outside the group' (p. 306). Inalienable possessions are so difficult to acquire and then to keep, that 'ultimate authority' is bound to be a brother's and sister's common achievement. Therefore, 'keeping while giving', which is linked to sibling intimacy and to inalienable possessions, is an elaborate response which ensures the reproductive capacity of society. It expresses an overall 'cosmological authentification of rank, mana, and gods' (p. 307), that constitutes the process which permits the establishment an ultimate authority. Such a process manifests a sphere of social activity which is situated beyond individual aims and calculations, that is, at the level where society fulfils the conditions of its permanence as a distinct social entity. 'Keeping while giving' must be placed among the few hierarchical constructs which clarify the coalescence of cosmos and society in Oceania, and probably elsewhere.

This brief outline of the articles composing this volume cannot do justice to the richness of the different contributions. Each of them deals with monographic or comparative ethnographic material, patiently adducing convincing proof of its central ideas while simultaneously enriching its arguments by the exploration of related issues.

We have furthermore chosen to stress certain common themes. But those selected represent only one set among others, and a different presentation would have resulted from an alternative selection of themes, or from the choice of a different theoretical standpoint. Our decision was not, however, arbitrary, since the different contributions gathered here were all originally offered as papers at a conference held in France in 1990 on the theme *Society and Cosmos, their Interrelations or their Coalescence in Oceania*. We trust that our outline shows how all the different studies contribute to exploring that particular question.

It may be objected that our outline blurs the diversity of the sharply contrasted theoretical positions expressed in the various contributions. Although the contributors to this volume do express diverse and original theoretical positions, the relative unity of the volume in our opinion remains one of striking characteristics. This unity emerges, not from theoretical criteria employed in selecting contributors, but rather from the fact that anthropologists today, contrary to what is sometimes asserted, are increasingly in agreement on their principal concerns. In our view, the field is now well defined, its methodological problems are increasingly clear, and most anthropologists agree on the nature of the difficulties we face, even if the hypotheses proposed to overcome them vary greatly.

In this volume, the kernel of agreement among the contributors is, we think, to be found in the common recognition that, in the Pacific, society and cosmos, as we understand them, are not distinguished. In each society studied other crucial global distinctions are, however, made. The relations which link the poles of these oppositions are each of the authors' central concern. It seems that in Oceania one never encounters simple opposition, but that, in each society, one of the poles contains the other, and that, simultaneously or alternatively, a category exists which combines the two poles. This complex configuration requires that an effort be made, with regard to each society, to disentangle the particular, and alien for us, organization of its cosmos. It may suggest as well that these societies are closer to each other than one would have imagined, and that a general comparative formula may eventually be revealed. But this would necessitate a reconsideration of all these societies, viewed each as a socio-cosmic whole.

Notes

1. The editors of this volume are grateful to Stephen J. Suffern, who has revised this introduction as well as Daniel de Coppet's paper.
2. As defined by the Webster *Dictionary*.

References

Detienne, Marcel and Vernant, Jean-Pierre (1979). *La cuisine du sacrifice en pays grec*. Gallimard, Paris.

Dumont, Louis (1970 [1966]). *Homo Hierarchicus. The Caste System and Its Implications*. The University of Chicago Press, Chicago.

—— (1986 [1983]). *Essays on Individualism. Modern Ideology in Anthropological Perspective*. The University of Chicago Press, Chicago.

Maine, H. Summer (1887). *Ancient Law*. London.

Mauss, Marcel (1974 [1925]). *The Gift. Forms and Functions of Exchange in Archaic Societies*. Routledge & Kegan Paul, London.

Read, Kenneth, E. (1955). Morality and the Concept of the Person among the Gahuku-Gama. *Oceania*, XXV (4), 233–82.

Weiner, Annette B. (1992). *Inalienable Possessions. The Paradox of Keeping-While-Giving*. University of California Press, Berkeley.

Chapter 1

Closure and Multiplication: An Essay on Polynesian Cosmology and Ritual[1]

Alfred Gell

The main features of Polynesian cosmological beliefs show a high degree of consistency and have become reasonably well known, through the efforts of a host of nineteenth-century writers, mostly missionaries or government officials, and subsequent re-working by Polynesia specialists. The Central–Eastern Polynesian culture area, comprising the Society Islands (Tahiti) the Marquesas, New Zealand, and Hawaii to name only the larger sub-regional systems, all maintained broadly similar systems of ritual and belief, which were founded on the cosmological scheme in which the creation of the cosmos came about through conflict and separation (Hanson 1982). The cosmos was originally one but this afforded no scope of action to the creator god (*Ta'aroa, Tane,* etc.) whose initial act was to bring about the separation of sky and earth, night and day, thus creating the 'bi-cameral world' of the Polynesians which was divided into the *po,* the other-world, the world of night (*po*), darkness the original gods, the dead, etc. and the *ao,* the world of light, day (*ao*) life, human activity, and so forth. This original separation was subsequently elaborated differently in different places, and might become formidably complicated, as is suggested by Figure 1.1, which shows a diagram of the cosmos created by a Tuamotuan informant for an inquisitive missionary in the late nineteenth century. The cosmos as a whole takes the form of a nested arrangement of 'shells' (*'apu*), each associated with a particular cosmogonic episode of separation; and pathways or ladders are indicated by means of which intercourse is possible between different cosmological levels.

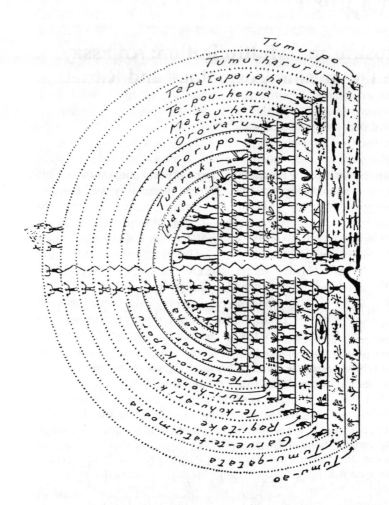

Fig 1.1 The Tuamotuan conception of the Cosmos by Paiore, c. 1820

Polynesian thought about the universe differed from Judaeo-Christian 'creationist' thought in that it was predicated, not on the creation of the universe *ex nihilo*, by God, but on the initial existence of everything in an all-embracing plenum or tightly-bound continuum. The creative epoch occurred as a process of 'differentiation' within this pre-existing plenum, undertaken by a God who made 'cuts'. The Tahitian creation chant, part of which I am about to cite, is really wrongly so called, because nothing whatsoever is 'created' in it. Instead, what the God does is to articulate, or differentiate, the world into its distinct components and qualities, but the substance of the newly-articulated cosmos remains what it always was, nothing other than the God himself. The name borne by *Ta'aroa*, the Tahitian creator god, actually means 'the sever-er'. *Ta'aroa* is called thus because he made the initial severance between the *po* and the *ao*, and he created the various natural phenomena by rearranging his own body:

> So he overturned his shell and raised it up to form the sky ... and he slipped out of another shell which covered him which he took for rock and sand. But his anger was not yet appeased, so he took his spine for a mountain range, his ribs for mountain slopes, his vitals for the broad fleeting clouds, his flesh for the fatness of the earth, his arms and legs for the strength of the earth, his finger-nails and toe-nails for scales and shells for the fishes, his feathers for trees, shrubs and creepers, to clothe the earth, his intestines for lobsters, shrimps and eels for the rivers and seas, and the blood of *Ta'aroa* got heated and drifted away for redness for the sky and the rainbows ... *Ta'aroa* had crusts, that is, shells, so everything has a shell.

> The sky is a shell, that is, endless space in which the God placed the sun, the moon, the sporades [the scattered or individual stars], and the constellations of the gods. The earth is a shell to the stones, the water, the plants which spring from it. Man's shell is woman, because it is by her that he comes into the world, and woman's shell is woman, because she is born of woman. One cannot enumerate the shells of all the things the world produces (Henry 1928: 339–40).

This projection of the body of the God into the phenomenal world, though developed in an exceedingly poetic way in the texts assembled by Teuira Henry, was not in itself an unorthodox conception of cosmogenesis. But it had profound consequences for the subsequent development and elaboration of indigenous religious thought. Because the *po* and the *ao* were originally emergent parts of a continuum, their separation had, for the Polynesians, only a provisional character, and they continually threatened to merge together again. Indeed the very instruments that kept them apart, kept them together and in communication. This was brought out most perspicuously in relation to the four props (*to'o*) which Ta'aroa positioned in order to keep the sky up and open a space (*atea*) for the *ao*, the world of light and of humanity. The props that separated the *po* and the *ao* also, by definition, joined them together, and thus became the exemplary prototypes of sacred objects, endowed with the power to communicate the divine presence. Society Islands politics revolved around rival claims to control certain ultra-sacred wooden billets, called *to'o*, which were counterparts of the 'props' of the cosmos as a whole. But, being so sacred, these wooden billets had themselves to be separated from the world, whose continued existence/differentiation they guaranteed; so they were confined to an elaborate ark, and were massively bound around with sennit cordage, and other wrappings, and were only uncovered on the most sacred and propitious occasions, requiring many human sacrifices to allay the danger they presented to mortals, however sanctified by birth and ritual preparations (Henry 1928; Oliver 1974).

The cosmogonic scheme of differentiation rather than creation *ex nihilo* and of immanent rather than transcendent divinity was, I think, the source of certain ontological anxieties that played an enormous part in Polynesian life. For us, the immanent *deus sive natura* of Spinoza represents an optimistic rather than a pessimistic deism, a blessed relief from the angry and punishing Almighty God of traditional Christianity, set apart from His creation and judging it harshly. But that is because the idea of an immanent God was never really naturalized in Christian Europe, however much eighteenth-century intellectuals may have hankered after one. In Polynesia the situation was the precise opposite; the immanence of the Gods was the source of continuous anxiety (the proverbial hedonism of the South Sea Islanders was founded on a sense of acute and abiding hysteria) and the rapidity and enthusiasm with which the Polynesians accomplished their conversion to Christianity stemmed from their untold relief upon discovering that God was, after all, transcendent, not part of this world.

In this essay, the theme I want to address is Polynesian anxiety about immanence, about differentiation, and some of the ways in which this fundamental anxiety shaped the patterns of their cultural life. That is to say, I want to explore some of the ways in which the underlying conception of the creation of the world through a process of differentiation (splitting, separation) gave rise to countervailing pressure towards fusion, absorption, collapse, etc., which had to be continually held in check through ritual action. In particular I want to identify the symbolic strategies through which social individuals sought to keep immanence at bay, while, at the same time, acknowledging the fundamental fact that immanence pervaded the world and constituted it. The essential strategy of counter-immanence (averting the danger of being absorbed, de-differentiated, etc.) was the recapitulation, in one form or another, of the process of separation on which both the cosmos in general, and the being of the individual, were founded. In other words, the cosmogonic activities of *Ta'aroa* the severer had to be recapitulated at the level of the individual subject; not out of a vainglorious desire to emulate the God, but certainly for the same reasons that the creative gods engaged in the original splitting, i.e. in order to open a space, to establish a difference. And just as the original cosmogonic act was the opening up of a domain, within the plenum, which was relatively non-sacred (the *ao*, the world of light) so the means of ritually securing the subject was the opening of a space between the subject and the sacred domain whence he originated.

Most important Polynesian ritual operated in precisely the inverse sense to Christian communion, i.e. the intention was to cause the divinity to leave (some part of) the world, rather than to induce the divinity to enter (some part of) it. There were no rituals through which persons (e.g. kings) were consecrated, because they were already all-too-sacred, but action in the world was impossible for persons of high intrinsic sanctity, because they did not truly belong to it, belonging, instead, to the *po*. Thus, for instance, the non-executive sacred ruler of Tonga, the *Tu'i Tonga*, was not mourned when he died, and his funeral mound was covered with excrement rather than offerings, because he had never lived (Bott 1982). Instead of being sanctified,

Polynesians of high intrinsic (i.e. genealogically-based) rank had to be elaborately de-sanctified. Thus, the main passage-rites of the Society Islands were the *amo'a* or 'head-releasing' rituals through which children, who were considered to be 'little gods' (and highly *tapu*) were made 'secular' by being offered blood drawn from the congregation, which replaced their sacred substance and freed them for ordinary worldly social interactions.

We can begin to consider the consequences of the cosmology of immanence for personal ontology by dwelling for a moment on the general Polynesian word for 'god', *atua*. This word is based on the morpheme *tua*, which means 'back', or the far, invisible, side of any object. The particularly sacred parts of a human being were the back (the spine) and the head – i.e. precisely those parts of the body that cannot normally be seen by their possessor. The *atua* (spiritual element) of the person was the *tua* (back) of the person. *Tua* also refers to elders and ancestors, the 'back' portions of time, and these were also sacred. Immanent divinity was not a contingent presence, but a categorical, dimensional, feature of objects, spaces, times. Ordinary human intercourse was front to front, expressed in western Polynesia (and Fiji) in the fundamental social morality of 'facing one another' (*fa'agaga*, cf. Shore 1982), while it was always strictly forbidden to move about behind some important person, invisibly to them. The back was the 'individual' as opposed to the cosmological *po*, the inaccessible, threatening, but ever-present unseen. But it was possible also to intervene so as to protect this aspect of the person.

I think one can identify two basic strategies through which the integrity of the person could be maintained against cosmological collapse, to which I have attached the labels of 'closure' and 'multiplication'. 'Closure' is the provision of extra reinforcement, hardening the target of spiritual danger, while 'multiplication' is the strategy of reduplicating the person in myriad forms. We can see both strategies at work in the cosmological myths referred to above: thus *Ta'aroa* multiplies himself by opening up the *ao*, assuming his myriad immanent forms; but also he closes it off with the 'shells' (secured by the 'props') so that it cannot fall in again. In fact, the entire cosmos consisted of such 'shells', as Figure 1.1 shows. But, as the chant also specifies, people were also 'shells', and so were their kin-groups. (In the eighteenth century, *'apu*, 'shell' was the standard Tahitian expression for the bilateral kindred, the basic unit of social organization, cf. Maori: *hapu*). But rather than continue with these general observations, let me turn to consider some more specific imagery of closure and multiplication in the context of Polynesian art traditions.

Polynesian carving is particularly rich in Janiform images (Figure 1.2), which, though they occur elsewhere (particularly in India), nowhere assume the importance they have in this part of the globe. Figure 1.2, which we may take as a typical instance, is one of a small number of images of Siamese twin goddesses carved from whales' teeth, all of which were actually collected in Fiji, where they were regarded as the consorts of *Ndeng'ei*, the main god; but they are known to have been carved in *Ha'apai*, (part of the Tongan group of islands), and they probably

Fig 1.2a Tongan twin deities carved in whale ivory. Collected in Fiji by Gordon (Haddon Museum)

Fig 1.2b Polynesian twin figures, Marquesas

Fig 1.2c Polynesian twin figures, Marquesas

Fig 1.2d Polynesian twin figures, Cook Islands

Fig 1.2e Polynesian twin figures, Cook Islands

Fig 1.2f Polynesian twin figures, Cook Islands

Fig 1.2g Polynesian twin figures, Cook Islands

originally represented the Tongan Siamese twin culture heroines *Nafanua* and *Tokupulu*. The Tongan Siamese twin goddesses (Colocott 1921; Reiter 1907), who play an important role in the Tongan creation myth (and were responsible for assuring plentiful catches for Tongan fishermen), have Samoan counterparts in the form of the twins *Taema* and *Tilafaega*, also known as *Nafanua* the goddesses of tattooing and warfare respectively (Kraemer 1902). I do not want to expand on the mythological detail, but I would like to offer some suggestions as to why Janiform images of this type had so much ritual significance in the area.

The Siamese twin archetype combines closure and multiplication in their most elementary forms. The most outstanding feature of a Siamese twin is symmetry about the vertical axis, not only in one plane (left/right} but also about the other vertical plane (front/back). In other words, a Siamese twin has no 'back', only a middle and a periphery. Such a being is protected, or encompassing, in a way in which no ordinary mortal can be. For merely one-dimensionally symmetric beings the back always remains the most vulnerable area as in Coleridge's lines:

> Like one who treads a lonely road
> And dare not turn his head
> Because he fears a frightful fiend
> Doth close behind him tread.

Siamese twins are immune from such dangers, and have therefore a kind of completeness which justifies their being considered among the immortals. Indeed, they seem to adumbrate creation (as splitting) itself, since their image seems to capture the moment at which the god created the world by splitting apart the plenum, which was himself. Siamese twins obviously qualify as 'multiplied' beings, but at the same time they are closed in that their twofold symmetry closes off that part of the ordinary being which is open to assault from the back.

It would therefore be natural to expect that one of the strategies through which ordinary mortals might seek to recapitulate, in themselves original cosmogonic splitting, and thereby assure the integrity of their persons, might be to imitate the twins, and attach a secondary person to their backs. We are

able to know that this possibility occurred to the minds of the
inhabitants of Western Polynesia, from where the statuettes of the
Siamese twin goddesses come, not because they practised
artificial twinning, but because they were specifically disallowed
from doing so. George Turner, a nineteenth-century missionary
ethnographer, recorded that in Samoa it was forbidden for
members of the family to sit leaning against one another back-to-
back, on pain of immediate fatal, divine retribution (Turner
1884). I believe that in contemporary Christian Samoa it would
still be thought very improper to adopt this posture. Turner also
noted that all fruit or vegetables that grew together to form a
fused pair (as happens sometimes with bananas, taro, yams, etc.)
were immediately to be offered to the gods and might on no
account be eaten. He makes both these observations in the same
paragraph, and leaves one in no doubt that they were connected;
but he offers no more specific explanation. In the light of what
has been said so far, I think one can reasonably infer that the
principle of the 'sacredness of doubles' and the prohibition on
back-to-back sitting relate to the image of divinities as protected,
encompassing back-less beings who escape from the
fundamental ontological deficit of ordinary mortals, i.e. an
asymmetrical relationship with *tua*, the back. To become such a
double being was to usurp a privilege afforded to the gods (or
goddesses) alone. It was sacrilege, in other words.

But although overt doubling-up was not a feasible symbolic
strategy, since it infringed too much on divine privilege (like
eating 'double' fruit of vegetables) there were other, more
indirect means of achieving a similar result. At this point,
multiplication and closure begin to diverge. Let me take
multiplication first. Returning to the Siamese twin image, one
possible reading of it is that it represents a mutual and
symmetrical parturition (note that the Western Polynesian
mythic twins are all female). There is a direct connection between
the idea of doubling and birth. Momentarily, at least, any woman
giving birth is a Siamese twin, and indeed in the Marquesas (if
not anywhere else, so far as I know) the word for 'birth' (*fanau*)
also referred to fused-double objects, such as double bananas,
etc. (Dordillon 1934–5). It goes without saying that there is a
strong relationship between cosmogony and birth, where
cosmogony is specifically not conceptualized as creation *ex nihilo*:
the God of the Old Testament does not noticeably 'give birth' to

the cosmos whereas the corresponding Polynesian texts, as has frequently been noticed, are permeated with procreative symbolism. Birth among mortals was also a process of cosmological significance recapitulating creation, in that children (in some places only the children of élite kindreds) were believed to come from the *po* and to be, in fact gods; exceptionally sacred, ranking higher than their parents (Oliver 1974). Because women were capable of recapitulating divine cosmogonic acts and were the means through which divinities entered the *ao*, it follows that women were not just more sacred, but also more protected against 'defilement' (which I construe as de-differentiation) than men. Women were 'naturally' *noa* (*me'ie*, etc.: various synonyms), i.e. 'clear', non-sacred in the sense of being not endangered by other persons, though very capable of harming others, especially males, by infringing their *tapu* (Hanson 1982).

Tapu (Tahitian *ra'a*) was the general quality of personal, sacred distinctiveness, which was continually subject, to dispersion. It is usually glossed as 'sacredness', and so much has been written on the subject, that I hesitate to embark on a discussion of it here. But, as briefly as possible, here are the salient points. Objects and persons were *tapu* in so far as they were held to be invested with *po*–derived, *atua*–derived attributes and qualities. Because these sacred properties were immanent, they were liable to dispersion: any object, or person invested with *tapu* quality remained so only in so far as that object, or person did not lapse back or become merged, with the generality of things. Immanent sacredness can be localized and preserved only via isolation from non-sacred things: it is quite different from our kind of sacredness, which is transcendental in which the sacred object is secular until it has been consecrated by ritual action. With immanent sacredness it is the object, or the person which is sacred simply by virtue of being that object or person because, in some way, it is itself an *atua*. Broadly speaking, things and persons contained *tapu* in proportion to the extent to which their existence recapitulated cosmogonic acts. Persons (especially of the élite) were sacred because their coming-into-being recapitulated the birth of gods. Creative activities, such as carving, canoe-building or tattooing were sacred because the activity of craftsmen is godlike, they cut things, make lines, hollow things out, and so on. Another way of putting this is to say that *tapu* is 'difference' in the sense that any thing or person that is non-substitutable, whose being there and then makes a difference, is characteristically *tapu*, and must be protected from indiscriminate contacts that diminish this difference. The effect of the philosophical attitude of immanence, just as is the case in India, is to place the whole weight of the religious system on the preservation of distinctions and boundaries (Dumont 1970). Where there is a god in everything, the need to keep things apart is overwhelming, because only this separation preserves essences, and essence precedes existence. Where boundaries are transgressed, annihilation follows.

To return to the question of the differential 'sacredness' of males and females. Male *tapu* qualities were intrinsically vulnerable, though they also had their means of defence, which I will consider shortly. But women, though no less imbued with *tapu* than males (sometimes more) were not vulnerable to quite the same extent, because a woman is, so to speak, a complete system of differences in herself, a microcosm, whereas males were irreducibly incomplete beings, dependent on women for their presence in the world (and their departure from it). Women were containers and conductors of *tapu* quality, whereas men simply possessed *tapu* like a static electrical charge, and could be much more easily deprived of it. As the Tahitian chant says, 'woman is the shell of woman, because she is born of woman'. On the surface this indicates a transitive relation

$$\text{woman (1)} \rightarrow \text{woman (2)} \rightarrow (3) \rightarrow (n)$$

in which one woman gives birth to another. But the phraseology suggests at the same time a recursive, self-referential relationship

$$\text{woman (1)} \rightarrow \text{woman (1)} \rightarrow (1) \rightarrow \dots$$

i.e. a woman giving birth recapitulates her own birth, *ad infinitum*. Whereas the schemes, also given in the chant,

$$\text{woman} \rightarrow \text{man}$$

admits of no such interpretation. Hence, I would argue, the procreative powers of women make them *temporally* 'symmetrical' beings (beings with no past and no future) in a way precisely analogous to the *spatial* symmetry of Siamese twins along the spatial axis front/back. They are thus, like the Siamese twins, both multiple and closed their *tapu* not lessened by the fact that it is in no danger from without.

For males this solution does not exist: they faced an acute problem in becoming sufficiently *noa/me'ie* in order to carry on a normal existence, while not dispersing their *tapu* quality in such a fashion as to lose their distinctiveness. They had essentially two possibilities: they could find other means of imitating the natural characteristics of Siamese twins, women, etc., which enabled them to contain their sacredness so that it was not in danger from without, or they could disperse their sacredness under 'controlled' conditions. I will consider instances of both of these.

One means that men could and did employ in order to convert themselves from mortals, with the fundamental ontological deficit that mortality implies, into 'complete' beings, recapitulating cosmogony, was tattooing, which was widely practised in Polynesia, especially by men (almost exclusively by men in Western Polynesia). Tattooing was an obligatory passage rite of late adolescence for males, particularly in Samoa, which produced tattoo artists for the Tongan élite as well. As was noted above, tattooing was thought to have originated from the Siamese twin goddesses, *Tilafaenga* and *Teama* (who brought it from Fiji). This mythical association of tattooing with Siamese twins underlines the latent equivalence between the strategy of multiplication-twinning and the strategy of tattooing which was predicated mainly on 'closure'. One is able to know this by making a study of tattooing ritual and the nomenclature of tattoo designs. Figure 1.3 shows tattoo designs, one from Western Polynesia (Samoa), the other from Eastern Polynesia (the Marquesas). Of the two, the Samoan example is the simpler, so I will discuss it first.

Samoan tattooing was a necessary preparation for war and for sexual life; untattooed males might not engage in either. Both of these were dangerous activities: it has already been made clear that women, by virtue of their position as mediators between the *po* and the *ao*, were a potent source of spiritual danger. Warfare was as well, indirectly, in that death in battle was never merely a matter of military incompetence, but would always be traced to spiritual debility. Tattooing strengthened young males and prepared them for warlike and amatory exploits. But how was

Fig 1.3a Samoan male tattooing (rear), by Kramer©

Fig 1.3b Samoan male tattooing (front), by Kramer©

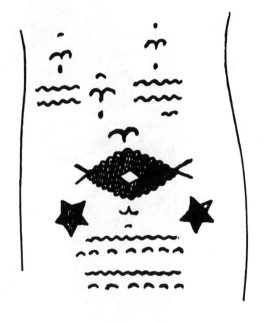

Fig 1.3c Samoan female tattooing

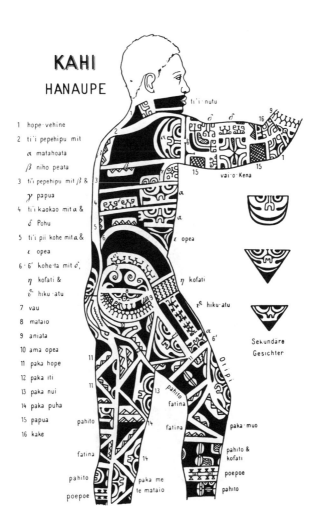

Fig 1.3d Marquesan tattooing (side), by Von de Steinen©

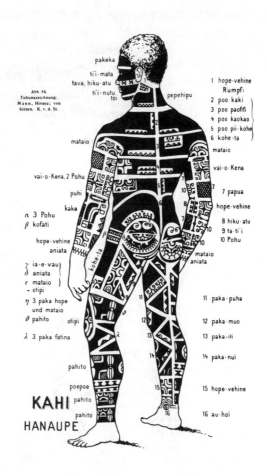

Fig 1.3e Marquesan tattooing (rear), by Von de Steinen©

tattooing conceptualized? To begin with, let us note that the area that was first tattooed was the lower part of the back, i.e. *tua*, and that over this vulnerable part were placed designs of a specifically protective nature (Buck 1930; Kraemer 1902; Stair 1897). The back-design as a whole was called *pe'a*, 'flying fox', alluding, among other things, to the motto of the King-making descent-group of *Sava'i*, the *Tonumaipe'a*, descendants of *Nafanua*, which was 'salvation comes from the flying fox'. More generally, the flying fox was a well-protected animal. anyone who has seen a flying fox securely wrapped in its enfolding wings will understand why. The design, which vaguely recalls the wing-shape of a flying fox, wrapped round the body. The back-design also has another name, *tapulu*, which means approximately 'tattooed wrapping' (*ta+pulu*). Other motifs are 'bindings' (*fusi*) 'beams' (*aso*), etc., suggesting that the metaphor of tattooing is the construction of a housing or defensive screen covering the body. Finally, the last and ritually perhaps the most significant tattoo was applied to the navel (*pute*). Horatio Hale (1846) enquired about this, and was told the navel had to be tattooed out of 'shame', because that was the part of the male body that was connected to the mother. One can certainly discount the idea that it was modesty as we would understand it that required the tattooing of the navel; everything suggests that it was the need to seal off the body, definitively, from the *po* and from the danger of dispersion via female 'conductors' of *tapu* quality. The mark over the *pute* was called a *fusi*, a binding, making clear that this was indeed the idea.

The metaphoric basis of Samoan male tattoo was therefore biased towards closure rather than multiplication. But the implicit identity between the two (Milner 1969) is none the less suggested in the famous proverb

> *Tupu le tane, ta le tatau*
> *Tupu fafine, fanafanau.*

> 'The man grows up, he is tattooed,
> The woman grows up, she gives birth.'

But the imagery of multiplication could also be incorporated into the general anti-dispersive prophylaxis of tattooing. In order to see this one has to turn from the elegant restraint of Samoan tattoo, to the more florid style of the Marquesas (Figure 1.3b). In the Marquesas, tattooing was called '_pahu tikl_, literally, 'wrapping in images' (_tiki_). It was obligatory for the same reasons as in Samoa, i.e. warfare and sexuality, and was applied in collective ceremonies which bear a strong resemblance to their Western Polynesian prototypes (W. Handy 1922).

The Marquesan tattooing style follows design principles which can be traced back 2000 years to Lapitan pottery decoration, in that it consists of delimited 'zones with decorative 'infills' (Green 1979). Between the zones there are narrow undecorated strips, so that the form as a whole articulates into distinct segments (in Marquesan, _paka_, 'crusts'). The effect of the zone-infill principle is to interfere with the perception of outlines, so that the body seems to dissolve into myriad fragments. This fragmentation, in turn corresponds to the non-unitary way in which the Marquesans treated their bodies conceptually, in that it was customary (for chiefs, especially) to have separate proper names for individual body-parts in addition to a personal name (Linton 1923). Thus a man (Roger, say) would have a head called Peter, a back called William, an arm called Charles and genitals called Henry, etc. Each of these separately-named members of the body would have its own life, be subject to its own _tapu_ restrictions, and so on. The same principle applied to important artefacts, such as canoes, which also had separate proper names for all their different parts. In this, one perceives the passion for distinctiveness which, I have argued, is the corollary of the religious premises of immanence; difference, non-substitutability, is at a premium because it is only provisional, and can be annihilated at a stroke.

The relative character of difference was itself subject to exploitation for social advantage: in order to lay claim to an object, it was only necessary to name it after (some part of) oneself, upon which the object became part of one's own person. Social identities could be merged and exchanged at will: craftsmen, who had to travel from place to place to execute commissions, would have a network of name-exchange partners, whose social identities (name, kinship affiliations, wives, property, etc.) they would assume when engaged in some foreign political district, extending the same privileges to their name-exchange partner when it was his turn to travel. A craftsman of this kind would thus regularly transform his social identity, even to its most intimate aspects, as he moved from place to place.

The effects of tattooing was to de-totalize the body into distinct fragments, exaggerating differences and conserving *tapu* quality. But the fragments themselves, the 'crusts', were a means of giving integrity to the body as a whole, by 'wrapping' it. Often this is brought out in the nomenclature of individual motifs, which metaphorically evoke certain well-protected, enclosed creatures, objects and spaces (W. Handy 1922; Von den Steinen 1925). The most important animal motif was *honu* or *kea*, generic name for testudinates, turtles and tortoises. These were particularly sacred creatures, which could only be eaten by chiefs, as a result of prestige conferred on them by their excellent armour, which corresponded to the ideal of 'closure'. Other 'closure' motifs were shellfish motifs (*poi'i*), crab motifs (*karu*), enclosed garden motifs (*papua*), and a large class of motifs based on *ipu* (calabash, bowl, dish, etc.). But inspection of Figure 1.3 also reveals that, besides 'enclosing' the body, Marquesan tattoo also protected it from immanence by multiplying it. The person was multiplied via an entourage of tattooed supernumeraries thronging his armoured integument. There are two types of such motifs: homunculi (*etua* 'gods') and tattooed 'secondary faces', as Von den Steinen calls them. There is a clear structural relationship between the tattooing style of the Marquesas, in which the self was furnished with a collection of subsidiary selves to surround and protect it, and the type of Siamese twin image found in Figure 1.2, and *n*-tuplet images of the type exemplified by the Cook Island staff-gods (Figure 1.2). The effect of the tattooing of '*etua*' motifs and secondary faces was to convert the body into such an *n*-tuplet. This is revealed particularly clearly in one Langsdorff's engravings of a young Marquesan Warrior sketched in 1801 by a Russian expedition (Figure 1.4). While mid-nineteenth-century Marquesan tattooing had become somewhat abstract, the more readable eighteenth-century style featured an important motif consisting of a death's-head positioned directly over the mid-line of the back. This design (*mata Komo'e*) had specifically military and protective functions, representing a dead (divinized) chief who was to be avenged. The Marquesan warrior, with his ghostly companion at his back, warding off harm, provides a striking male counterpart to the female Siamese twin images we consider earlier (cf. Figure 1.2).

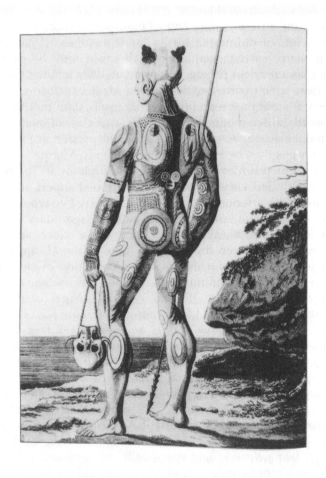

Fig 1.4 Marquesan tattooing (incomplete), by Von de Steinen©

The Marquesans were less inhibited than the Samoans in directly emulating the multiplicity of the gods in their tattooing. They also permitted living individuals to combine in multiple configurations, at least under ritual conditions. None the less, it was sacrilegious to assume these configurations casually, or in play – thus, we learn from the traveller Christian (1910) that Marquesan children were explicitly forbidden to give one another piggy-back rides. Why this should have been forbidden one can easily infer from the prevalence of carved representations of multiple *atua* in Central–Eastern Polynesian art in the piggy-back configuration, of which both Society Island and Marquesan art furnish copious examples, where they often combine with the back-to-back configuration (Figure 1.2d). But even if these carved representations did not exist, one would still know that this configuration has religious implications from the material in Marquesan ritual.

Figure 1.5 is a reconstruction, from descriptions and a photograph taken by Von den Steinen (E. Handy 1923; Von den Steinen 1925) of the physical configuration assumed by the groom and his retinue at Marquesan marriage ceremonies (the bride was similarly carried). Marriage involved the establishment of intimate relationships between persons outside the sphere of close consanguinity and was consequently ritually dangerous, especially to male *tapu*. Therefore sacredness, which could not be preserved indefinitely, or there would have been no possibility of forming alliances, had to be dispersed under ritually controlled conditions, which is what happened at marriage ceremonies. *Tapu* (taking the groom as the focal subject of the ritual for the present) was dispersed among a specific category of relatives, the groom's *pahupahu*. It will he recalled that '*pahu*' in the expression for tattooing (*pahu tiki*) meant 'wrapping'. *Pahupahu* is a reduplicated form of the same word, and referred to close real and classificatory 'cross' relatives, mother's brothers and father's sisters and their spouses. These cross relatives were ego's social 'wrapping'. *Pahu* also means a 'prop', 'support' etc., and the groom was duly borne into the arena by his main 'prop', i.e. his closest mother s brother.

The giving of piggy-back rides to honour the bride and groom at weddings is something one sees among the poorer classes in India (for lack of a horse); but in Polynesia it has a significance which goes beyond the merely honorific, and of course the idea

Fig 1.5 Marquesan groom riding on mother's brother (reconstruction
by A. Gell after Von de Steinen and W. Handy©)

of riding on animals was traditionally unknown there. I think the reference is to the cosmogonic notion of the 'propping up' of the cosmos during the creative epoch. But there is an important ambiguity, which I touched on before about 'props', which also applies to wrappings. That is to say, from one angle, the mother's brother who does the propping prevents the sister's son from touching the ground, and thus losing his contagious sacredness (this is the standard interpretation of bearing chiefs aloft in Polynesia); but this interpretation is insufficient by itself, because inevitably, by virtue of carrying the highly-*tapu* focal subject of the marriage ritual, the mother's brother in question is suffused with his *tapu* and is himself therefore a sacralized being. The situation is analogous to the one mentioned earlier in connection with the ultra-sacred *to'o* of the Society Islands, the wooden props of the cosmos, whose sacredness came from the fact that they were interposed between the *po* and the *ao*, and which were moreover, distinctive primarily by virtue of their 'protective' sennit wrappings, which the priests manipulated in order to disseminate divine power, in carefully metered amounts, into the world. The prop which supports, the wrapping which covers, do not keep divinity out of the world, they simply intervene so that sacred power is diffused in forms and quantities that do not bring about the ultimate cosmic implosion.

So it is with the ritual assemblage depicted in Figure 1.5. The function of the *Pahupahu* relatives is both to contain and to disseminate the dangerous *tapu* of the groom. We can see the concurrent functions of containment and dissemination very perspicuously in relation to the sacred loincloth (*hami*) worn by the groom as he rides on the shoulders of his mother's brothers. This loincloth (which bore analogies to similar strips of sacred cloth wound around images of the gods as, for example, in Figure 1.2g) is a 'containment' device, not unlike a tattoo; but it was also provided with a long train, which was passed over the heads of the procession of *pahupahu* relatives following the groom and his mother's brothers. While the bindings constrained the groom's sacredness, the function of the train was to diffuse it. In effect the *hami* made the assemblage of groom, mother's brothers and *pahupahu* relatives into a single composite being, a kind of sacred version of a pantomime horse (perhaps a less demeaning analogy would be with a Chinese New-Year dragon). Into this composite being (once again, I would refer this to the *n*-tuplet

carved representation of fused *atuas* in Figure 1.2) the sacredness
of the groom could be safely diffused. In effect, there took place a
loss of *tapu* – no worldly business could proceed without there
being a diminution of *tapu*, which only isolation and inactivity
could preserve completely intact – but this necessary derogation
was compensated for by the multiplication of the groom into a
composite being, which was, in itself, a complete microcosm, a
system of differences. This effect was heightened at the climax of
the nuptial rites, during which the groom's *pahupahu* procession
encountered the *pahupahu* procession of the bride, which was
similarly constituted. At this point the two processions merged,
the bridal party passing under the train borne by the groom's
party and vice versa. I do not know how, precisely, this mutual
enfolding was choreographed, but even from the bare
descriptions that have survived the underlying intention is
plain enough. There was a generalized merging of *tapu* qualities,
out of which, by virtue of the alliance established, a new
pahupahu 'wrapping' would be constituted for the united
kindreds.

The marriage ceremony I have described, both dissipated
individual *tapu*, reduced individual distinctiveness, and yet at
the same time conserved it by constituting a kind of collective
being, a multiple person or Siamese *n*-tuplet, innumerable yet
protected within the 'closed' bindings of sacred cloth. A happy
outcome indeed! – but then, marriages are supposed to be
optimistic occasions. But, to conclude this essay, I intend to
darken my palette somewhat and explore a number of more
melancholy themes.

My general argument, up to now, has been that Polynesian
cosmology is correlated with the religious attitude of immanence.
The world is a space within the deity (the plenum of deity) that
is kept apart through the preservation of difference. But
everything in the *ao* has only a relative – one could say, 'an
embattled' – existence, and must eventually be consumed by the
night, as the Maori culture-hero Maui was crushed within the
grinding genitals of *Hine-nui-te-po*, in his vain attempt to confer
immortality on himself, and on mankind (to have achieved this
he would have had to pass right through her, exiting through her
mouth into the unimaginable country beyond the night). The
Polynesians' refusal of transcendence explains both the
extraordinary passion of their mourning ceremonies, and the

unbounded relief, which I mentioned before, afforded them by Christian eschatology. What I want to turn to now is certain Polynesian mortuary practices that reflected the underlying religious attitudes to which I have referred.

The outcome of ordinary deaths, in most Polynesian belief systems, was that the dead person would return to the *po*, a journey which was usually imagined as going under the sea, towards the west and the setting sun. On arrival in the pitch-black underworld, the dead person would be eaten by the *atua* there, who would gradually scrape and gnaw the flesh away until only the bones were left. Only then would the deceased (on the most optimistic assumptions) become an *atua* himself or herself. The images of darkness, submersion, excoriation, cannibalization and extinction – not as punishment, but as a consequence of the mere fact of death – relate to the fundamental nemesis that must await the person in a cosmos pervaded by immanence. Death assumes a particularly terrifying shape in this type of intellectual milieu, and it is surely true that the Polynesians went further than most in increasing its terrors in the here and now in the treatment they meted out to the weak and captive whom they made into cannibal victims and human sacrifices.

The typical pattern of Polynesian mortuary practices (in Central and East Polynesia, anyway) was, first of all, exaggerated mourning, usually involving self-scarification by the bereaved, especially women, and the dispatching of funerary victims, in the case of great chiefs. There followed the exposure of the corpse and 'mummification' (so called, though it was not really comparable to the ancient Egyptian variety), followed eventually by the final disposal of the dry remains, usually only the bones, in secret places, most frequently caves. Some bones were kept in family temples, and some were turned in ornaments, weapons and tools; but it would not be true to say that they ever became significant cult objects.

The only aspect of these mortuary practices that I propose to discuss here is the middle phase of the sequence, i.e. the desiccation or mummification of the corpse. And the point that I want to make about this phase of the mortuary sequence is that, once again, it reflects the basic cosmological scheme of immanence. Here I have one final illustration (Figure 1.6), to which I now turn. This illustration is a reconstruction of a scene

Fig 1.6 The flaying of Iotete witnessed by Aimable Petithomme (A. Gell)

witnessed, in 1844, by the missionary on the left, Père Aimable Petithomme – I hope this man's remarkable name has not unduly influenced my notion of his physical appearance – and reported to his superiors (Williamson 1933). In this year died Iotete, in his hey-day called 'le roi de *Tahuata*', a Marquesan chief of great stature, cunning, and renown, who sought to attain the status of the *Pomare* 'Kings' of Tahiti, but who was eventually humbled (Thomas 1986). Petithomme, visiting the widow of this chief shortly after his death, was surprised to discover her stripping the skin, bit by bit, off his body.

The missionary asked the queen why she was obliged to remove her late husband's skin in this way. She replied that the goddess *Oupu*, who ruled over the afterworld, had decreed that none who had tattooed skins might enter the '*Havaiki*' inhabited by the gods themselves, 'a land of delights planted with all sorts of excellent fruits and adorned by the waters of a blue and calm lake', but would be consigned for ever to a swamp where the sun never shone. This obligation to excoriate the corpse (together with the obligation to feed the gods of the *po* with numerous mortuary sacrifices) had to be fulfilled in order to assure a 'desirable' afterlife.

One can easily see that excoriation of the corpse simply pre-empted the 'scraping' that the dead were expected to undergo at the hands of the *atua* in the *po* according to the standard conception of the afterlife in Polynesian religion. Indeed, the corpse was also 'eaten' in the course of Marquesan mortuary rites (E. Handy 1923). The strips of the skin that had been removed from the body were placed in a special calabash which incorporated a kind of strainer-device, so that the fats and juices from the strips of skin and flesh would drain into a sump at the bottom (Linton 1923). These juices would then be eaten 'with fresh green taro leaves, as a delicacy' by the same women as were charged with the duty of excoriating the corpse. Here, one can see an attempt to short-circuit the 'long-cycle' of transactions between the *po* and the *ao* – in which the dead were consumed by the *atua* – by a 'short cycle' in which the de-construction of the dead was assigned, not to the *atua*, but to the female mourners, who both produced life and consumed it, confining the cycle to the *ao*, in microcosmic form, and thus making it possible for the dead to depart to the *po* already 'scraped' and 'eaten' and thus fully transformed into divine beings. Only by recapitulating the cosmic cycle of *po–ao* interactions in the here and now, was it possible to avert their eschatological consequences. Or rather, that was one necessary part of the procedure. The other was the need to feed the gods, who would be deprived of sustenance if the cycle was short-circuited in this way. The poor had no option – they were simply eaten; but the rich could, and did, escape from the consequences of immanence by replacing their own substance with copious sacrificial offerings. In the Marquesas, enormous quantities of wealth were invested in reciprocal mortuary feasts (which were conducted competitively, very much like New Guinea Highlands pig-feasts) to honour the famous dead and ensure that they reached a desirable *Hawaiki* (Thomas 1990). These feasts had secular political purposes as well as religious ones; but from our point of view the important thing about them was, once again, that they symbolically acted to neutralize 'inimical hunger' (the appetites of the enemy chiefs and their supporters who were given the food symbolically equate to the appetites of the hungry *atua*). The void had to be filled with food, with wealth; and the more dreaded consumption was, to that extent, obviated.

But why did the queen specifically state that it was necessary to efface the tattooing on the skin of her dead consort in order to assure his place in paradise? Here the argument of this paper comes full circle. We saw earlier that tattooing was conceptualized as 'wrapping' (*pahu*) – wrapping that preserved the integrity of the self and prevented the diffusion of difference and *tapu*. Tattooing was necessary part of worldly existence, part of a battery of essentially 'defensive' structures that constituted the Polynesian ego – 'character armour', to borrow a very apposite phrase from the ego-psychology of W. Reich (1950). But tattooing was incompatible with unmediated sacredness. For all the effort and inventiveness that the Marquesans lavished on the art of tattoo, they explicitly believed that their gods were *not* tattooed.

Finally, when the fragile defensive structures on which they depended caved in, and life was at an end, it was necessary to dismantle the defences bit by bit, in order fully to achieve the fusion and de-differentiation of absolute death. Not to attain a subsequent state of immortality, but an antecedent one: to make it as if the living individual had never been at all. Hence the mortuary sequence is essentially a playing out of the cosmogonic process in reverse, enacting gestation and birth in reverse (or 'de-conception': cf. Mosko 1983) at the hands of the female mourners/cannibals. The incremental logic of the passage through life's stages was replaced by a subtractive logic of remorseless exposure, desiccation and dissipation. This was not a 'new birth' as Dante imagines it, in his famous lines on the flaying of Marsyas, who finds everlasting life *'Traeste dalla vagina delle membre sue'* – 'dragged from the sheath (vagina) of his own limbs – so much as birth undone, life stripped away, and a return to the *status quo ante*, in which the creation of the universe and all its consequent effects had been cancelled and annulled.

Notes

1. Further discussion of the topics raised in this essay are continued in a book written by myself and published by Clarendon Press entitled *Wrapping in Images: A study of Polynesian Tattooing.*

References

Bott, E. (1982). Tongan Society at the Time of Captain Cook's Visit. *Memoirs of the Polynesian Society*, 44. Wellington.

Buck, Sir P. (1930). Samoan Material Culture. *Bishop Museum Bulletin*, No. 75. Honolulu.

Colocott, V. (1921). Notes on Tongan Religion. *Journal of the Polynesian Society*, 30, 152–63, 227–40.

Dordillon (1934–5). *Dictionnaire de l'homme des îles Marquises*. Société des Océanistes, Paris.

Dumont, L. (1970). *Homo Hierarchicus*. University of Chicago Press, Chicago.

Green, R. (1979). Early Lapita Art. In: S. Mead (ed.), *Exploring the Visual Art of Oceania*. University of Hawaii Press, Honolulu.

Hale, H. (1846). *United States Exploring Expedition 1838–42 under the Command of Captain Wilkes . . . Ethnology and Philology*. Lea and Blanchard, Philadelphia.

Handy, E. (1923). Native Culture of the Marquesas. *Bishop Museum Bulletin*, 9. Honolulu.

Handy, W. (1922). Tattooing in the Marquesas. *Bishop Museum Bulletin*, 1. Honolulu.

Hanson, F. (1982). Female Pollution in Polynesia. *Journal of the Polynesian Society*, 91, 335–81.

Henry, T. (1928). Ancient Tahiti. *Bishop Museum Bulletin*, 48. Honolulu.

Kraemer, A. (1902). *Die Samoa-Inseln*. E. Schweizerbart, Stuttgart.

Linton, R. (1923). The Material Culture of the Marquesas. *Bishop Museum Memoirs*, No. 8 Part 5. Honolulu.

Milner, G. (1969). Siamese Twins, Birds and the Double Helix. *Man*, NS 4, 5–24.

Mosko, M. (1983). Conception, De-conception and Social Structure in Bush Mekeo culture. *Mankind*, 14, 24–32.

Oliver, D. (1974). *Ancient Tahitian Society*. University of Hawaii Press, Honolulu.

Reich, W. (1950). *Selected Writings*. Vision Press, London.

Reiter, F. (1907). Traditions Tonguiennes. *Anthropos*, 2, 743–54.

Shore, B. (1982). *Sala'ilua : a Samoan Mystery*. Columbia University Press, New York.

Stair, J. (1897). *Old Samoa*. Religious Tract Society, London.

Steinen, K. Von den (1925). *Die Marquesaner und ihre Kunst*. D. Reimer, Berlin.

Thomas, N. (1986). Le Roi de Tahuata. *Journal of Pacific History*, 21, 3–20.

—— (1990). *Marquesan Societies*. Oxford University Press, Oxford.

Turner, G. (1884). *Samoa 100 Years Ago and Long Before*. Macmillan, London.

Williamson, R. (1933). *The Religious and Cosmic Beliefs of Central Polynesia*. Cambridge University Press, Cambridge.

Chapter 2

Cosmogonic Aspects of Desire and Compassion in Fiji

Christina Toren

This chapter concerns the interplay of desire and compassion and how, for Fijian villagers, it informs relations between people and the ancestors, and people and the Christian God. Desire and compassion between people constitute the ideal emotional axis of Fijian kinship; in the more inclusive domain of relations between the Christian God, ancestors, chiefs, and people, desire and compassion become cosmogonic. Here desire references the old Gods' oral and sexual desires for people, and compassion is a residual category – one that becomes dominant in the relation between people and the Christian God.

The field data discussed here were gathered in Sawaieke country on the island of Gau, Fiji.[1] To establish the context for my analysis I first summarize some conclusions from earlier papers. I then relate two myths that show how the old Gods' carnal appetites are ultimately cosmogonic. These myths are contrasted with a story of the origin of Sawaieke village and the idea of a compassionate Christian God to show how carnal desire becomes a residual category, partly because it is only implicit in the Christian God's relations with people and partly because it is 'devilish' (*vakatevoro*), a malign aspect of the old Gods. Moreover, Christian notions of God and the supernatural can suggest that hierarchy is an encompassing value. This relatively new idea makes it appear as if the ritual contexts in which hierarchical relations are constituted and expressed are projected on to the Fijian collectivity as a fixed and bounded unit. But Christianity too is being subtly transformed 'in the Fijian way', for when desire as well as compassion is attributed to the

Christian God's relation to humans, he becomes associated with competitive equality, which is antithetical to fixed hierarchy and prevents its becoming an encompassing value.[2]

The Interplay of Compassion and Desire in Kinship Relations

The affective aspect of kinship is constituted in and through the interplay of *veilomani* – mutual compassion, and *veidomoni* – mutual desire (Toren, 1994). Fijian kinship relations – and ideally all Fijians are kin to one another – are properly relations of mutual compassionate love. Compassion seems of its nature to be hierarchical, since its paradigmatic reference is to the household, and relations *within* household are by definition relations of inequality. But *across* households, between cross-cousins, *veilomani* is associated with competitive equality. For while relations between cross-cousins are also informed by *loloma* (compassion, love, pity, mercy), the behaviour expected of them is joking, competitive, intimate, friendly, and exchanges between them are reciprocal and balanced over time – all these behaviours being constitutive of the explicit equality between cross-cousins within and across sex.

Cross-cousins are potential spouses or siblings-in-law; *veidomoni*, mutual sexual love or desire, is proper only to cross-cousins across sex and, like all other behaviour between them, is associated with equality and balanced reciprocity. An incest taboo applies to all other categories of kin, between whom day-to-day relations require varying degrees of respect and avoidance. It is axiomatic that a wife is subordinate to her husband, so when cross-cousins marry (by definition one always marries a cross-cousin) their equal relation becomes a hierarchical one.[3] This shift is evident in betrothal and marriage ceremonies and further established, at least in part, by the young man's periodic violence towards his wife. Not *all* young married men beat their wives, but violence does seem to characterize the early years of marriage and is attributed by both women and men to male sexual jealousy.[4]

Loloma (compassion) and *dodomo* (desire) tend to be spoken of as independent of each other. This is easy enough, because only in marriage is *veilomani* – the mutual compassionate love proper to hierarchical kinship, confronted by *veidomoni* – mutual desire between equals, within a single dyadic relationship. And only in marriage can each kind of love be seen to be the grounds for the other, such that hierarchical and equal relations can be understood as mutually constituting. In the course of married life, the connotations of the two terms are reversed: the jealous anger fuelled by *dodomo* (passionate desire) is the vehicle of a wife's fear of her husband's violence and helps to create her subordination; the loving trust that emerges in *loloma* (compassionate love) becomes the grounds for a possible, but publicly unacknowledged, equality and mutual respect between spouses. This is important, for the marriage relationship is the crucial site for the constitution of Fijian hierarchy (see Toren 1990: 50–64).

Marriage and Hierarchy

Within Sawaieke country (*vanua*), the chiefly village of Sawaieke ranks above seven other villages that owe it tribute; people often describe relations within and across villages as if the heads of ranked households are ranged in ranked clans, in ranked *yavusa* (groups of connected clans), in ranked villages.[5] This notion of a pervasive hierarchy is constituted in *yaqona* ritual, where tribute is made *apparently* to encompass day-to-day exchange relations of balanced reciprocity across households, clans, *yavusa* and villages.

The apparent dominance of tributary hierarchy in the face of thorough-going balanced reciprocity depends on men's being seen to be the heads of households. This is effected by a woman's marrying into her husband's house, where by virtue of age and kinship-relation she is subordinate to her husband's parents, and by ritualized aspects of the public face of her relation to her husband. In production and exchange, husbands and wives have equal obligations and are equal partners – with a single important exception: in respect of food products and cooking, husbands' contributions seem to be valued above wives', and at every meal in every house, wives take their places nearest the common entrance *i ra*, below, and wait upon their husbands and eat after them. So 'every man is a chief in his own house' and women refer to their husbands and to other men as 'leaders of households' (*liuliu ni vale*); whenever I questioned this I was told that 'it is right that [married] men should lead' (*e dodonu me ra liu na turaga*).

The axiomatic ritual subordination of wife to husband is historically attributable to the way that marriage deprived women of direct access to ancestral Gods; but their attendance on the Christian God gave women direct access to divine power on the same basis as men; and they are included too in *yaqona*-drinking, from which they used to be excluded (see Toren 1988). But in *yaqona*-drinking, a woman takes her position with reference to her husband: she sits *i ra*, below, near the common entrance. Even if she be wife to the paramount chief and high-ranking in her own right, she sits *i ra* in the presence of her husband; but as she is of higher status than other women, they all sit below her. So, in *yaqona*-drinking, it *appears* as if all women are below all men, even though, in their natal households, many women as elder sisters not only have a formally higher status than their younger brothers but may also have significant effective authority over them.

Women's status as elder sisters poses a problem for the ranking of households, clans, and *yavusa* against one another; but with women as subordinate wives effectively removed from consideration, these collectivities can be ranked in respect of their obligations to chiefs (*turaga*) – a term that can refer to married men, to people of chiefly birth irrespective of gender or, more exclusively, to the chiefs of *yavusa*, also called *na malo*, 'the cloths'. On a day-to-day basis in *yaqona*-drinking, it is with respect to *na malo* and a few other senior and high-status men that elders, married men, young men, and women can all apparently be ranked on the above–below axis that describes any space where *yaqona*-drinking takes place. The authority of *na malo* – including the paramount chief – is at once expressed and constituted in *yaqona*-drinking, and especially in the drinking that instals a chief as *yavusa* head, or as paramount of a country (*vanua*).

The presentation of *yaqona* (*sevusevu*) and the drinking of it are paradigmatic of sacrificial tribute: the root is presented raw to the chiefs, under whose aegis it is ritually prepared and re-presented as drink to the people; the *yaqona* cannot now be further transformed. It is, as it were, 'cooked', and must be accepted if one is not to give offence.

In the current politico-economy of rural Fiji, *yaqona*-drinking is crucial for the constitution of the authority of chiefs. Chiefs are held to be essential for the moral well-being of the country at large and for prosperity; they are the locus of exchange across collectivities, and so may seem to give more than they receive and to deserve people's attendance on them. But the material power of the chiefs of small *vanua* is limited; it is the drinking of the installation *yaqona* that makes a chief 'truly effective' (*mana dina*) – because then those who disobey him or are wanting in respect are likely to fall ill and die. By contrast, in pre- and early colonial times, a properly installed chief had the literal power of life and death over his people, and his *mana* was manifest at once in his people's prosperity and in his warriors' victory in war; a truly powerful chief struck terror into his followers according to the strength of his warlike attributes and his carnal appetites. But more of this below.

In the developmental cycle of love, as it emerges from an analysis of representations of what is appropriate at different stages of life, compassion and desire are mutually constituting. *Veilomani*, whose paradigmatic reference is mutual compassion between kin within the hierarchical household, comes into being as the ultimate artefact of the passion of *veidomoni*, which can only describe mutual desire between cross-cousins as equals across households. Thus *loloma* (compassion) and *dodomo* (desire) are opposite ends of a continuum of meaning in which each can be seen to be the grounds of the possibility of the other. This analysis can be extended into the religious domain, for, according to one preacher, the Christian God has both *loloma* and *dodomo* for his people: 'God wants to put a wedding ring on your finger.'[6]

Here the Christian God's desire motivates the marriage whereby the congregation become his wives; the marriage constitutes him as the omnipotent husband and father in a vast, hierarchically-ordered household. In this image the Christian God contains within himself the creative tension between *loloma* and *dodomo*, and makes both aspects inform his relation to people. Thus he takes on something of the nature of the old Fijian Gods – in their benign aspect, 'the founding Gods' (*na kalou vu*, lit. 'origin Gods') or 'the ancestors' (*na qase e liu*, lit. 'the old ones before'), and in their malign aspect 'devils' (*tevoro*). Despite this covert suggestion of syncretism in the imagery of the Christian God's love for humanity, Fijians are able to assert their practice to be eminently Christian. This is because, in an earlier Fijian

cosmology, *mana* was manifest less in compassion than in the
violence of desire; and compassionate love was rendered a
fugitive by-product of a violent and cosmogonic carnal desire.

Cosmogonic Desire

Carnal desire was focused in orality as much as in sexuality. To
consume a sacrifice demonstrated the power of the consumer; the
efficacy, the *mana*, of Gods and chiefs was constituted and
expressed in sacrifice. So Sahlins argues that, in myth, the origin
of cannibalism is also the origin of culture, and that in his
installation a chief becomes at once the feeder of the people and
their food (Sahlins 1983). These ideas are also present in the
following story of Tui DelaiGau, King of the Heights of Gau (for
the original, see the monograph by the Methodist missionary,
Waterhouse 1978 [1866]: 379–83).

> At odds with their fellow villagers, two men decide not to attend the
> games at Muana [a promontory near Sawaieke]. Angry at this, their
> wives go alone to the games. The two men go to picnic elsewhere on
> the coast and there, while looking for landcrabs to eat with their root
> vegetables, they see a handsome and gigantic man coming towards
> them.
>   When he reaches the beach this man says, 'Arms, go and bathe'
> and the arms detach themselves and go to wash. Having thus
> instructed all his body parts, his head goes up into a tree until the
> parts return and reassemble. Seeing he is a God, the two men follow
> him to the top of the highest mountain in Gau, where he ascends
> into a tree.
>   Next morning the two men take a large root of *yaqona* and present
> it formally at the foot of the tree. The God appears and asks what
> they want. The bolder man replies that, having seen and recognized
> his power, they want him to adopt them as his children and become
> their God. The God is pleased and tells them to prepare *yaqona* for
> him. When he has drunk, he summons from the tree a spade, which
> begins on its own to dig an oven. The men are terrified. The God
> calls down cooking stones, and wood which ignites itself and heats
> the stones. When the oven is ready, the God asks which of the two
> men is to be cooked and eaten. The bolder one says he is, leaps into
> the oven, is covered by leaves that pour from the tree and earth that
> is heaped up on the oven by the spade.

Later the God says that all is cooked and calls the spade to open the oven. In it are piles of mats and barkcloth, and under them the man, who jumps out quite unharmed. The God gives the two men all this property and they go home. The next day they return with the product of their own labours – four large baskets of fish, which they leave under the tree as a thank-offering.

The next day the two men go to the games and are insulted by the crowd because they are not well-dressed. One goes to the centre of the dancing-ground, announces that he will make a feast for the chief, and calls above for a spade to dig an oven. A spade descends as before, and the man imitates all the God's commands. His fellow, who was before the onlooker, leaps into the oven, which is covered with earth by the spade. The man then goes to bathe, and returns dressed in the beautiful cloth given him by the God. He calls for the spade to open the oven, revealing a vast number of mats and under them the other man, now dressed superbly in barkcloth with white cowrie shells on his arms and ankles. The property is carried formally to the chief and then the men go home. They have been preceded by their wives and are followed home by other women who also want to marry them, but their wives drive these women away, saying they want no polygamous marriages.

Here the two men's augmented effectiveness results from their willingness to attend on one who is greater than they are, even to the extent of becoming his food. By sacrificing themselves to the God, they are able to become like chiefs. This is evinced by the beauty of their new clothing for, in pre- and early colonial Fiji, the length of a chief's barkcloth train signified his rank, and by the cowrie shells, also a mark of chiefly rank, that adorn the second man's arms and legs. The God's *mana* is manifest in his acts and, more importantly, in the men's very willingness to attend on and to obey him. Cosmogonic power is prefigured by the God's ability to dis-member and recreate himself as a new whole; the men's sacrifices oblige him to manifest his power on their behalf.

One current idiom for witchcraft is *sova yaqona*, lit. 'pouring *yaqona*', which is supposed to take place behind closed doors or in the bush. One who wishes to gain a magical efficacy performs *yaqona* ritual alone, pours a libation to an ancestor God, and asks his aid; the person then has to name a close relative as a sacrifice to the God; the naming itself effects the sacrifice. The God then gives his follower what he or she wants. In the story of Tui DelaiGau the two men offer *yaqona* to the God and his acceptance of it is followed by his asking which one of them will become his food. Here the interplay of kinship and oral desire becomes crucial, for the men had asked not only to be allowed to attend on the God, but to become his children. In the Fiji of cannibal sacrifices, the eating of one's close kin was *tabu* and said to cause one's teeth to fall out. The men became the God's children when he accepted their offering of *yaqona*. Thus when the bolder man volunteers to become his food, he shows himself to be truly subordinate even while he relies on the God's compassion for one who is now his son.[7] This man is then able to provide for his own kin, as is his fellow who enters the oven dug on the dancing-ground. There is no malign act of witchcraft here; the story reveals the compassion that a good father, a good God and, by implication, a good chief has for those who augment his power by willingly attending on him and doing as he says.

So when the oven is opened, its contents have become those of a grave whose occupant is still living. Today, as in old Fiji, a dead body is dressed, wrapped in barkcloth and fine mats and buried in a grave lined with mats. The grave is dug on *yavusa* or clan gardening land and, when it is filled, the earth is heaped up on it and banked with stones or, today, covered with a concrete platform. In appearance it is a miniature *yavu*, house foundation. In earlier days, and apparently especially in the case of chiefs, the corpse was interred in the house foundation itself. The ancestors are *kalou vu*, 'founding Gods', and the term *yavu* is the base for *yavusa*. That the benign Tui Delaigau has truly adopted the two men as his children is plain in his acceptance of their sacrificial tribute and in his raising them, still alive, from the oven – here made analogous at once to the grave and the house foundation.

House foundations are private to those who have rights in them, and should not be walked across, even if they are not built upon; their names are permanent. The varying height of remaining house foundations still signifies the status of those who live in the houses built on them. Those that are *yavu tabu*, 'forbidden house foundations' are usually situated in the bush on clan and *yavusa* gardening land; their names form the honorific titles of clan and *yavusa* chiefs.

At the outset of the story of Tui DelaiGau the two men hardly appear to be heads of households; their wives are able angrily to defy them and to go off to the games alone. Indeed the women neglect to provide, as is their duty, the *i coi* (the meat, fish or other element of a meal) to go with the cooked vegetables already provided by the men. By the end of the story, having shown themselves to be *mana* – 'effective', the men go home to wives who have, rightly, preceded them; what is implied is that the women will now attend properly on their husbands. The two men are followed by other women, who want too to become willing wifely subordinates. That the men's wives shoo away the other women, saying they want no polygamous marriages, is perhaps the missionary's flourish, but it also suggests that their initial disrespect for their husbands was warranted, and so they can rely on their husbands' forbearance. A wife is *obliged* to attend on her husband only so long as he shows himself deservedly able to command her.

Thus the god's cosmogonic act in transforming the oven at once into grave and house foundation makes it possible for the men, via their marriages, to become the heads of effective, hierarchically ordered households – households in which husbands and wives fulfil their reciprocal obligations to one another, and wives are seen to attend on their husbands.[8]

In the story of Tui DelaiGau, the God's oral desires are overt: the men give him *yaqona* to drink and their own bodies to eat; that he does not eat them does not alter the fact that his *mana* is constituted in the consumption of sacrifices. The great baskets of fish that the men leave as a thank-offering are substitutes for their own bodies and for human bodies in general; men whose clan is that of fishermen (*gone dau* or *kai wai*, lit. 'seapeople') were, in old Fiji, also often warriors, fishers of men, who provided human sacrifices for both Gods and chiefs. Here the satisfaction of the God's oral desires is ultimately constitutive of the ordered hierarchical household.

The story of the *yavu* (house foundation) called *Na i vinivini* – a great mound covered with stones that stands near the sea front of Sawaieke village – also shows how oral and sexual desire can be *mana*, effective. It was told me by a Sawaieke chief whom I asked to tell me some stories of 'earlier times' (*na gauna e liu*); here I give an outline of it.

> At that time Sawaieke country was led by Ravuravu (Killer With a Club – a warrior God, one of the earliest Sawaieke ancestors). The people went to serve him at his hilltop dwelling near the shore. He was always cold, and they had to drag firewood up there; whole

trees like the *dawa*, mango and chestnut were consumed in warming him.

Then a war began between Sawaieke village and one of its tributary villages, Nukuloa. Nukuloa sent a man to ask the help of Radikedike, who was chief of Bua (in Vanua Levu – an island to the north of Gau). He came to help Nukuloa, but by chance he entered through the reef at the opening near Sawaieke and mistook the *tavola* tree that marked Ravuravu's dwelling for one that was supposed to show where the Nukuloa chief lived.

He came ashore and climbed up the hill, but when he got there no one took any notice of him and he could see he was not expected. Radikedike had brought 100 chestnuts which hung from his arm. He wanted to roast and eat some of his chestnuts, so he went to the house of Ravuravu and asked him for some firewood. Ravuravu said that if he could carry the firewood away, then he was welcome to it, and was astonished to see his visitor take up a whole tree, strip off its leaves and take it away – a tree that had taken fifty Sawaieke people to drag it up the hill. He said to himself 'I am getting old, I shall give him the country, hand it over to him so that he may lead it.'

So Ravuravu made way for Radikedike. But Radikedike was always wanting women and so asked that he might build his *yavu* at the spot where the ladies ceased to sing *meke* songs on their way home from reef-fishing. So he built his house foundation, *Naivinivini*, there at that spot, which later became the new site of Sawaieke village.

Here, in proper Fijian fashion, an ageing but still powerful chief, recognizing a stranger's *mana*, makes him leader of the country. Ravuravu's warlike power is waning, for he has always to be warmed by fire, but the size of the fruit-bearing trees that are consumed in warming him shows his power has still to be reckoned with.[9] Radikedike is in his prime; the man who told me the story said, 'He carried here 100 chestnuts . . . huge chestnuts – but if 100 hung from his arm, what about the size of this chief, this victorious chief?' Radikedike wants firewood, not to spend its fruitfulness in stoking a passion for war, but to roast chestnuts. The chestnuts denote his own fruitfulness, as well as his strength, and eating them gives him the heat that is proper to men, the heat that makes a man desire women.[10]

The leadership of Radikedike and the attendance of the Sawaieke people upon him is implicit in their allowing him to build his *yavu* at the spot where the women ceased to sing as they came home from fishing – the story suggests that he took many wives; moreover, it was in relation to Radikedike's *yavu* that the new village took shape. Today, the house foundations of the old village said to have been under the sway of Ravuravu can still be seen at some distance from the present village of Sawaieke, as can the impressive mound of Radikedike, which stands to one side of the village, beside the road.

In the stories above, the Gods' manifest powers are benign. Tui DelaiGau desires to drink *yaqona* and to eat men and, in return for the men's sacrificial tribute, presents them with superb goods; these make the men both providers of valuables and, implicitly, sexually powerful; so they become effective husbands and household heads. Radikedike, in return for being allowed ready access to many women, accepts the leadership of the country and so enables Sawaieke to retain its paramount position.

Devilish Desire

A husband's legitimate sexual desire for his wife is expressed not as *dodomo* (passionate love) but as the desire to eat what is his, *sa via kania na kena*. When people refer to the old Gods as *tevoro*, 'devils', they are usually referring to the Gods' sexual or oral desire to consume humans. *Ko-i-rau-na-marama*, The Two Ladies, are known for both their sexual and cannibal appetites. In Sawaieke they are said to be ancestors of the chiefly *yavusa* Nadawa. They were implicated in one of the two cases of suggested witchcraft that occurred during my time in the field. A man in his late 30s had an apparently incurable illness – one that did not respond to herbal remedies or prolonged Western medical treatment. Speaking of this man's illness, a woman of chiefly birth, aged about 30, said to me:

> It is because of our ancestor Gods; it has been a long time since those two devil women, our ancestor Gods, have appeared. They were seen before Y married and again before Z married [this being at least 16 years earlier]. Perhaps someone is attending on them, someone wants this man to die.

She said that the sick man was plagued by visions (*rai votu*) of The Two Ladies, who took the form of chiefly women whom he knew. Once he heard them say, 'Come, let us throw X outside that he may be killed'; he was sure then that witchcraft had caused his illness, for the ancestor Gods are not usually supposed to act on their own. Speaking of this case, the chief who told me the story of Radikedike's mound, said:

> Those two can't just go and kill a person. There is a reason for it, it may be that someone is doing something in order to kill X. They can't just kill people [on their own account]. Their *yavu* is in the old village at Nadragugasau. Someone has prepared *yaqona* and asked them to do something, perhaps to kill him. Actually they [The Two Ladies] were here last week. My younger brother understood; he was angry, our house smelled bad. He said to me he knew the meaning of it; he was angry – nowadays it's not liked.

In cases of witchcraft-induced illness, an effective cure requires *yaqona* to be drunk in a ceremony where the *dauvagunu* – 'giver of drink' – prepares the *yaqona* and calls on the winds to beg the ancestor God to remove the curse; sometimes he or she places a *tabua* (whalestooth) on a Bible and calls on Jesus Christ as well as on the ancestor God; but whatever the specific form of the ceremony, the tributary offering of *yaqona* is essential.

In the course of the *yaqona*-drinking accompanying a wedding, the man referred to as Z in the woman's remarks above (a married man in his mid-40s) told me, unprompted, about his encounter, about 16 years before, with The Two Ladies. He was returning alone from his gardens when he saw two women whom he greeted politely, though he did not know them; they greeted him in return and began a flirtatious dialogue, remarking on his coming marriage and saying that he would be better off to marry them, at which point he realized they were devils and fell in a faint to the ground. He woke up hours later, knowing that had he gone with them, they would have consumed him.[11] In Sawaieke one can detect their invisible presence by a bad smell for which there is no usual explanation; this smell may hang in the house for days, but one must not remark on it, for if one does The Two Ladies will be offended and misfortune – illness or even death – will strike the household.[12]

The old Gods are held still to visit their malign power upon people and, specifically, to be eager to consume them sexually and orally; to dream of having sexual intercourse is to know that one has been possessed by a God. Several times young women told me they had been visited during their sleep by Daucina (The Lamp-Bearer) in the form of a handsome young man. This God haunts coastlines and possesses women who are foolish enough to bathe alone after dark – a warning of his likely presence is often the subject of a joke directed towards a woman who bathes late. I never heard men's dreams or behaviour in bathing similarly remarked on, though men often say that one of the praiseworthy attributes of *yaqona* is that it ensures a dreamless sleep – which suggests that they are as ambivalent about their dreams as young women seem to be.[13] Young men also tell tales about two female devils (perhaps a manifestation of The Two Ladies) often seen dancing in a Suva nightclub – one frequented by villagers on holiday in the capital. Young men have been attracted by their beauty to dance with them, only to realize that they had to be *tevoro* – devils – because their feet did not touch the floor when they danced. The association between sexual intercourse and European-style dancing in nightclubs suggests that these female devils intend to seduce the young men.

That the old Gods are still killers (and cannibals) is implicit in a tale about the first children to board at the Gau Junior Secondary School; the ancestral owner of the site is said to have been angry at the people's temerity in building there (in spite of previous *yaqona* ceremonies to placate his wrath) and to have attacked the children, who woke in terror in the night to find this 'devil' on their chests, trying to choke the life out of them. More ceremonies had to be performed. Thus the old Gods still inhabit the places where once they ruled, though their power is diminished, 'because no one attends on them any more'.

The Coming of the Light

Attendance on a God or a chief is what actually empowers him. Here one may contrast the story of Radikedike's *yavu* with that of the founding of Sawaieke village as it is today. I was told this story several times; the version below is that of a well-educated commoner in his 60s, much respected for his past achievements and his devout Christianity:

Before, the people of this village did not live together in the manner of kinship [*vakaveiwekani*]. No. Each little village stood alone and

there were many quarrels and fights between them . . . During the
old time, in the time of the devils [*gauna vakatevoro*], the church came
here; civilization came here. It brought the light to us [*vakararamataki
keimami*]. Before, all the old villages on this piece of coastline had
stood alone; then they wanted to be nearer each other because if all
the villages moved here it would make easier their attendance on
one another [*veiqaravi* lit. 'facing each other' – their mutual ritual
obligations].

The owners of this village, of this land, were *yavusa* Sawaieke –
Nakorolevu eh? [The Big Village, a name for *yavusa* Sawaieke]. They
called the people of the little villages to come here: 'Takalaigau, come
here' – and they came; 'Tui Navure, come here' – and they came.
And the Voda people came too. The Buli [officer of the colonial
administration, usually a traditional chief] decided that house-
building should begin. Then they built the church and this was the
beginning of true kinship.

Other versions did not mention the Buli, but all agree that the
church brought forth the present village of Sawaieke. *Yavusa*
Sawaieke, whose chief instals (and some say selects) the
paramount, invited the chiefly *yavusa* denoted by Takalaigau to
reside on its land along with his landspeople – *yavusa* Navure,
and his fishermen – 'the Voda people'. Both priests (*Bete*) and
warriors (*Bati*) are conspicuously absent. This may be a function
of particular historical conditions, but even so it is fitting that
neither figures in the founding of the new village, where chiefs
and people dwell in harmony in the sight of the Christian God.[14]
For this is no story of cosmogonic carnal desire; rather it recounts
the acts of literally enlightened chiefs whose 'attendance on each
other' implies their concerted attendance on the Christian God.

The story seems to suggest that Christianity imposed an
encompassing hierarchy on 'the little villages'. Before 'the
coming of the light' they had a certain autonomy; they owed
tribute to Sawaieke village, but they might (as Nukuloa did)
hope to rebel and to establish the supremacy of their own Gods
and chiefs. So the old stories may tell of Gods making way for
Gods and chiefs for chiefs – always on account of acts of *mana*
that show them worthy of being 'attended on'. Both Gods and
chiefs were represented as striving to establish paramount
positions, but the relations between chiefs or between chiefs and
people were not fixed, for they were *always and inherently* open to
the challenge given by the equality of cross-cousins, a relation

that is also played out across countries.

Two countries that attend on the same ancestor God are *veitauvu*, 'of the same root'; Sawaieke and Bua are *veitauvu* because of their common attendance on Radikedike. To be *veitabani* is to be 'mutually branching', and relates countries whose ancestors were cross-cousins. These are both joking relationships, like that between cross-cousins. Even where people say that countries *should* be ranked according to their relative positions in a notional hierarchy, they acknowledge that no such ranking is really possible because people would not agree on what it might be. So, when the Provincial Council for Lomaiviti met in 1982, the seating positions of paramount chiefs in the *yaqona*-drinking that accompanied each day's meeting and the ceremonies that marked each night, shifted as if by mutual but probably unspoken consent; it looked as if each of the chiefs was allowing each of the others a turn in the top, central position of paramount authority. This is a product of earlier times when chiefs (and implicitly their Gods) warred against one another to establish their relative statuses and at the same time gave their sisters in marriage to secure the alliance of some possibly rebellious tributary village. But the hierarchy they vied to establish could never be quite secure – at every level it was challenged by the equality residing in balanced exchange between cross-cousins as affines and equals across generation and across households.

Yaqona-drinking, as an integral part of all *cakacaka vakavanua* (lit. 'working/doing/acting in the manner of the land'), seems to fix hierarchy. But a fixed hierarchy can only be momentarily achieved, for the tributary relation it denotes is manifested only in *yaqona* ritual, where the balanced reciprocal relation between *yavusa* chiefs who stand to one another as 'land' and 'sea' is itself suggested by the order of the drinking (see Toren 1990: 90–118). Thus *yaqona* ritual contains the tension between tribute and balanced reciprocity but does not resolve it; the ritual itself becomes the site of the dynamic play of relationships. That it suggests to a European the image of a hierarchically ordered whole, is at once an artefact of European predilections and of the articulation of Christian and indigenous ideas of the relations between humans and gods.

Church teachings, as given in prayers and often in sermons, make Christianity all-encompassing. So the story of the origin of the present village of Sawaieke makes the church the foundation for the acknowledgement of mutual ritual obligations and for the 'true kinship' that is their product. Like most rural churches, Sawaieke's is built to one side of the village green; it is literally and figuratively at the centre of village life. The Christian God is at the peak of the hierarchy of names derived from sacred places, so prayers often address the Christian God as follows: 'To heaven, to the holy dwelling place, you the true God, you the God who alone is served.' Further, the speeches for *sevusevu* (presentation of *yaqona*) to chiefs, while they always begin with a recital of the honorific titles of the chiefs – i.e. the names of their *yavu tabu*, lit. 'forbidden house foundations' – often end by expressing the hope that the following of the chiefs and the Methodist minister might 'grow ever greater'.

Death as Sacrifice

For nearly a century and a half people have attended on the Christian God. He is supernatural in a sense that was not – and is not – true of the old Fijian Gods. The *kalou vu* were different in quality from humans, but not utterly different in kind; their domains were on earth in known places. So the old paradisal island of Burotu could be moved about at will by its spirit inhabitants, on top of or below the waves, and after death the spirit travelled across known territory and encountered spirits whom he or she now resembled in substance (Hocart 1929: 195; Thompson 1940: 115; Williams 1982 [1858]).

The old Gods were more powerful than humans, but an installed chief himself instantiates godly power by virtue of the installation *yaqona*, which in Gau means that an installed Takalaigau 'has at his back all the ancestor Gods of Gau'. In the installation the high chief becomes at once the object of the people's sacrificial offering of *yaqona* and the sacrifice itself, for when he has drunk he is *mate ni yaqona*, lit. 'dead from *yaqona*' (Sahlins 1983). So his effectiveness is rendered paramount: because the people attend on him, their ancestors are compelled to 'stand at his back'. The power of installed chiefs resides in the godly power they instantiate; in the story of Radikedike's *yavu*, Sawaieke emerged triumphant from an impending war with

Nukuloa because its god-chiefs were the more powerful. Winning a war meant that one's own God had (if only temporarily) ousted another.

Today the ancestors are, in their benign aspect, made to attend on the Christian God who, omnipotent and all-knowing, confers chiefship upon men as 'a godly gift' (*na i solisoli vakalou*). So prayers by a church minister are important in chiefly installations, and chiefship seems to have been encompassed by the Christian church. The power to instal a chief is itself held to be from God, even though what is conferred with the chiefship is an efficacy whose source is also ancestral. But chiefly installations are rare, precisely because the chiefship is itself open to competition between clan chiefs within the chiefly *yavusa*.[15]

It is death that makes apparent the power of the Christian God and his relation to the indigenous Gods; the Christian God made the world and everything in it and appointed each thing, including humans, to its proper place.[16] He appointed too the day of each person's death, and so each death is implicitly a sacrifice to the Christian God.

In a description of *reguregu*, the last rites for the dead, that forms part of an account of Fijian traditions for secondary school children, it is written that:

> In their speeches of offering [lit. of 'holding in the hand' – the whalesteeth or other goods presented by mourning kin] they will emphasize how the living look out for one another, and love one another, and they will emphasize in their acceptance and their invocations their earnest wish that death will delay in coming to us, or that this [death] might be the last of our troubles.

But given that, even while one wants to put it off, each death is a sacrifice, one should not be made angry or resentful by it, partly because it is God's will and partly because in being willed by God each death makes kinship relations across groups take on their proper form 'in the manner of the land' (*vakavanua*). Thus in a speech accepting a *sevusevu* (presentation of *yaqona*) that was part of the initial four days of mourning for a high-status man of chiefly birth, the speaker referred to the occasion of the death as 'that morning that God had concealed from us, it happened so that today the chiefly establishment would have to take form . . .'.

Addressing the assembled chiefs who had brought the body from the capital city, Suva, to Sawaieke, he went on to say:

> We know there is a moral that God had already hidden in this day... By coming here, you have met with what stood ready for you [you willingly took on your pre-ordained obligations] – this is just according to the chiefly path followed by *yavusa* Nadawa. You were there to meet the trouble when it arrived, it laid on the burden where it was proper that it should be laid, we are very grateful for that. We know this is a thing from God, it followed you, our chiefs, wherever you went – and so I am praising your coming here.

This idea of predestination is likely to be of Christian origin, for while the old Gods could foretell the future or cause particular states of the future to be brought about – as for example in predicting how many of the other side might be killed in a war – there is no suggestion in the old stories that they caused people's futures to be embodied in them on the day of birth.[17] Here I quote a further speech made on the same occasion; a much-respected man of chiefly status was presenting two fine whalesteeth to the land chiefs whose task it is to preside over the mourning ceremonies for the dead of the chiefly *yavusa*:

> This is a difficult day, a day we had not appointed ... our father on high knows we are met together in kinship this morning in this chiefly establishment. We greatly respect the chiefs' coming here because of our child [chief] who has gone away in atonement and whom you have carried here ... Different tasks are appointed to us by God. Truly he has said, you did not choose me, only I chose you ... His [the dead man's] task in our land is already performed; we should rightly be thankful for it. A good-tempered chief and a determined chief, God has called him, we should rightly be very thankful for it ...

The idea of death as sacrifice pervades the above speeches and, as with a sacrifice to the old Gods, death makes material the relations between collectivities and gives them form; *yaqona*, whalesteeth and food are amassed according to clan or *yavusa* (*vakamataqali, vakayavusa*) and presented as such by their chiefs to the chiefs of the mourning *yavusa*.

Associated with predestination is the idea that the Christian God chooses his own people. In the speech, God's choice refers to the hearers' 'obligations in the manner of the land' (*i tavi vakavanua*); but the wider implications of the words are that in choosing for them their duties, God has also chosen them as his people; certainly they do not choose him. One might contrast this with the old Gods, on whom people may decide to attend; as far as the Christian God is concerned it seems one has no choice in the matter.

That Christianity is inescapable and all-encompassing is contained in an uncompromising view of the necessity of church membership as represented by a young man of 25 or so:

> In the Fijian way, if a person is not a member of a congregation – not a churchgoer – then that person is not a member of a household, not a member of a clan, not a member of a *yavusa* nor a member of a village. The meaning of this is that s/he is not counted as one of the people of this land.

He had asked me about my religious affiliation, and this was his response to my saying that in London I did not go to church. He went on to question the legality of my marriage and my residence in the United Kingdom. Because my husband cannot be described as even nominally Christian and because we are of different nationalities and neither of us is British, my questioner could not credit that either our marriage or our living in London had been properly ratified in any sense with which he was familiar. The young man's demand for consistency in respect of nationality, religious affiliation, marriage and residence was relatively unusual – but it does show how Christianity *can* be held to be an encompassing value.

On first meeting, villagers in Gau always ask foreigners certain stock questions; these concern one's country of origin, whether one is married, how many children one has, and what church one belongs to. One's acceptability as an adult and moral person is predicated upon marriage and Christianity. One cannot deny being a Christian. People are so dismayed. Once, in the company of a group of women, such a denial on my part met with the shocked response: 'So you live just like that – just anyhow?' I felt compelled to add that as a child I was a Catholic, and this brought sighs of relief and a general relaxation in the tension that had resulted from my earlier denial.

Hierarchy, Equality, and Ritual

Church membership constitutes one domain of social relations, and when Christianity is being talked about it seems to be understood to be a superordinate domain and a superordinate value.[18] But this is true too of kinship and chiefship; it all depends on which domain of relations is presently being made the focus of ritual or discussion. Behaviour according to the church (*vakalotu*), to kinship (*vakaveiwekani*), to chiefs (*vakaturaga*) and to the land (*vakavanua*) are mutually constituting; and in each domain, relations which are either hierarchical or equal are the very grounds of the possibility of the opposing form. In respect of the processes of daily life, any given person is the locus of both the equal and unequal relations which constitute the different domains.

In personal experiential terms, the relation between cross-cousins is essential for passionate relations across sex and for intimate, friendly camaraderie within sex, and is highly valued for these reasons. One can demand anything of a cross-cousin and one should never refuse him or her anything, for one's cross-cousins give zest to life; in other words, this competitive relation between equals is valued as highly as the hierarchical relation between siblings or between parent and child, and is the basis for the possibility of marriage which, in daily domestic life, is constituted as *the* crucial hierarchical relationship.

In their ritual practice Fijians succeed momentarily in the struggle to contain the equal, competitive relation between cross-cousins, and the threat of disorder it sometimes represents, within the bounds of hierarchical kinship. That this struggle is in principle unending is a product of the fact that all dynamic, fertile and affective processes are *founded* in the relation between cross-cousins. Fijians represent social relations in terms, not of fixed structures, but of certain ways of behaving – the chiefly way, the way of kinship, of the land, of the church, of the government, of the law; in so far as each way is associated with certain ritual behaviour (*yaqona*-drinking, meals, life-cycle ceremonies, church services, village council meetings and so on) this behaviour projects particular images of social relations as fixed structures: tributary relations between chiefs and people in *yaqona*-drinking, hierarchical kinship within the household as a commensal unit, the community either as the children of God's cosmic household in church services, or, in council meetings, as the children of chiefs.

But ritual can only momentarily fix social relations as hierarchical, for ultimately, given that all Fijian ritual has recourse to the imagery of the household as the foundation (*yavu*) of all social relations, they suggest too the hidden imagery of the balanced, reciprocal relations between cross-cousins across households, and the dynamic of their sexuality, which is at once permitted and threatening. For the household depends for its very existence on the relations between cross-cousins, who alone can bring into being a new household or ensure the continuance of an existing one.

Today Christianity is taken to be one with 'the Fijian way', and thus *seems* to be an encompassing value. But 'the Fijian way' is being forged in contradistinction to 'the European way', or 'the way of money' (see Toren 1989). The contrast operates on difference and hierarchical value in such a way that all that is morally proper is associated with the Fijian way and all that is amoral with Europeans; but if we bring the church into this ideal international contrast it inevitably mediates it by introducing likeness and equality – Fijians as a Christian people alongside other Christian peoples – and suggests relations across boundaries, which are always, at least initially, like relations between cross-cousins. From this perspective Christianity too can be seen as yet another product of the dynamic, cosmogonic play of competition and desire that for Fijians fuels the competitive relations between households, countries, nations, peoples, and underlies their very existence. Here the play of value between dynamic equality and static hierarchy is pushed out beyond the bounds of nations theoretically to encompass the cosmos, where desire and compassion become dual aspects of a new, Fijian, formulation of Christianity.

Notes

This article was substantially revised and rewritten during my 1992–3 tenure of the Research Fellowship in the Politics of Tradition in the Pacific, funded by Macquarie University and the Australian Research Council.

1. Fieldwork in Fiji occupied 20 months in 1981–3 (funded by an SSRC Studentship and the Horniman Trust) and four months in 1990 (funded by a Brief Award from Brunel University). In 1990, the chiefly village of Sawaieke had a shifting population of around 270 and Sawaieke country (*vanua ko Sawaieke* – all eight villages) had a population of about 1500. The economy is mixed subsistence (gardening and small numbers of pigs, cows and poultry) and cashcropping, *yaqona* being the most lucrative crop. Fiji Indians make up almost half the population of Fiji, but on smaller islands like Gau the population is often almost entirely Fijian.

2. In Fiji, hierarchy is what Dumont would call a 'value' and is routinely evinced in people's disposition *vis-à-vis* one another in the internal space of any building inside the village. These internal spaces have mapped on to them a spatial axis whose poles are given by the terms 'above' and 'below' (in reference to a *single* plane); people of higher status are always seated above those of lower status. So, when gathered together in any space, villagers are always seated such that their relative status (derived from an interaction between rank, gender and seniority) is apparent. This and other ritualized behaviours have led analysts such as Hocart and Sahlins to describe Fijian hierarchy as if it is Dumontian in form – that is to say, as if 'chiefliness' is the ultimate encompassing value in a hierarchy of values where an opposition between 'chiefs' and 'people' generates all other sets of binary opposing values. I argue that, on the contrary, hierarchy in Fijian social relations can never become an encompassing value because it is always and inevitably opposed by competitive equality as an equally important and antithetical value. My argument for this thesis is prefigured in Toren (1990) and directly addressed in Toren (1994).

3. One may marry someone to whom no actual kin relation can be traced, but in this case the in-marrying spouse, usually the wife, learns to address her husband's kin *as if* the two of them had been cross-cousins before marriage; anyone he calls sibling she calls cross-cousin, anyone he calls cross-cousin she calls sibling, etc.

4. From the analyst's point of view, male violence in the early years of marriage may be attributed to any one of a number of causes; however, it seems significant that jealousy is the most usual reason given by Fijian villagers.

5. The *yavusa* is made up of clans that are closely connected by affinal and ritual-cum-political ties. In pre-colonial times the *yavusa* was co-terminous with the village; today Sawaieke contains five *yavusa*.

6. This observation was made by Pamela Peck, who worked in Lovu, another village in the *vanua* of Sawaieke, and is quoted in her doctoral thesis (Peck 1982).

7. One could not eat close kin; cross-cousins might be close kin, so in earlier days marriage was allowed only between second cross-cousins (a notion that is still in force in many parts of Fiji, but not in Sawaieke). The marriage taboo itself suggests the degree of relationship where 'eating' might perhaps begin, so there is a covert suggestion here that the god is initially to be thought of as perhaps a cross-cousin to the two men. But the god's manifest *mana* is such that the men cannot approach him as his peers, for then he might eat them; they disavow the possibility of cross-cousinship and opt for the hierarchical parent–child relationship.

8. The very dwelling of Tui DelaiGau implicates the domestic life; his home is reported by Waterhouse to be 'a very lofty cowrie-tree'; this is the *dakua*, which grows to great heights and whose wood was used for many everyday and yet important purposes. Thus Seeman says, '*Dakua* is used for mats, booms, spars, for flooring houses and for all those purposes for which deal is usually employed by us.' He also reports that its gum was burned as a torch, or used to fuel lamps, and that a dye made from the burning gum was used for the hair, for printing barkcloth, and for tattooing the skin of women not of chiefly clans (Seeman 1862: 358–60).

9. Heat is associated with anger and thus with a warlike spirit. The old Fijian gods often had their abode in trees, and the nature of the tree and its uses always accords with the nature of the God who lives there, or whose dwelling is marked by the tree's proximity. A *tavola* tree marks Ravuravu's dwelling; its wood is used to make the great slit drums with which, in pre- and early colonial times, the people of one group might challenge another to war and beat out the rhythms of their success in killing and eating the enemy (Clunie 1977: 25, 27; Seeman 1862: 363).

10. Sexual desire in men manifests as heat; so during the football season young men are strictly forbidden 'to go with'

girls lest they lose their strength – football practice being referred to as *vakatakata*, lit. 'making hot'. A full analysis of the myth of Radikedike's *yavu* is to be found in Toren (1995).

11. His tale accords with one related by Waterhouse (1978 [1866]: 387–8), where the Two Ladies are said maliciously to kill all solitary travellers in revenge for having been poorly treated by the people of Vione (a Gau village – not part of the *vanua* of Sawaieke), whose chief one of them had married and to whom she had born a son.

12. Shortly after I was told about this I remarked on it in conversation with a young man of 23, unthinkingly telling him that oddly enough, I had noticed a bad smell in my own house during the previous few days and been unable to find out what was causing it. He was clearly angry that I had referred to it, and hissed at me *sotto voce* not to talk about it; 'Those two will hear you', he said.

13. Dreams are often accorded validity in that they are considered either to be 'messages' from God or the ancestors or to be 'out of the body' experiences. See Herr (1981).

14. *Yavusa* Koviko, which traditionally supplied both priests and/or warriors to the Sawaieke chiefs had, for many years before this story was told me, been subsumed as a clan (*mataqali*) within the chiefly *yavusa* Nadawa; it was reconstituted as a *yavusa* in its own right during the period of my first fieldwork in 1982.

15. Thus I was told by a high-status man of chiefly birth past middle age (one who was an interested party in respect of the paramount chiefship of Sawaieke, even though he was rather too young to be given that office): 'You see here we have Takalaigau [title of paramount chief of Sawaieke country] but he has not drunk, the power has not been given to him. But that will just be up to Raitena [the elders and especially the chief of Sawaieke *yavusa*]. If they will see that he is a good chief, that he cares for the country, they will not delay in making him drink . . . The previous Takalaigau went around all the villages in an effort to make it so that if someone was to be installed as paramount [*Tui*], this country [i.e. all eight villages] should be of one voice. If not, each one will just go its own way. In the manner of the land, the status of one who is installed is such that he is promised the people,

the earth, the grass, that he may be their only leader. This [present situation in Sawaieke] is called the *Sauvi* – meaning to be marked down or to stand waiting. Here Sawaieke is just marked down, waiting . . . I understand that Europeans also install the Prime Ministers of governments like that.'

16. The old gods are held to have created particular areas in Fiji and to have given form to the country itself. It may be that the Christian God delegated to them this task, or that they indeed formed the land and the Christian God revealed himself later as the true source of their power; I have heard both views expressed by different people, and on two different occasions by the same person.

17. The ancestors are the source of one's identity as a member of a particular clan, etc.; they are also often said to be the source of various powers, abilities, etc. with which people are born, but this refers to what particular ancestral sources can pass on to their own descendants; these are not notions of predestination.

18. Virtually all Fijians (as opposed to Fiji Indians) are practising Christians, the overwhelming majority being Wesleyans; 'the church' (*na lotu*) denotes Christianity in general. Sawaieke villagers held explicitly that while they were all Wesleyans, other forms of Christian practice were perfectly acceptable; what was important was that one professed oneself to be of some Christian denomination. For accounts of early missionary activity in Fiji, see, for example Williams (1982 [1858]), Clammer (1976). Missionary success was assured when the powerful paramount chief Cakobau converted to Wesleyanism in 1854; his conversion (like that of lesser paramounts) led to mass conversions by those who were subject to him. Calvert (1982 [1858]: 401) quoted in Geddes (1948: 334) claimed 54,000 conversions by 1856 – one-third of the population. Cf. Burton (1910: 127), who described the Fiji of his times as only 'nominally' Christian – despite its 80,000 Methodists in a total population of 86,000 Fijians.

References

Burton, J. W. (1910). *The Fiji of Today.* Charles Kelly, London.

Calvert, J. (1982 [1858]). *Fiji and the Fijians,* Vol. 2. Mission History, Fiji Museum, Suva.

Clammer, J. R. (1976). *Literacy and Social Change.* E. J. Brill, Leiden.

Clunie, Fergus (1977). *Fijian Weapons and Warfare.* Fiji Museum, Suva.

Geddes, W. R. (1948). An Analysis of Cultural Change in Fiji. Unpublished Ph.D. thesis, London School of Economics and Political Science.

Herr, B. (1981). The Expressive Character of Fijian Dream and Nightmare Experiences. *Ethos,* 9, 331–52.

Hocart, A. M. (1929). Lau Islands, Fiji. *Bernice P. Bishop Museum Bulletin,* 62. Honolulu.

Peck, P. J. (1982). Missionary Analogues: The Descriptive Analysis of a Development Aid Program in Fiji. Ph.D. Thesis, University of British Columbia.

Sahlins, Marshall (1983). Raw Women, Cooked Men and Other 'Great Things' of the Fiji Islands. In: P. Brown and D. Tuzin (eds), *The Ethnography of Cannibalism,* Special Publication, Society for Psychological Anthropology. The Society.

Seeman, Bertholdt (1862). *Viti: An Account of a Government Mission to the Vitian or Fijian Islands.* Macmillan, Cambridge.

Thompson, L. M. (1940). Southern Lau, Fiji: An Ethnography. *Bernice P. Bishop Museum Bulletin,* 162. Honolulu.

Toren, Christina (1988). Making the Present, Revealing the Past: The Mutability and Continuity of Tradition as Process. *Man,* 23, 696–717.

—— (1989). Drinking Cash: The Purification of Money in Ceremonial Exchange in Fiji. In: J. Parry and M. Bloch (eds), *Money and Morality.* Cambridge University Press, Cambridge.

—— (1990). *Making Sense of Hierarchy. Cognition as Social Process in Fiji,* London School of Economics Monographs in Social Anthropology, 61. Athlone Press, London.

—— (1994). All Things Go in Pairs or the Sharks Will Bite: The Antithetical Nature of Fijian Chiefship. *Oceania,* 64, 3: 197–216.

—— (1994). Transforming Love – Representing Fijian Hierarchy. In: P. Gow and P. Harvey (eds), *Sex and Violence. Issues in representation and experience.* Routledge, London.

—— (1995). Seeing the Ancestral Sites: Transformations in Fijian Notions of the Land. In: E. Hirsch and M. O'Hanlon (eds), *Anthropology of the Landscape.* Clarendon Press, Oxford.

Waterhouse, J. (1978 [1866]). *The King and the People of Fiji.* AMS, New York.

Williams, Thomas (1982 [1858]). *Fiji and the Fijians* (ed. G. S. Rowe). Fiji Museum, Suva.

Chapter 3

An Essay on the Symbolic Construction of Memory in the Kaluli *Gisalo*[1]

Nancy D. Munn

La mémoire est l'invention de conduites particulières relatives a l'absence, destinées à triompher des objets absents et des hommes absents . . .

Janet (1928:231)

Introduction

In some of his most telling passages about the social construction of memory, Halbwachs (1950)[2] develops his argument by establishing a narrative space within which persons move, reminding each other of past events. This space with its objects is not merely a 'container'. Traversed by persons and events of a subject's or collectivity's past, the space encodes these traversals as meanings capable of actively engaging in the mnemonic process. Halbwachs frequently returns us in one form or another to this vision of remembering in which persons, objects and spaces external to the subject enter into consciousness as mnemonic agencies. In this aspect of Halbwach's work, there is, as Duvignaud (1950: xi) points out,the sense of an 'ensemble', a co-ordination of elements. Remembering is shown emerging in and through this ensemble.

The present analysis of a particular mode and arena of memory construction among the Kaluli of the Great Papuan Plateau in Papua New Guinea's Southern Highlands is also concerned with remembering as a relational process, but in a more complex sense. On the one hand, we shall see different ways in which the mind itself is being constituted as a social space–time or virtual landscape. The source of this landscape is an actual, lived landscape invested with consociative relations or meanings, which is being symbolically 'detached' from its spatiotemporal locus (Basso 1988: 102; cf. Munn 1986: 117), and reconstituted in the mind by the mnemonic agency of songs. On the other hand, this mental space–time is being formed through and encompassed within the space–time of the immediate consociative context – the people, location, and generalized media of these specific mnemonic transactions. The entire ensemble of social, spatial and temporal relations being created *and the mnemonic process of creating them* define what I take to be the symbolic field of the 'present', with its particular modes of incorporating both relevant pasts and the sense of their pastness into experience. The overall formulation of the relations characterizing this symbolic (spatiotemporal) field is the level at which the problematics of Kaluli remembering – i.e., its tensions and contradictions in this particular context – are implicated and can be analysed.

The Kaluli example illustrates that kind of memory Husserl (1964) called 'recollection' rather than 'primary remembrance', since it entails conscious representation of the past, and not simply the ongoing engagement of the past within present moments operating below the level of consciousness. Furthermore, in contrast say to Bergson's (1988: 80ff.) 'habit memory', the memory's content is not divested of its quality of being past: instead, the pastness of the contents remembered is integral to the memory in the present. Thus we deal with the well-known contradiction of memory as an attempt to draw what 'no longer exists' (Augustine of Hippo 1960: 288) into the 'now' of the present. My subject pertains in particular to certain more intense efforts at 'reliving . . . from within' (Casey 1987: 109) in which, as we shall see, the contradictions of remembering seem most radically construed.

The aims of this paper are thus twofold. On the one hand, it examines some aspects of the cultural dynamics of remembering in one Melanesian example of collective practices involving, in this case, a deliberate effort on the part of some people to make others remember certain past relationships. On the other hand, I use the analysis of these particularities to address certain general issues familiar in the academic literatures concerned with memory, and to suggest a model in which such broad phenomenological conditions and dimensions of human societies as spatio-temporality, sociality and mnemonic processes are drawn into a unitary analytic framework for talking about the construction of remembering.

The Kaluli *Gisalo*

The world inhabited by the Kaluli is framed by the tropical forest; within its dark cover they clear areas for their longhouses and swidden gardens, hunt, and extract sago from palms growing by the many streams that configure the forested landscape (Schieffelin 1976: 29ff.). Kaluli longhouse communities (each usually including more than one patrilineal clan) tend to shift around within a limited part of the longhouse territory (ibid.: 40). The longhouse set in a clearing; current garden clearings; the remains of previous gardens and longhouse locations; and the dark forest with its waterfall pools thus provide fundamental spaces of Kaluli existence.

A notable feature of Kaluli society is the concern with arousing biographical memories[3] of past co-presence with absent others – sometimes a currently absent person, but prototypically, the dead – through the medium of a song genre depicting place-named forested scenes of the Kaluli landscape; these scenes convey the presence of nameless actors who travel through them. Kaluli sing these songs in major exchange feasts and séances; women's 'sung weeping' (Feld 1982: 129) also employs the basic song genre at burials, but has a different relation to the biographies of singers than the *Gisalo* dance singing discussed here; the latter is performed in Kaluli longhouses by male visitors participating in major exchanges between different longhouse groups.

Since Kaluli say, 'song is in your head' (Feld 1982: 160) or 'mind' (*asugo*, Schieffelin, personal communication), we may think of these songs as creating virtual social landscapes in the mind that are being transacted from the interior (*sa*) of the singer to that of the listener. The Kaluli term for head, *mise*, (Feld, pers. comm.), is also the general term for surface appearance;[4] we shall see later that Kaluli construal of visible appearance as an exterior surface creating interiorized spatializations of hidden (inside, *sa*, or underneath, *hega*) elements or spaces ramifies to form a fundamental Kaluli structuring of 'presence'.

Songs innovated for each such event by the dancer-singers are intended to 'ferret out' (Schieffelin 1976: 183; 1979: 130) male and female hosts in the audience who have lived associations with now absent others (especially the dead) at the places named in the songs. Although the hosts may feel that their attention is 'caught' by the song, they are also actively 'searching' (Schieffelin, pers. comm.) to establish connections it may have to their own memories. Thus listeners are not simply hunting among the prior contents of their own minds for something they are trying to recollect (cf. Yates 1966: 34, on Aristotle), but simultaneously in the generalized content of the song produced within the mind of a visitor, an outside 'other' (who should not be too well-known to the hosts, Schieffelin 1976: 166) to see if it indeed evokes their own past experiences. Conversely, the outsider does not compose a song to encode his own biography nor does he necessarily know the personal associations of the place-names he mentions in the *host's* territory. He aims to evoke other people's remembrances (sometimes a specifically intended person, sometimes not), and make them weep (cf. Schieffelin 1976: 178). If remembrances of particular (frequently recent) dead (Feld 1982: 136) are aroused, the rememberers (who might be more than one person per song) are likely to rise in grief and anger to burn the singers: thus they transpose their interior mental pain onto the bodily surface of the outside singer, to pay him back.[5] As we shall see, a complex of transpositions between inside or hidden and outside or visible emerge in the formation of the spatiotemporal field of the present in these transactions.

At a later time, the visitors will receive the current hosts as 'singing detectives' of their own pasts. One's own remembering contains, in effect, the future potential for evoking the remembering of others, as formulaic songs depicting real landscape space circulate against particular biographical memories of past events, and both are transacted between communities.

In addition to their capacity to ferret out memories of particular dead, songs also invite listeners to dwell within them to take sad landscape journeys in the head.[6] Overall, we are dealing with what Poulet (1964: vii) describes as 'an ambient milieu, a field of union' within and between minds that defines in particular ways the relations of subjects – here, both singers and listeners – not only to their own interior being, but also dialectically, to the interior being of others.

Songs as Memory Worlds

If the *Gisalo* songs are not themselves biographical memories, they can nevertheless be seen as what I shall call 'memory worlds'.[7] By this I mean a template realized in verbal or visual genres suited to social circulation. The template *iconically* renders basic culturally informed experiential structures or *principles* of biographical memory, and enables remembering or memory-like experiences. In any given moment of its realization a memory world *may or may not* be identified with a given subject's biographical memory, but it contains the potential for activating particular biographical memories which then themselves take on critical features of the template, and in this sense become 'memory worlds'. Thus, the memory world is a 'metamemory' – a particular kind of iconic language *about* memory – as well as a 'formative' operator that has the capacity to shape the particularized biographical memory; and a mnemonic medium or 'agency' with the capacity to trigger this remembering in given contexts.

To be a 'world' – the model must entail minimally a *mise en scène* – what Casey (1976: 50) calls the 'world frame' of 'imaginative presentation' which 'function[s] in a worldlike way by giving . . . [imagined content] a local habitation' – an *'imaginal space and . . . time'* (emphasis author's). As a virtual 'world' the instantiated model invites subjects to live in it, just as it inhabits their minds as its own locus, constituting mental space–time in its image.[8]

In distinguishing 'biographical memory' and 'memory world', 'I am *not*, of course, contrasting the individual and the social. I assume that biographical memory is culturally/symbolically constituted in its ongoing social production in daily life. In fact, we may infer that public transactions of memory worlds are themselves among the sociocultural processes structuring a Kaluli's biographical memories. However, part of our problem in the case of Gisalo is to understand in what sense the songs are memory worlds, but not biographical memories; and how the move is made in the singing from the former to the latter.

I focus on two critical features that characterize the songs as memory worlds: some aspects of the spatiotemporal frame – in particular the use of place-names, which Kaluli stress; and the mode of constructing social relationships between persons that is typical in the songs.[9]

The song landscape is located by place-names of actual Kaluli localities and concretized with landscape qualities and features such as streams,pools, or trees. Songs focus on places known to residents (or one-time residents) in the region of a Kaluli longhouse. The 'path' (*tok*) sequence of place-names in a song, 'mapping' a section of the Kaluli land, defines a place-to-place movement, evoking the possibility of such movement in the listener's mind (Feld 1982: 151; see also Schieffelin 1976: 183ff.). Songs simulate a unified space and time of the successive movement of persons from place to place. These movements may be indirectly conveyed, as, for example, through the singer rhetorically questioning a generic addressee (or addressees), as in 'Do you see? Do you see the Galinti pool?'(ibid.: 180).

The place-names are the primary clues and 'emotional movers' in the mnemonic leap across the divide of the memory world into biographical memory, from the conventional details of the song to the *recognized* particularity of biography. 'Hearing the names of familiar localities' in the context of songs makes people 'nostalgic and sorrowful ... remind[ing them] ... of the past' (Schieffelin 1979: 130); the sung names seem to be 'effective by themselves' (Schieffelin 1976: 183; 1979: 130) and to propel any necessary further search for specific losses.

We must consider then, the power of place-names[10] to transpose the form of experience from the generalized sense of pastness of the memory world to the particularized and finitely centred modality of 'my past'. This turn is crucial in the conversion of any symbolic form into the form of memory. As the philosopher William Earle (1956: 13–14) has put it:

When I ... remember, I do not *infer* that the past event happened to me, but rather *recognize* it as mine ... It is always the I *now* which says that the past experience *belongs* to it, not that it once belonged to it: the 'mine' therefore is the name of the relation which unites past with present (emphases author's).

Here I build on Earle's concept to suggest something slightly different: just as the 'I now' joins the past and present by recognizing that 'the past experience belongs to it', so simultaneously experience of this unification acts back on the self of the rememberer to create a sense of disjunction – namely to constitute the self in terms of the discontinuity created by grasping this past's 'no longer' as 'mine'. So we shall see that, in *Gisalo* remembering, the uniting of past and present as 'mine' occurs only in the recognition of separation from or loss of co-presence with *close* others (aspects of the rememberer's self), realized in contrast to the current co-presence of external, *distant* others (the 'not-self'), who yet sing one's place-names. Remembering is thus a complex constitutive act in which the subject's 'self' is redefined in this discontinuous form in the 'moment' of exerting its continuity and conjoining power – i.e., in recognizing the past as its own.

The condensation of these contradictions within the rememberer's body is grief and anger – the interiorized, bodily 'subjective correlative' (to twist T. S. Eliot's phrase) of the contradictory symbolic field. One could say, for reasons emerging later, that these contradictions have their verbal 'objective correlative' in the outsider's singing of the place-names which initiates the mnemonic cycle. In general, the structure of remembering in *Gisalo* is the whole symbolic field of the present being produced in this cycle.[11]

Schieffelin and Feld both examine Kaluli emphasis on place-names and the binding of persons to the inhabited landscape. Bambi Schieffelin (1990: 84) notes that such connections are manifested in childhood language–socialization practices which repetitively engage the children in a verbal exchange conjoining particular linguistic forms 'with a set of socially meaningful place names (where family members garden, hunt, and fish together). Small children through these language–socialization sequences come to identify activity, persons, and locality with each other.' Kaluli discussed places with E. Schieffelin in terms of 'who had lived or gardened there' (1976: 45). And in discussing *Gisalo* one man said: 'When the dancer sings about [the place] Alimsᴐk . . . I am reminded of my dead wife, Yano, who planted pandanus and breadfruit there with me' (ibid.: 190). Thus people cannot be disentangled in experience and in biographical memory from the named places through which they move.

Bonds of persons and places are also implicit in the semantics of forest place-names. Although some names refer simply to landmarks, the terms typically combine the name of a local stream with a suffix specifying a landscape feature or some aspect of the stream: for example, *Kidensagu*, the waterfall at Kiden stream. Kaluli use the streams to orient and locate themselves when travelling (Schieffelin 1976: 30; 1979: 131). If, as Schieffelin states, a name 'carries ... its own geographical coordinates ... [fixing the locality] in determinate relation to the ... brooks and streams' (Schieffelin 1976: 30; 1979: 131);[12] so also, we may say that it connotes the travellers' bodily co-ordinations which place them in determinate, oriented relations to the region. In this respect it connotes the operations of establishing these relations of 'hereness' and 'whereness' of the moment.

Thus a complex of place-situated, bodily being and self–other relationship is ongoingly created in daily life as an *integral unit* in Kaluli experience and biographical memory. Songs present icons of this unitary structure, emphasizing the spatiotemporal situatedness of social experience and memory. Such structures reflect general phenomenological frameworks of memory construction. Casey (1987: 182) puts it thus: 'As embodied existence ... *takes place in place* ... so our memory of what we experience ... is bound to place as its own basis (emphasis author's).'

However, the bodily locatedness embedded in the landscape (i.e. 'where I am') is mapped on to the person at another level as 'who I am (or we are)': the name of the region where a longhouse is built stands for the longhouse community. Members use these names 'in ... [both friendly and aggressive] interaction with people of other communities' (Schieffelin 1976: 43). 'A person's name is in the ground' (ibid.: 44), one Kaluli put it. Thus names make available not only 'place' as 'situatedness', but also 'place' in the sense of a homeland 'where one belongs' (Grene 1982: 56). A homeland, in the sense used here, is a more complex order of symbolic space, since it incorporates locatedness into the construction of identity: in effect it is the self in its located form, or conversely, a location of the self – the kind of place (whether now or once lived in or not)[13] where one may go virtually or in reality to find oneself. Furthermore, others identified with these landscapes are part of the self one is contacting there. *Remembering* a homeland is one form of virtual visiting or recontacting of the self. In *Gisalo*, such recontacting simultaneously foregrounds the loss of the co-presence of those close others who are integral to the formation of these charged social landscapes of the self.

In sum, place-names in songs occupy a special position in this process of self-construction. One could say that they precipitate a mnemonic leap not only because they make particular landscapes out of general ones – giving, as Feld says, 'uniqueness and singularity through locales' (1990: 262), but because they encode a self-related or 'centred' space – a space not merely particularized but also 'possessed'. It is on this basis that Kaluli place-names become personal names, and can be used as the pivot of an intersubjective dialogue in which the verbal ferret of one's own memory is an aspect of oneself.

Indeed, it is just in the listener's self-construction in remembering that the relation between particular listener and singer becomes an angry opposition: Schieffelin (pers. comm.) suggests, 'there is an implicit . . . provocation in the song: "Who is he to say I am alone? Who is he to sing those lands [i.e., my/our lands]?"'[14] So the man grieving for his wife Yano later explained his feeling as he went to burn the dancer: 'Why do you [the dancer] sing about my gardens? Why do you say I am alone? What do you mean?' (Schieffelin 1976: 190). This provocation is initially implicit in the knowledge that *Gisalo* performers sing the hosts' place-names. Significantly, the singing reverses what happens in battle contexts, when longhouse members call out their own names, asserting their identities in battle (ibid.: 43–4). But the provocation's poignancy emerges as the listener converts the song into memory – as if reappropriating the alienated name by converting it back into the self-related meanings for which it is a currency. Moving towards completion of this self-constructive process by defining him or herself in opposition to the outsider, the rememberer converts interiority (i.e.'myself', my mental pain of memory in which past co-presences come to mind) into the exterior pain (burning) of the currently co-present other. Without considering the significance of this mnemonic cycle here, I note merely that the cycle may conclude with the griever wailing as he embraces the burned singer (ibid.: 190), implying perhaps, a return from the remembered, interior past to the outside other, exterior to that past – hence, it would seem, a resynthesis of the self in the present.

In contrast to places, people are typically denoted in the songs by pronouns or kinship terms rather than proper names. Deictic and relative usages allow latitude for different interpretations, emphasizing relations *between* persons rather than particularized identity. Interactions figured in the songs[15] are characterized by current absence between persons who (it is implied) were previously 'co-present' to each other; or by absence between persons and places (which would be imbued with past consociative meanings for relevant hosts). People are, in effect, 'gone' from each other and gone from places. Absence from places is expressed, for example, in the song phrase 'He has gone from the spring of the Waido stream' (ibid.: 183); similarly, spirits of the dead are called 'gone men' (*ane kalu*, ibid.: 97; i.e., 'gone people', as I shall gloss this expression here; see Feld 1982: 251, glosses for *kalu*).

The dynamic of this relation is what forms absence in its full sense: a co-presence once enjoyed, which is no longer. For instance, in one case (Schieffelin 1976: 183), people who burned the singer/dancer took the lyric 'I' of the song to refer to their recently deceased kinswoman. She conveyed her socio-spatial dislocation in mourning 'I have no brother. Where shall I go?' The song aroused her living kinsmen to burn the singer, carrying out, in effect, the interactions of loss. Thus a song's landscape, with its named places and its place-to-place movement, is formed into a space–time of social relationships pivoted on the *absence* of persons from each other and of people from inhabited places. This pattern (among others), imbuing the landscape with the differentiation of present and past, introduces the 'now' into the landscape as a depleted state. So the griever for his wife Yano explained that the dancer was saying to him as he sang: 'Now you go alone to pick from the gardens you planted with your wife. Now there is only you.' This 'now alone, once together with X at Y' is the underlying spatiotemporal and inter-subjective frame of the memory world, construed here as a particular remembrance shaped in its form. I take this frame itself to be a basic spatiotemporal structure of Kaluli remembering.[16]

Gisalo memory worlds do not refer directly to past events or interactions but to a generalized *current* state or space–time in which loss has entered as the defining feature. By this means, the mnemonic process that introduces different pasts into the present – working against the direction of ongoing time or temporal transience in the effort to generate temporal and self continuity –

actually incorporates this transience, a mode of discontinuity, into the template of remembering.

Modes of Co-presence in the Kaluli Present

Nevertheless, this absence does *not* mean that the Kaluli dead can no longer be co-present with the living and communicate with them. Rather, a changed *mode* of possible co-presence defines their absence: '"Becoming a bird" . . . [defines] the passage from life to death' (Feld 1982: 218).[17] Assuming the bird's surface appearance (*obe mise*, ibid.: 252), the dead communicate with the living by means of song coming down from the trees (cf. Feld 1990: 20). Birdsong is the speech of 'gone people' whose long-houses are trees (and who also frequent the pools) (Schieffelin 1976: 97).

This distancing is an *interiorization* in the *external* non-human domain: the deceased, no longer visible as people, take on bird form;[18] birds themselves are relatively invisible inside the forest cover from which their voices emerge (cf. Feld 1982: 45; Schieffelin 1976: 96). The dead thus become much less perceivable through vision than through their voices.[19] They have literally gone away from the people and their longhouse habitations within the forested world. Their absence consists of this transposition: a movement of distancing – outside human habitation, upward and inside the external domain that is 'out and around' – which defines the loss of their previous ground-based, overt, human mode of spatial co-presence with the living. This spatial distance reflects a temporal history of change or transformation.[20]

However, in *Gisalo* performance space, this very mode of *distanced co-presence* is being *made close*. It is not the dead that are brought up close (as they are in Kaluli séances where the manifestations, *mama*, of the dead enter into the living medium) but *the distanced mode of their co-presence – i.e., absence or loss itself –* that is brought into the longhouse and hidden interior (*sa*) of the human mind.

Thus certain spatial transpositions occur through the song composition and performance. To create a *Gisalo* song, words (*sa-gisalo*) drawn from the interior of the composer's mind are fitted to melody (*gisalo*) 'that comes into mind [as bird songs] from the ["outside and around"] of the surrounding air' (Feld 1982: 167). Song melody surrounds or covers the most interiorized human dimension with the interior element (birdsong) from the arboreal 'outside and around' where the distanced dead dwell. Song words are also said to enter composers' and listeners' heads like a waterfall (*sa*, with its 'tucking under', 'moving inside' motion [ibid.: 93], an epitome of forest 'innerness') 'swirl[ing] around in the pool of melody' (ibid.: 160–1). Human words then condense the dynamizing temporal motion of the *forest* interior with the *human* interior.

Just as bird-like melody surrounds song words, which are its inner meaning and dynamic, so the human singer-dancer's surface is decorated to simulate a bird at a forest waterfall pool. Artifice brings the distant 'outside and around' *in* (to the human mind and body), and turns the external inside or underneath *out* (on the bodily or song surface).

But these singer-dancers are also the human longhouse outsiders who draw all this distance into the longhouse. Embodying it both on their bodies and in their minds, they transmit the hosts' *own* lands saturated with distance from the outside into their interior beings. Kaluli themselves say, the singing 'brings the forest up close' (ibid.: 180). People feel as if they were 'off bush' or at a waterfall, journeying dreamlike 'from place to place' (ibid.: 180) in their heads. In sum, the mode of spatial co-presence which characterizes the dead, and defines their absence, pervades the spatiotemporal field of the present.

So far I have spoken of modes of co-presence in *Gisalo* primarily in terms of spatial rather than temporal distancing. Of course, the dead are *spatially* distanced because of their *temporal* life history: once close, they were changed away. In their past mode of co-presence, when they could be communicated with in their own *particular* human forms, face to face, they are now present only within the virtual space–time of biographical memory. In *Gisalo*, this *temporally* distanced mode of co-presence is experienced in the most radically contradictory form of remembering: i.e. by being brought back into the subject's sense of self ('*my* past') as that aspect of self that has become '*other*' and can be apprehended only by being sung into the mind by the outsider who has verbally appropriated the self (i.e. its place-names).

Significantly, the category label for place-names means literally 'ground/land' names (*hena wi*, Feld 1982: 251; cf. also my Note 2); and ground dwelling (*hena sab*) is contrasted with arboreal living (*iwalu sab*) (ibid.: 251). Place-names seem to connote not only the bodily orientations of movement in the landscape, noted earlier, but also the bodily position of ground living which distinguishes human co-presence from that of the dead.

When, therefore, these *ground* names are embedded in the *arboreal* melody of birds;[21] and human *outsiders*, simulating bird manifestations of the dead, sing a living person's or group's *own* names, the naming condenses in its most marked form the contradictory space–time which characterizes the symbolic field of the present in *Gisalo* remembering.

Summary and Conclusion

This analysis of the Kaluli *Gisalo* has considered aspects of certain general issues familiar in the study of memory and relevant to its cultural analysis. Mnemonic procedures; the connection of memory and identity; the contradictory construction of time in remembering and ways in which social and spatial relations enter into the mnemonic process are all subsumed here under a view of remembering as both a formative process and a formation of a particular field of the present. Thus I have not considered remembering simply as a subjective process triggered by an objective mnemonic medium ; or as a particular activity going on *within* a *given* spatiotemporal field. Instead, I have argued that in any given instance remembering is a particular 'configuring' of this field, and that its form consists of the relations of the field that are being produced. In the Kaluli case, *Gisalo* is only one part of a wider paradigm of remembering involving sung (or wept) memory worlds. *Gisalo*, other feast contexts, séances, and burial rites entail different spatiotemporal formations – i.e., each produces a somewhat different configuration of the field of the present.

What I have called a 'memory world' is not, of course, limited to the specific characteristics taken by the Kaluli genre. For instance, the various forms of the well-known 'arts of memory'

(Carruthers 1990; Yates 1966) can be described as 'memory worlds' in the sense defined, although they are very different from the Kaluli example, and involve another kind of remembering. Thus the arts of memory are described in didactic texts which instruct the would-be rememberer to encode verbal information into images, placed according to a sequential principle within an architectural or other patterned mental space; the aim is to 'store' the images there for later mental visits for retrieval and decoding.

The space involved need not necessarily be drawn from a particular lived space of the rememberer, although it might be. Indeed, in some instances an instructor recommended 'real places, which can be visited and re-inspected frequently in preference to wholly imaginary ones', in order to ensure that the relevant array is held in mind with fixity and clarity (Carruthers 1990: 131). Thus visits to real places are themselves aimed at refreshing the rememberer's mental memory code, keeping it intact as a locus for specially encoded information. This information has no *necessary* connection to meanings with which the place may itself be invested from lived relations and events identified with it by the rememberer, and/or occurring there in the past. The latter have, as it were, been 'displaced' from focus or backgrounded by assigned referential meanings which do not require them for their semantic elaboration. By contrast, in the Kaluli case, *mental* visits to a place through the memory worlds of songs are concerned with persons and events in one's own life. Thus places may operate as the landscapes of memory worlds in quite different ways.

However, it is interesting to consider an instance of the art of memory in which we can see the biographical power of lived places retake the memory world for itself, converting it into a kind of charged semanticity more like that of the Kaluli memory worlds I have discussed here. Thus we have the case of the Russian psychologist Luria's subject Shereshevski (whom Luria calls 'S.'), whose remarkable memory feats were built on the ancient principles of the arts of memory (Carruthers 1990: 75). This man memorized by converting written or orally received verbal material (for example, word sequences) into images which 'he would distribute along some ... street ... visualized in his mind'. For example, selecting a familiar Moscow street, he would 'take a mental walk along that street "distributing" his images at houses, gates and store windows. At times, without realizing how it had happened, he would suddenly find himself back in his hometown ... where he would wind up his trip in the house he had lived in as a child' (Luria 1987 [1968]: 32; also cited in Carruthers 1990: 76).

Shereshevski's different memory worlds involve the use of personally known, lived spaces. However, in accord with the aims of the art of memory, these lived spaces merely served as frameworks mediating the retention of verbalized information unrelated to them. Nevertheless, Shereshevski's procedure sometimes triggered a Proustian 'involuntary memory': for instance, in the above example, S.'s remembrance of his childhood street inserts itself seemingly unbidden, so that he then walks along it as if it were continuous with the other (Moscow) street. Moreover, S.'s images of lived places might also encroach on his reading about other places outside his own experience: 'If I'm reading a description of some palace [he said], for some reason the main rooms always turn out to be those in the apartment I lived in as a child ... Even when I read about [new] circumstances ... if there happens to be a description, say of a staircase, it turns out to be one in a house I once lived in. I start to follow it and lose the gist of what I'm reading' (Luria 1987 [1968]: 116). In these examples, either the biographically based mental streets of a memory world or the non-biographical spatial images in some written source (the staircase, the rooms of the palace) evoke other places that are charged homelands of the self; within these homelands, Shereshevski momentarily travels. In contrast to the Kaluli case, however, biography is not being searched out, but is emerging involuntarily through the power of the images.

Although the streets of Shereshevski's memory worlds have names, names are not themselves key agencies of the mnemonic or triggers of his involuntary memories. His memory worlds (like the art of memory in general) convert words into visual formulae (for example, streets).[22] In this respect the names of streets or squares may sometimes be treated as features of these locations providing an analogical basis for the conversion: for example, 'poetry' becomes 'Pushkin Square' (Luria 1987 [1968]: 40). All of this is obviously very different from the Kaluli verbal art, in which place-names are the privileged agencies for sparking the transposition from the otherwise relatively general *mise-en-scène* of the songs into biographical memories.

Nevertheless, in both instances, place-names appear as verbal aspects of space; and space is itself an aspect of activity and bodily movement. In the Kaluli case, we have seen that names systematically 'detach' and circulate in concise linguistic form, not simply space, but space in Merleau Ponty's (1945) sense, as an aspect of bodily being and activities – as particularities of spatial and temporal locatedness which also convert into the constitution of self.

The Kaluli exemplify a culturally widespread emphasis on place-names in song and narrative as media of these connective powers (see for example the discussions in Basso 1986, 1988; Kuipers 1984; Weiner 1991).[23] If *places* are those necessary aspects of the self which are its most immobile dimension and mode of being – to and from which a person may go, but which cannot themselves go to and from the person – place-*names* may be seen as concise interlocutors in this asymmetric relationship. They speak to us, as it were, from both sides of this passage: as identifying aspects of the external place, and as its signifiers held within us, which travel where we go.

Like place-names, the Kaluli memory worlds of song can be seen as part of a larger anthropological problem involving the social circulation of memories and memory-like experiences of homelands by means of what Helsinger (1989: 272), in a recent examination of Constable's paintings, has called 'portable representations', which make it possible for 'home [to] ... be moved'. Constable's paintings, she points out, are 'objects made to be circulated among those who, like Constable himself, have left the places of their rural origins [for the city]. As such the paintings testify that the local and the rural [are] ... reproducible anywhere' (p. 272).

In this instance, the media are material objects, and Helsinger is talking of portability in the context of people's urban displacement from a particular rural world that was increasingly becoming the stereotyped epitome of pastness and loss, while also entering into a nationalist discourse about England as a homeland. The Kaluli are not displaced from their homelands (although some individuals may be); but they create verbally detachable or portable landscapes which they envelop in pastness and loss in order to be reminded of those distanced within their forested world – in effect, to put their displaced dead back in place and re-identify with them by remembering them *where they used to be.*

Notes

1. The ethnographic materials on the Kaluli are drawn from the research of Edward Schieffelin and Steven Feld, except where otherwise noted. I have used Feld's transcription of the term for the ceremony (*gisalo*), rather than Schieffelin's (*gisaro*). I am greatly indebted to the generosity of both authors in answering my queries and providing critical comments in connection with earlier versions of this paper.

   My interest in basing a study of memory on the Kaluli derives from a commentary I gave on the session 'Memory and Exchange in Melanesia' (in which Stephen Feld participated; see Feld 1990) at the meetings of the American Anthropological Association, Phoenix, 1988. As originally prepared for the conference organized by D. de Coppet, and A. Itéanu on 'Society and Universe in Melanesia', Tours, April 1990, the present chapter was developed as part of a wider analysis of memory that included both a rethinking of some aspects of the *malangan* of the Masei people of New Ireland studied by Susanne Küchler, and a brief discussion on 'debt memory' based on my own Gawan work. The study took on a form closer to the current one as a presentation at the meetings of the Society for Cultural Anthropology, Boston, May 1991, which were held on the topic of 'Culture and Memory'. I am indebted to Edward Casey for his careful reading of this version.

2. I refer specifically here to the posthumously published 1950s study rather than the 1925 work (*Les cadres sociaux de la mémoire*). The former maintains a more intimate connection between concrete space and social memory in the examples used throughout the study, as well as in more explicit notions about the relation between them (discussed especially in the section on 'space and collective memory'). The intensity of Halbwachs's concern with the fundamental role of places in the constitution of historical recollection is most apparent in his remarkable study of the legendary topography of the evangelists (Halbwachs 1941).

3. The Kaluli term corresponding to remembering, *asul*, means 'to understand' or 'think about'; being reminded is simply 'being made to think about' (Schieffelin, pers. comm.; Feld, pers. comm.).

4. One term for mind or brain (*tugus*) also carries the sense of a 'hard shell outside that covers a . . . living inside' (Feld, pers. comm.).

5. Finally, the singers must recompense the hosts with small gifts because they are responsible for having pained them, and to assure return 'for the things . . . [of one's] life . . . [one] has lost' (Schieffelin 1976: 206). The cycle thus concludes with an overt substitution of non-bodily goods (some of which appear to be connected with body décor – for instance, shells, a mirror or paints) for the interior suffering of loss. In this respect, the cycle of transpositions from interior to exterior, covert to overt, concludes with a common Melanesian move from losses of persons to the substitution of things *via* exchange – a reconstruction of loss in terms of material exchange items. The logic of this cycle is only partly worked out here.

6. Songs are closely associated with dreams and, like them, located in the mind (Feld, pers. comm.). In a well-done *Gisalo* hosts should seem to lose their senses until dawn (Schieffelin 1976: 168). For lack of space, I do not deal here with the states of consciousness involved in these mental landscape journeys, despite their relevance to the argument.

7. For simplicity, I use the label 'memory world' for both the model and particular instantiations. Kaluli song is a genre which has different kinds of instantiations. Unlike *Gisalo*, in women's 'sung weeping' (more literally 'inner-texted-weeping', *sa-yelema*, Feld 1990: 242) at funerals, the memory world coincides with the biographical memories of the singer-weepers. This affects the construction of the spatiotemporal field of the present.

8. Memory worlds may take different cultural forms, and these I will comment on briefly in the conclusion.

9. Schieffelin (1976: 179–81) has published several *Gisalo* songs in translation. Feld provides the Kaluli text and translation of a long *Gisalo* song performed at a séance rather than a *Gisalo* song dance (1982: 194–9). My analysis is based on these songs and relevant accompanying commentaries.

10. It is *only* within songs that place-names make people grieve.
11. The particular contradictory form of the singer–rememberer relation in *Gisalo* is not characteristic of all contexts in which songs (or sung weeping) occur. The field of the present being constituted and the modality of self-construction in other modes of Kaluli collective remembering, such as mortuary rites, thus require separate analysis.
12. More recently Feld (In press: pp. 20–1, ms) has suggested that 'while this might slightly overstate the primacy of water forms ... the experience and naming of Bosavi lands and waters is always interpenetrated'. In this account, Feld (In press: p. 23, ms) also discusses additional kinds and complexities of place-names, pointing out that many also 'open out to biographical or historical stories'.
13. There are many different kinds of 'homelands' of the self, and a person may have more than one. Some *loci* of identity can be places (real or unreal) one has never been (like the 'unattained place' of Edwin Muir's poem, around which 'there is a line ... And all inside is home' [Muir 1953]).The relations to memory are obviously other than in the current case, where the homeland is (or was) also one's residential home.
14. Compare one man's expression of his anger at the failure of dancers from a currently visiting longhouse to pay compensation at a previous dance: fiercely burning one of their dancers, he called out, 'You should not sing our ground names if you don't pay compensation' (Schieffelin 1976: 207). (On compensatory payment, see Note 5 above.)
15. The conventional use of second person, direct address (e.g., 'Do you see the Galinti pool?' Schieffelin 1976: 181) and imperatives (e.g., 'Come see the Saeluwai stream,' ibid.: 183) suggests that the audience is the addressee absent from the song protagonist and the landscape, to whom the singer directs his lonely soliloquy. Thus the phrase 'Come see the Saeluwai stream' seems to call the absent living back to the deceased's location (in the song's space–time) – as if the song's protagonist would bring herself and this landscape back into their vision. Other interactions of absence are conveyed through the use of the first and third persons, as in 'He has gone from the spring of the Waido stream ... I will sleep under the *dona* trees' (ibid.: 181).
16. Compare the similar framing of remembrance in one man's

explanation of his taboo on eating a particular food at the death of his wife: 'She brought it home to eat with me – now I will have to eat it alone' (Schieffelin 1976: 160). As in the *Gisalo* case, the man remembers consociation of the past (here in connection with food-sharing, a crucial Kaluli symbol of social connection) in relation to the aloneness of the present. Consider also that in women's sung weeping, in which the texts convey biographical memories, the standard way of citing a place-name is 'my [relation], you and I were together at [place-name]' (Feld 1990: 261; see also the long example in Feld 1982: 116–21).

17. Although the dead may also appear as fish in the forest pools (Schieffelin 1976: 97), I deal here with their prototypic manifestation as birds.

18. This appearance has a more complex conceptualization than I analyse here. When a person is alive, his or her manifestation in the bush is a wild pig (men) or cassowary (women) – both ground-dwelling creatures who wander, however, 'invisibly' on the slopes of Mt Bosavi (Schieffelin 1976: 96–7). These manifestations are called *mama*, a shadow, or reflection (as in water). When a person dies, his or her *mama* becomes an *anemama* (ibid.: 212–13), or 'gone shadow–reflection' – visible only as a bird or fish manifestation – now, it would seem, joined into one with his or her person (who has become a 'gone person', *ane kalu*).

19. Schieffelin (pers. comm.) has suggested to me in conversation that for Kaluli visual perceivability may in general be less emphasized in the dark forest environment, where sounds are paramount perceptual signs. Cf. also Feld (In press).

20. Transformation into birds is regularly asserted in certain standard rhetorical directives in women's sung weeping at burials. These directives tell the deceased to say (or sing) back to the singer 'always look up to the top branches of the tree' (Feld 1990: 261–2). Thus the deceased as bird is to tell the *mourner/singer* to continue their relationship in its now spatially transposed form.

21. Some birds are classified as ground-dwellers, but these are not the *Gisalo* birds or those manifesting the dead (see Feld 1976: 46ff.).

22. Luria (1987: 30ff.) discusses Shereshevski's 'visual quality of

recall' as a general feature of his memory.

23. Weiner's (1991) study of the poetry of the Foi, who are neighbours of the Kaluli, is directly concerned with some of these connectivities.

References

Augustine of Hippo, Saint (1960). *The Confessions*. Image Books (Doubleday), Garden City.

Basso, K. (1988). Speaking with Names: Language and Landscape among the Western Apache. *Cultural Anthropology*, 3(2), 99–130.

—— (1986). 'Stalking Stories': Names, Places and Moral Narratives among the Western Apache. *Antaeus*, 57, Autumn, 95–116.

Bergson, H. (1988 [1908]). *Matter and Memory*. Translated by N. Paul and W. Ortner. Zone Books, New York.

Carruthers, M. (1990). *The Book of Memory: A Study of Memory in Medieval Culture*. Cambridge University Press, Cambridge.

Casey, E. (1976). *Imagining: A Phenomenological Study*. Indiana University Press, Bloomington.

—— (1987). *Remembering: A Phenomenological Study*. Indiana University Press, Bloomington.

Duvignaud, J. (1950). *Preface* to Halbwachs, *La mémoire collective*. Presses Universitaires de France, Paris.

Earle, W. (1956). Memory. *Review of Metaphysics*, 10 (1), no. 37, 3–21.

Feld, S. (1982). *Sound and Sentiment*. University of Pennsylvania Press, Philadelphia.

—— (In Press). Waterfalls of Song: an Acoustemology of Place Resounding in Bosavi, Papua New Guinea. To be published in a volume on place, expression and experience, eds S. Feld and K. Basso. School of American Research, Santa Fé.

—— (1990). Wept Thoughts: the Voicing of Kaluli Memories. *South Pacific Oral Traditions*, 5(2–3), 241–66.

Grene, M. (1982). Landscape. In: R. Bruzina and B. Wilshire (eds), *Phenomenology: Dialogues and Bridges*. State University of New York Press, Albany.

Halbwachs, M. (1925). *Les cadres sociaux de la mémoire*. Alcan, Paris.

—— (1941). *La topographie légendaires des évangiles en terre sainte: étude de mémoire collective*. Presses Universitaires de France, Paris.

—— (1950). *La mémoire collective*. Presses Universitaires de France, Paris.

Helsinger, E. (1989). Constable: The Making of a National Painter. *Critical Inquiry*, 15(2), 253–79.

Husserl, E. (1964). *The Phenomenology of Internal Time Consciousness.* Indiana University Press, Bloomington.

Janet, P. (1928). *L'evolution de la mémoire et de la notion de temps.* A. Chahine, Paris.

Kuipers, J. (1984). Place, Names, and Authority in Weyewa Ritual Speech. *Language in Society,* 13, 455–66.

Luria, A. (1987 [1968]). *The Mind of a Mnemonist: A Little Book about a Vast Memory.* Harvard University Press, Cambridge, Mass. and London.

Merleau Ponty, M. (1945). *Phénomènologie de la Perception.* Gallimard, Paris.

Muir, E. (1953). The Unattained Place. In his *Collected Poems 1921–1951.* Grove Press, New York.

Munn, N. (1986). *The Fame of Gawa: a Symbolic Study of Value Transformation in a Massim (Papua New Guinea) Society.* Cambridge University Press, Cambridge.

Poulet, G. (1964). *The Interior Distance.* The University of Michigan Press, Ann Arbor.

Schieffelin, B. (1990). *The Give and Take of Everyday Life: Language Socialization of Kaluli Children.* Cambridge University Press, Cambridge.

Schieffelin, E. (1979). Mediators as Metaphors: Moving a Man to Tears in Papua, New Guinea. In: A. L. Becker and A. Yengoyan (eds), *The Imagination of Reality: Essays in Southeast Asia Coherence Systems.* Ablex Publishing Corporation, Norwood.

—— (1976). *The Sorrow of the Lonely and the Burning of the Dancers.* St Martin's Press, New York.

Weiner, J. (1991). *The Empty Place: Poetry, Space and Being among the Foi of Papua New Guinea.* Indiana University Press, Bloomington.

Yates, F. (1966). *The Art of Memory.* The University of Chicago Press, Chicago.

Chapter 4

On 'Grandmothers', 'Grandfathers' and Ancestors: Conceptualizing the Universe in Mono-Alu, Solomon Islands

Denis Monnerie

'Cosmologies (and I include cosmogonies under this rubric) are the classifications of the most encompassing scope. They are frameworks of concepts and relations which treat the universe or cosmos as an ordered system, describing it in terms of space, time, matter, and motion, and peopling it with gods, humans, animals, spirits, demons and the like.'

(S. Tambiah 1985: 3)

Introduction

In this chapter[1] I would like to focus on the cosmology of the society of Mono-Alu, established on the island of Alu, in the Solomon Islands, a few kilometres off the south coast of Bougainville. Several ethnographers and travellers have written about this area, but a special mention should be reserved for British anthropologist G. C. Wheeler, who carried out fieldwork in Mono-Alu in 1908–9.[2] His published and unpublished ethnographic and linguistic data contain a wealth of information (see bibliography in this chapter). By close attention to his own material we can get much more out of his evidence today than could be done by Wheeler himself.

I will begin with the analysis of the relations of the Mono-Alu people with the ancestral figures of the social groups they call *latu*. As does much of the understanding of this society, this

requires a detour via the funeral rites, which eventually proves
to be the shortest road to the understanding of what these
ancestral figures are and especially of their relevance to the
conceptualization of the universe. I will then proceed with
another notion, *nitu*, which refers to 'ancestors' in another way.
The second part of this paper will be devoted to the presentation
of the articulations between two fundamental aspects of the
notion of *nitu*: the *nitu* of the recently dead and the 'original' *nitu*
(*nitu talu*). These various sorts of 'ancestors' are among the
building blocks of the Mono-Alu cosmology, which, as a matter
of interest, have a characteristic tendency to overlap most of
Tambiah's own vast heuristic categories: space, time, matter,
motion, gods, humans, animals, spirits, and demons. My general
argument is that the relations between the living and the
different notions corresponding to these different forms of
'ancestors' account not only for much of the social life of the
Mono-Alu people, but also for some very important features in
the way they conceptualize the universe.[3] Thus I will conclude
with a description of some basic features of the socio-cosmic
system of the Mono-Alu society.

'Grandmothers' and 'Grandfathers'

The Mono-Alu people are ranked into the nobles (men: *lalaafa*;
women: *mamaifa*)[4] the commoners (*soi*) and the *toniga*; the latter
are acquired on nearby Bougainville in exchange for shell money.
The village and local 'chiefs' (*lalaafa*) are noble men. All the
Mono-Alu people – including most *toniga* – belong to 12 different
latu. One belongs to one's mother's *latu*. This is commented by an
informer, unfortunately in Pidgin English: 'Woman makes the
line. Man he no carry picaniny. Man he nothing' (MS[5] 436). The
people who belong to the same *latu* are in a *fanua* relationship.
The term *fanua* is an important relationship term and has several
other meanings (see below). In each village, several *latu* are
represented. The *latu* are not territorial units. No ritual or ritual
sequence gathers together all the members of a *latu* and, apart
from the one remarkable exception I am going to deal with, the
people taking part in a ritual always belong to more than one
latu.

Marriage within the *latu* is said to be prohibited; this prohibition is called *uloulo*. Such unions are frowned upon as being *paitena* (bad, worthless, of no account, etc.) and people make fun of those who do marry within their *latu*. One informer even says that the *uloulo* may cause death through a skin disease (boils: *maula*). However, from his genealogies (which are unfortunately lost) Wheeler noticed a trend towards in-*latu* marriage among noble families. I will now examine more precisely the inner workings of these *latu*.

We have a list of 13 *latu*, one of which is extinct. Each *latu* is associated with ancestral figures, most of them animal species, called *tua* and *tete* (see list, pp. 127–8). Besides applying to these ancestral figures, the words *tua* and *tete* have other meanings. *Tua* and *tete* are the kinship terms for, respectively, male or female kin from the grandparents generation (+2) upwards. *Tua* and *tete* also are used by a married woman respectively for the father and uncles, mother and aunts of her husband (this is the only case of skewing in the Mono-Alu kinship vocabulary). In the kinship vocabulary, one basic feature of the distinction between *tua* and *tete* is that it is made in terms of absolute sex. The reciprocal term, *fabiu*, does not distinguish sex. The word *tua* also means old man, and *tete* old woman. I render *tua* by 'grandfather', *tete* by 'grandmother' and *fabiu* by 'grandchild'. Wheeler calls these ancestral figures 'totems', but I shall not use this word nor shall I use the expression 'matrilineage' to define the *latu*, for reasons which will soon become clear.

Each *latu* refers to one 'grandfather', who is known to everyone. Most 'grandfathers' are birds, with four interesting exceptions. Each *latu* also refers to at least one, often several 'grandmothers', who are shrouded in secrecy. In the cases when we know the different 'grandmothers' of a *latu*, one of them usually is a fish or a subaquatic creature, the other one(s) being land animals.

Wheeler's attempt to understand the relationships between the people and the 'grandfather' or the 'grandmothers' of their *latu* focuses on the prohibition on consuming them as food – a standard approach at the time. The words which describe this prohibition are either *olatu*, a very general word for prohibition, valuation and sacredness (which can be rendered by 'taboo') or *tabu* and *tabutabu* which are exclusively used for food prohibitions either in this context or during a period of mourning.

However neither of these words is reserved for the prohibition on consuming as food the 'grandfather' and (or) 'grandmother' of a *latu*. As a matter of fact, while some *latu* eat both 'grandfather' and 'grandmother' (which is the case for *karoua* people) others do not eat them (thus *talapuini* and *tabooti*), but can kill them. There are also cases in which the people of a *latu* can kill and (or) eat one of its animal 'grandparents' and not the other. There is no systematic correlation between these food prohibitions. They are at best fragmentary manifestations of a system that should be considered in a more global way. As C. Lévi-Strauss (1962) demonstrated in his classic refutation of the theories of totemism, another type of approach is required. Whereas Lévi-Strauss's purpose is the discovery of universal mental categories or processes, my own approach will differ from his, my aim being to account for a specific society. We shall see presently that a food relation *is* relevant, but it is a different food relation, in a different context and with far-reaching consequences for the global understanding of this society.

I shall first deal with a sequence of the funeral rites which involves several beings called 'grandmothers' of the dead person. This will help delineate some basic features of the notion of 'grandmother'. With these findings in mind, the next step will be to take up again the 'grandmothers' and 'grandfathers' of the *latu* in order to contrast them and thus complete our understanding of the basic tenets of the two contrasted notions of 'grandmother' and 'grandfather'.

The Funeral Role of 'Grandmothers'

The funeral role of a subaquatic creature which is also called a 'grandmother' (*tete*) and which is also linked to the *latu* provides a clue to the understanding of the notion of 'grandmother'. At this point a word should be said of a few basic facts which cannot be fully developed here (see Monnerie 1988, 1995). According to Mono-Alu conceptions, there are three components of the person: the 'name' (*lea*), the 'image' (*nunu*) and the 'body' (*uli*). These components of the person are best understood not as homogeneous substances but as constituted by relations. Besides, in Mono-Alu as in other parts of the Solomons, there are several ways of disposing of a dead person. *Toniga* are immersed in the sea, commoners usually buried. The sequence of funeral rites which I am going to analyse pertains to the most prestigious and complex funeral treatment, cremation, which is performed mostly for the nobles, men and women.[6]

Just after a cremation, the 'remains' (*apasa*) of the 'body' (*uli*), fragments of charred 'bones' (*suma*), are picked up, gathered and put in a round-shaped basket or pottery vessel[7] held by an old woman, who is a classificatory 'grandmother' (*tete*) of the dead person's *latu*. For several days, a series of ceremonies involving a 'funeral spear dance' (named *sagini*) focuses on the pot or basket containing the bone remains. At night and between ceremonies a classificatory 'mother' (*nka*) of the *latu* of the dead person sleeps next to this container. The whole spear dance exhibits a rivalry over the bone remains of the deceased's body between, on the one hand, the *latu* of the dead person's 'father' (*apa*), and, on the other hand, the *latu* of the mother, potentially assisted by all other *latu* (excluding that of the father). The end of the spear dance shows the necessity for the *latu* of the deceased's father to forfeit all pretensions to recapture the bone remains, which eventually are left in the care of the dead person's *latu*.

All these facts show that the body is composite. It is worth mentioning here briefly that the word used for the bone remains of the body can be glossed as 'with the father' (*apa* + *sa* together [+poss.]), and that some aspects of the funeral treatment of the body after a cremation evoke and probably reverse the role of the father during the gestation – as distinct from conception – of a child (see Monnerie 1988, 1995; compare and contrast with the Bush Mekeo 'de-conception' process described in Mosko 1985).

Until approximately the second half of the nineteenth century,[8] after these ceremonies, the bone remains of the body were fed to a subaquatic creature which was called the 'grandmother' of the *latu* of the dead person. This was done even for *latu* whose 'totemic' 'grandmother' is not a fish. We know about five of these subaquatic 'grandmothers'. The only one which is clearly identified is the eel, *toloo*, also mentioned as the 'grandmother' of *latu* Baumana Karoua, which was given the remains of the dead of this *latu*. Two other 'grandmothers' were large man-eating fish of the *maguili* and *kitoma* species (unidentified). Another one, called *marimari*, is 'something which looks like a large personal netbag' (MS: 545); yet another of these 'grandmothers' is described as 'something which comes up to the surface' (*beampeu mamatate sana*, MS: 546) in order to eat the remains. These 'grandmothers' were specifically connected to one or several places called *keno*. Each *latu* was related to one or several *keno*, often together with other *latu*. The word *keno* also means 'sea water', and 'the sea'. Most *keno* were in the sea, close to the shore, a few of them in a widening in a river. Apart from this ritual, the *keno* were strictly 'forbidden' (*olatu*) and no one would go there or even look at a *keno*, as this would lead to death (*korausi*).[9]

The ritual feeding of the remains of the body to the 'grandmother' was performed by a group of people belonging to the *latu* of the dead person. After the funeral spear dance, they carried the container to a place on the coast, whence several men of the *latu* embarked in a canoe and took it to their *keno*. Having reached the *keno*, first they had to attract the 'grandmother' of their *latu*. For this purpose, one of the crew made an 'offering' (*fasagi*, see p. 117) of areca to the dead (pl.) and said: 'Here is an areca nut, do ye make a fish to come up here; grant it me here; do not refuse; then I shall give his (her, its) bone remains' (MS: 533). The 'grandmother' was then addressed: 'If thou comest we will give thee thy grandchild (*fabiu*). ... When it comes up and reaches them, and opens its mouth they cast in the bones. It swallows them and goes away; it goes below the sea; and the people go away' (MS: 539). Note that in this circumstance, the dead person was not referred to by name but in kinship terms as the 'grandchild' of the subaquatic 'grandmother' which eats the dead person's remains. After the canoe had come back to the shore, the man who had done the first offering made another one, dedicated collectively to all the dead of their *latu*. Then he gave an areca nut to the man who had offered the remains to the 'grandmother'. Finally the whole bunch of areca nuts was shared between the men and women of the *latu* who had taken the remains of their dead *fanua* to this ceremony. In some cases at least, the container which was used to hold the remains after cremation and carry them to the *keno* was hung on the branches of a nearby tree (*siing*, a sort of banyan) reserved for this purpose and associated with the *latu*. This can be interpreted as a residual offering to the domain of the 'grandfather' (see Monnerie 1988, 1995). The same day, back in the village, a mortuary meal of fish and vegetable food called 'hiding the remains' (*funiapasa*) was held. Before this meal, a 'sacrifice' (*sisifala*, see p. 117) to the original *nitu* was made, with an invocation declaring 'Here is a sacrifice; we have come and laid his bones there, we have brought and given them to the original *nitu*; yea look after him' (MS: 537). Thus the feeding of the bone remains of the deceased's body to the 'grandmother' of the *latu* was an intermediate step towards a gift to the original *nitu*.

I can now sum up the ritual sequence which follows a cremation. It should be stressed that, for the time being, we are concerned with the destiny of one of the components of the dead person, the 'body' (*uli*). The image and the name receive a different funeral treatment. Just after cremation, the remains of the body are collected in a container held by a classificatory 'grandmother' of the deceased's *latu*. This is followed by the funeral spear dance which reaffirms the ultimate rights of the *latu* of the dead person over the bone remains of the dead person's body. During this dance and the *keno* ceremony which followed, the people of the *latu* set in motion a sequence in the circulation of the bone remains aimed at their ingestion by a subaquatic 'grandmother' related to their *latu* and eventually at their rejoining the original *nitu*. The *keno* ceremony is the only Mono-Alu ceremony in which only one *latu* is participating, it is clearly *latu* business. Thus (i) characterizing the *latu* merely as a matrilineage is insufficient and can be misleading, as belonging to a *latu* does not merely imply matrilineal transmission, or even the common reference to the 'grandfather' and 'grandmothers' of one's *latu*. For the nobles, it also implied, after death, the reaffirmation of the primacy of the mother's and grandmother's *latu* over the father's – and at the same time the indispensable albeit subordinate contribution of the latter. (ii) This primacy was expressed in the ingestion of the remains of the body by a subaquatic 'grandmother' related to the *latu*. (iii) There was a close and direct relation between the *latu*, its subaquatic 'grandmother' and the original *nitu*, which are all linked through the oriented circulation of one component of the person, the body.

The study of this offering of the bones to the 'grandmother' led Wheeler to reconsider his early appraisal of the 'grandmothers' of the *latu* as being merely 'secondary totems'. His first impression was no doubt a consequence of the secrecy surrounding the 'grandmothers'. Wheeler was later led to believe that there was a 'grandmother' ... conception which covered both aspects' (MS: 563), that is the subaquatic creatures which eat the bone remains at the *keno* and the 'totemic' aspect. What Wheeler calls a 'conception', I call a notion, a notion being a complex of ideas and values informing both thought and action.

These data concerning the funeral rites will now enable me to investigate and develop systematically various aspects of the notion of 'grandmother', and then contrast it with the notion of 'grandfather'.

From Relations to Spatial Domains

One point of interest is that the rite at the *keno* shows that a spatial principle underlies the notion of 'grandmother' (*tete*) which can be contrasted with the spatial principle underlying the notion of 'grandfather' (*tua*). What is the domain of the 'grandmothers'? The 'grandmothers' acting in the *keno* were all subaquatic creatures. In the sense of 'grandmother' of a *latu*, we have fish, reptiles or insects. Mostly, when a *latu* has several 'grandmothers', they belong to two categories: subaquatic animals and land animals linked to the underground. The small (unidentified) *habubusu* bird (*tete* of Baumana and Baumana karoua) is a problem. Its case may be related to that of another 'grandmother' which is also a bird, the megapode (*tete* of Hanapara, Malatigeno and Talapuini). For the megapode a close association to the underground is clear in the way it lays its eggs on the ground, then covers them with sand or vegetables, hiding them under the surface to be hatched by the heat of the sun or of the decaying plants. Thus these 'grandmothers' are creatures which spend a significant part of their existence in the water or underground, with more or less frequent excursions to the surface. These spatial features of the domain of the 'grandmothers' also hold for the subaquatic 'grandmothers' which have to 'come up to the surface' to eat the remains of their dead 'grandchildren' (*fabiu*). Thus the domain of the 'grandmothers' combines the underground and subaquatic worlds in a wider conception, that of a world below, bordered upwards by the surface of the ground and of the sea.[10] All this suggests that the secrecy surrounding the 'grandmothers' of the *latu* is an echo of the very strong secrecy attached to the subaquatic 'grandmothers' and their *keno* and/or may have to do with the opacity of their domain.

In contrast, most 'grandfathers' of the *latu* are birds. In this context, the Pidgin translation for *tua* is 'bird'. There are a few exceptions though. The iguana *sabau*, which is said to hide in trees, is one. Another, *pausape* (the *tua* of Oita) is a volcanic stone, probably linked to (or even brought by an eruption of) the nearby active Bareka volcano of Bougainville (see below). Whereas not all the 'grandfathers' are birds – the flying fox is for us a mammal – they are flying creatures or live in trees, or are related to the world above which is their domain.

In contrast, again, men and women mostly remain on the surface (*peta*: also ground, land) which is the domain of the 'living' (*salena*) (MS: 992, 995). Men do climb high trees,[11] but these forays are fraught with danger, and there is a special ritual for those who lose consciousness after a fall from a tree.

One now sees more clearly one of the features underlying the contrast between 'grandfather' and 'grandmother': the former inhabit the world above, the latter the underground or subaquatic worlds. The world above is that of the 'grandfathers', the birds, the high trees and, generally, of all that which is or lives upwards from the surface. The world below is that of the 'grandmothers', where insects, reptiles and fish live, most of the time hidden from the sight of the living. This is confirmed by the fact that burial replaced immersion as a form of treatment for the bone remains of cremated bodies some time during the second half of the nineteenth century.[12] Both burial and immersion achieve a similar aim: 'hiding the remains' in the domains of the 'grandmothers'. As regards the immersed bodies of the *toniga* and the buried bodies of commoners, they also disappear under the surface into the domain of the 'grandmothers'.

The surface being the domain of the living, the association in a *latu* of its living members with a 'grandfather' and one or several 'grandmothers' is an echo of the conceptualization of the universe. In a fashion which is characteristic of this society, the distinctions between these three domains are not conceived as clear-cut separations. For instance, spatially, both 'grandmothers' and 'grandfathers' can make incursions to the surface, the world of the living, who themselves can make the occasional foray into the world above, or the subaquatic world. Interestingly, many of the significant processes of interrelation of this society, especially the rituals, display comparable features, in which contrasted entities, although clearly distinguished, are at the same time connected or interacting.

We may now consider what may appear as an exception, that is the peculiarities of *latu* Talili, which, remarkably, has the swordfish and (or) the *habubusu* for 'grandfather', which, in relation with other *latu*, are 'grandmothers'. This special relation to its 'grandfather'(s)' corresponds to an inversion in the behaviour of the male members of the *latu*, as contrasted to the attitudes of the male members of all other *latu*. Talili men do not go to the common house, a place which is normally reserved for men and is closely associated with male values. Besides, the Talili people do not go to the annual *biloto* ceremony. This shows that the notions of 'grandmother' and 'grandfather' can be subjected to a sort of logical play, and that their relationships can be inverted, as exemplified here, or transformed, as we shall see when describing the great platform ceremony.

Towards the Conceptualization of the Universe

The two notions of 'grandfather' (*tua*) and 'grandmother' (*tete*) are contrasted in other ways. One of them is revealed when one considers different extensions of the *fanua* relation. The people of a *latu* are *fanua*, and should not kill each other at war. But the people in the following three groups of *latu* are also considered *fanua* and also spare each other: Malatigeno and Karoua; Baumana and Baumana Karoua; Simea, Simea Pegata and Oita. However these *latu* are considered distinct and can intermarry. As a matter of fact, as was noticed by Wheeler (MS: 452) these *latu* have in common at least one 'grandmother'. How can we analyse these different relations, which are usually glossed as 'segmentation'? First of all, the use of the term *fanua* shows that the *latu* are thought of in terms of relations in their internal structure as well as in their relationships to one another. It should then be emphasized that in the cases just mentioned the *fanua* relation is a relation between 'grandchildren' who relate to the same 'grandmother', whereas when the *fanua* relation refers to people belonging to the same *latu* it is more narrowly associated with a relation between the 'grandchildren' of one distinctive 'grandfather'. Thus the notion of 'grandmother' is not merely symmetrical to that of 'grandfather', it has a tendency to extension, a tendency to spread beyond the divisions between the *latu*. This is further confirmed by the fact that both the *keno* and the subaquatic 'grandmothers' which ate the bone remains of the body of their dead 'grandchildren' at a *keno* were often common to several *latu*. In contrast, the *latu* do not share their 'grandfathers' which are specific to a *latu*, its distinctive feature. Furthermore, the 'grandfather' of a *latu* sometimes gives its name to the *latu*,[13] and the Mono-Alu material shows a close association of the notion of 'grandfather' with name-giving. In short, a 'grandfather' (*tua*) expresses the specificity of a *latu* and distinguishes it from other *latu*. In contrast, the notion of 'grandmother' (*tete*) in its relation to the *latu* and in its ritual role tends to spread beyond these divisions between *latu* and create links between them. To put it broadly, two contrasting roles in the segmentation of the *latu* system pertain to the asymmetrical notions of (i) 'grandmother', with its tendency to *relate* and spread beyond distinctions and (ii) of 'grandfather', with its tendency to *distinguish*.

With its asymmetrical complementary opposition between its 'grandfather' and 'grandmothers' and the relations with their living *fanua*, each *latu* refers to three basic notions in the conceptualization of the universe. The relations between the 'grandmothers' and 'grandfathers' and the people of a *latu* are embedded in a rich and complex system which expresses both the disjunction and the complementarity of three contrasted domains of the universe that are conceived in terms of sex, kin, ancestors and animal species as well as spatial domains.

We can now sum up the most important features of the notions of 'grandmother' and 'grandfather'. In the kinship terminology, the terms *tete*, 'grandmother', and *tua*, 'grandfather', refer to ancestral generations applying to 'living' persons (*salena*) as well as to dead ones (*nitu*). Another feature of the opposition between 'grandmother' and 'grandfather' is that it refers to the relations between male and female in terms of absolute distinction of sex.[14] When applied to the ancestral figures of the *latu*, these terms refer to the distinctions between two categories of animal species which are themselves contrasted not in terms of sex but in terms of their spatial domain. Spatially, whereas the domain of the living is the surface, the domain of the 'grandfathers' is the world above and the domain of the 'grandmothers' is the world below, encompassing the subaquatic and the subterranean. The world above and the world below are contiguous with the surface, and this corresponds to a characteristic emphasis on interactions between the living and various aspects of the notions of 'grandfather' and 'grandmother'. Then the notion of 'grandfather' is associated not only with the world above and the male principle but also with tendencies towards distinction and specificity, whereas the notion of 'grandmother' is associated with the world below, the female principle, and principles of inclusion, extension and secrecy. Thus, these notions are elements of society *and* of the universe, which is conceived in the same terms and organized in a structured socio-cosmic system. The importance of the components of the person in this system is shown in the funeral rites, during which the circulation and transformation of these components establishes some essential links in this system. Shortly after death, the funeral circulation of the body takes a downward direction through the surface into the subaquatic/subterranean domain of the 'grandmothers'. The *keno* ceremony shows that with this *oriented* movement, the body rejoins the original *nitu*. This can also be viewed as an attraction exerted by the domain of the 'grandmothers' and the original *nitu* over the body.

The Notion of *Nitu*

Let us now take a step further into another dimension of the Mono-Alu cosmology and inquire about the notion of *nitu*, which will reveal its own complex polysemy at a glance at Wheeler's glossary:

> *nitu*: heart ... probably identical with *nitu* = ghost, etc.
> *nitu*: any supernatural being; especially, the ghost of a dead person. Any deadly *leako* [magic preparation] ... ([in the language of] Simbo, *tomate*) ...
> *nitu*: seed of a fruit (probably identical with *nitu*= heart and *nitu*= ghost etc.) (MS, glossary: 52).

An attempt to comprehend this notion should take all these meanings into account; this is not my aim within the limited scope of this paper, and I shall especially concentrate on the distinction the Mono-Alu people make between two broad categories: the *nitu* of the recently dead and the original *nitu*, with only cursory references to the other meanings of this word.

The *nitu* in these two categories can assume any form and can manifest themselves in human guise or as flying creatures, or as creatures living under the ground or under the sea. They are held to be the providers of food for the living. The living perform numerous 'sacrifices' (*sisifala*) and 'offerings' (*fasagi*) to the *nitu*, which, in turn may prove to be more or less generous. During a sacrifice, the officiant, usually a man, calls the *nitu* and then announces the purpose of the sacrifice, simultaneously burning a small amount of food on a fire. This food can be either the meat of an animal which has just been killed or the food which is about to be eaten, which is done before a meal. The other type of relationship, the offering, can be permanent or temporary. It is very often an offering of areca, which can be suspended or thrown into the sea, as was the case mentioned before the giving of the bones to the 'grandmother' at the *keno*. It can also be shell money, calico, tobacco or pipes.

All things and beings have an 'image' (*nunu*: reflection in the water, shadow).[15] Both in the case of offerings and sacrifices, the *nitu* seize the image of what is offered or sacrificed. In the cult to the original *nitu* the offerings and sacrifices follow the same pattern.

At the turn of the century, in their daily life, the Mono-Alu people were very busy interrelating with the *nitu* of the recently dead. 'The attitude towards the Dead is one of submission: they are besought or prayed to' (Wheeler 1912: 40). In the majority of cases described in the ethnography, the word *nitu* has the meaning of 'ghost' or 'spirit of a dead person'. The *nitu* of the recently dead are the transformation accomplished by the funeral rites of the image of the dead nobles and commoners (for the *toniga* there is no funeral treatment of the image or name). Funerals are among the longest, most complex and most spectacular ritual undertakings of this society. In their maximum development, for the high-ranking nobles, men and women, and especially for village chiefs (*lalaafa*), they reverberate throughout the society and into several neighbouring societies, not only in the Shortlands, but also in southern Bougainville. The death of a chief and his funeral rites have far-reaching and long-drawn-out consequences. The dead chief becomes the tutelary *nitu* of the village as a whole. The common house, slit drums, chief's house and large canoes are destroyed or abandoned. The new chief is usually a 'son' (*natu*), 'brother' (*kai*, male speaking) or 'uterine nephew' (*manai*) of the dead one. In most collective ceremonies he will be the officiant of the *nitu* of the dead chief, which has become the tutelary *nitu* of the village. Step by step, under the leadership of the new chief, the construction of a new common house, slit drums, chief's house and canoes is undertaken. Each stage of these complex enterprises is accompanied by sacrifices and offerings to the tutelary *nitu* of the village. Feasts and dances on these occasions and others often link several neighbouring villages. Raids to Southern Bougainville also are part of this scheme. Thus a good deal of the collective life of a village can be seen as a continuation of the death rites of the last chief, and the cycle of life and death of the chief is an important element in the cycle of life and renewal of the village. In contrast to this collective cult, each house is home to a more limited domestic cult of one (sometimes several) recently dead person(s) – all of them close kin – who is (are) the domestic *nitu* of the inhabitants of a house. The *nitu* of some noble men who were not chiefs and of noble children (of both sexes) can also have a specific cult, which usually extends beyond their close kin. A compound cult of several *nitu*, among then the *nitu* of noble people and the personal *nitu* of the fishermen, is related to important collective fishing expeditions, mostly for turtle. The cult of the *nitu* of the recently dead is in large measure a male business. In almost all cases, the officiant is a man: the head of the family in the domestic cult, the chief of the village in the cult to the tutelary *nitu* of the village. The *nitu* is in most cases a 'father' (*apa*), a 'brother' (*kai*, m. s.) or a 'maternal uncle' (*manai*) of the officiant. A few cases are mentioned of sacrifices and (or) offerings to a 'mother' (*nka*) and 'sister' (*fafine*, m.s.) and to a 'daughter' (*natu*).[16]

The 'original' *nitu* (*nitu talu*) are all the *nitu* which 'appeared with the earth' (*imera poro petaang*). This includes named or unnamed *nitu* linked to places of the land or the sea, some important mythical heroes, the *nitu ialele* which carry epidemics, the *nitu* of the forest (*nitu ome* and *nitu sakusaku*). Many of the celestial bodies also are original *nitu*. The *nitu* of the dead which are no longer venerated by name eventually move into this category, in which their name and personal identity are erased. In contrast with the pervasive cult of the *nitu* of the recently dead, a cult dedicated to the original *nitu*, collectively, is attested in only four cases, but all of them are crucial. They are the *keno* ceremony which was presented in the beginning of this paper, the first great sacrifice during the death rites, which will be described presently, and the annual *biloto* rite, as well as the great platform ceremony, which will be summarized later.

The *Nitu* of the Recently Dead

I shall now describe in some detail the funeral transformation of the image of a dead person (noble or commoner) into a *nitu*. One of the main features of this transformation is that it is conceived as a journey into the crater of Bareka, an active volcano in the Southern part of the neighbouring island of Bougainville. This journey is said to be made up of a sort of zigzaging in the vertical dimension: it is a series of jumps from high cliffs into the sea in which the *nitu* progresses from one jumping point to another before reaching the southeastern coast of Bougainville. There, an original *nitu* shows the way up to the crater of the volcano. In Bareka, it is also original *nitu* which confirm the 'death' (*matena*) and inform the new *nitu* of the reason why it died. The process of transformation of the image of the dead into a *nitu* involves alternating upward and downward movements towards or into the world above and the subaquatic and subterranean worlds. Its new expanded spatial domain, unbounded by the surface, now encompasses the domains of the living as well as those of the 'grandfathers' and of the 'grandmothers'.

This journey of the *nitu* is accompanied by a series of funeral ceremonies performed by the living and called 'great sacrifices' (*sisifala kanegana*). Most of these are death meals taken at sunrise or sunset and alternating opossum meat and fish meat, i.e. meat from the domain of the 'grandfathers' and meat from the domain of the 'grandmothers'. Thus the transformation process of the image of the dead is accompanied by similar alternating movements of the hunters, their prey and the sun during the great sacrifices. At the same time, the new *nitu* learns its new condition and its role as provider of meat for the living.

The starting point of this process of transformation and learning is the first great sacrifice, which is called the *tiputipulu*. It is held immediately after the bone remains have been collected from the base of the funeral pyre. Simultaneously, the spear dance described above (p. 109) begins, performed around the site of the funeral pyre where the *tiputipulu* is being held. The officiant breaks a 'dead' (*matena*) coconut over a small fire, also called *tiputipulu*, which has been lit in the middle of the rectangular area where the funeral pyre stood. He addresses both the *nitu* of the dead person and the original *nitu* in these words: 'This is a sacrifice. We shall get meat (*sanaka*) by hunting. Do you grant us plenty of fish, you original *nitu*, do you grant us plenty of fish' or 'This is a sacrifice, the *tiputipulu*. Do thou [the dead person] grant us food seekers plenty of meat. You original *nitu* do you grant us plenty of meat. Yes, it will be good. All men and women will eat fish and opossum. It will be ever good.'[17] This first great sacrifice is the only one which is not a meal and in which no meat is sacrificed. It is also the only one which is addressed to the original *nitu* as well as to the dead person. The following great sacrifices will be dedicated solely to the *nitu* of the dead person. Later the same day, fish having been caught, the next great sacrifice takes the standard form for all great sacrifices of a funeral meal with an invocation to the *nitu* of the dead person. Thus the beliefs related to the journey of the dead and the first great sacrifice show the essential role of the original *nitu* in enabling the transformation of the image of the dead person into a *nitu*. Their role is manifold: (i) they enable the image/*nitu* of the dead to reach Bareka; (ii) they inform it about its death; (iii) they enable the ritual hunting and fishing which will provide opossum and fish meat for the subsequent great sacrifices and establish the new *nitu* as a provider of meat.

The Original *Nitu*

I can now give an overall view of the role of the original *nitu* in funeral rites, before presenting their role in two important ceremonies. First I shall consider the parallelisms and differences in the funeral treatments of the body and the image, and especially their relations to the original *nitu*. The death rites perform a de-constitution of the person, and then proceed with the differentiated treatments of the body and the image of the deceased (we are not concerned here with the treatment of the dead person's name). After only a few days, formerly during the *keno* ceremony, later through burial, the remains of the body rejoin the original *nitu* (see p. 111). The first great sacrifice opens the transformation of the image of the dead person into a venerated and named *nitu* which will undergo a period of worship that will generally last until the death of its officiant. In this first great sacrifice, the original *nitu* are conceived as originating the cult of the *nitu* of the recently dead person. At the same time they will be its final destination and repository when the officiant of this *nitu* dies and the first great sacrifice is performed for him. Thus, after a death, there is a gap between, on the one hand, the short time-span of the destiny of the body, which is limited to a maximum of four days before it rejoins the original *nitu*, and, on the other hand, the longer time-span of the venerated *nitu*, which generally corresponds – and is linked – to the remaining life of the officiant. In other words, after death, the body does not endure and is very quickly depersonalized – it is a 'grandchild', and through a *latu* relationship with its 'grandmother' is soon to rejoin the original *nitu*. In contrast, the enduring *nitu* will be invoked by a personal name during the time-span of its cult, and will only be depersonalized and rejoin the original *nitu* when its officiant dies. Taking care of these intricate movements of circulation of body and image is one of the main tasks of this society. It could be argued that much of the social life of Mono-Alu is sustained by the discrepancy between the time-spans of body and named *nitu*. This is especially clear of the life of a village which focuses on the cult of the *nitu* of the last chief, whose officiant is his successor; but food relations can also be analysed in this framework.

As we remember, the differentiated funeral treatments of body and image simultaneously imply a complex combination of relations and spatially interlacing oriented movements of the components of the person, of the living, of the 'grandmother', of the opossums and fish and, in the eschatology, of the zigzag journey of the image/*nitu* to Bareka. During the death rites, the movements of the body and the image and their different time-spans are oriented in reference to the three spatial domains, the surface, the world above, domain of the 'grandfathers' and the world below, domain of the 'grandmothers'. This is another way in which people, their components and society are conceived as being in constant interaction with the rest of the universe, in different ways, during their life and after death. Thus a person is regarded as a temporary, socially constructed, combination of components that are also at work in the rest of the universe.

Two important ceremonies show other important aspects of the role of the original *nitu* in this socio-cosmic system. I shall now sum up these ceremonies and the relevant aspects of my analysis (see Monnerie 1988, 1995). The aim of the 'great platform ceremony' (*aia*) was to confirm the high rank of a 'great chief' (*lalaafa kanegana*), his eldest daughter of *mamaifa kanegana* rank and, usually, his sons, as well as to bless them with good health. For the great platform ceremony, a large vitex tree was uprooted, carried towards the village and replanted upside-down. On top of its roots a platform was installed. Two ladders (*tete*)[18] were placed on each side of the inverted trunk for the actors of the ceremony to climb up and down the platform. The villagers remained on the ground, whereas the actors of the ceremony, a 'seer' (*dondoro*), the great chief, his eldest daughter and his sons climbed to the platform. There, an invocation and an ointment were made by the seer in order to bestow good health upon the chief and his children, who were said to be the 'grandchildren' (*fabiu*) of the *nitu* of the ceremony, an original *nitu*. In this ceremony, we see that the high rank of the chief and his family as well as their health are due to the original *nitu*. Interestingly, this confirmation of high rank through original *nitu* linked past, present and future generations. The original *nitu* were again associated with aspects of the notion of 'grandmother': the underground, supporting the monumental ceremonial construction, is the domain of the 'grandmothers'; the upturned roots supporting the great platform usually belong in this domain, and the ladders enabling the ritual movement up and down the platform are called 'grandmothers' (*tete*).

In a myth (MAF 64: Dudueri) the boat carrying the large tree which is to be used in the construction of the great platform capsizes. After throwing the food of the ceremonial meal into the sea. Dudueri, the great chief who has ordered the ceremony, kills himself by drowning. Here the failure to hold the ceremony is perceived not as an accident, but as a socio-cosmic manifestation of disharmony. This precipitates the death of the chief, who disappears with the food of the ceremony into the domain of the 'grandmothers'. Dudueri is a *nitu*, said to still reside where he disappeared.

Finally, the annual *biloto* ceremony. It is performed simultaneously in all villages, when the Pleiades reappear over the horizon, a moment which is called *matinale*. The canarium (*kai*) nuts, which by that time are mature, can only be felled and eaten after the *biloto* ceremony, which is held the day following the reappearance of the Pleiades. The first four nuts are given in sacrifice to the original *nitu*, which the invocations associate with the annual cycle of the canarium nuts, the fertility of gardens and the abundance of vegetable food, *darami*.[19] Associated with the regular yearly reappearance of the Pleiades over the horizon and the two seasons, *matinale* and *belafa*, the original *nitu* are related to phenomena which encompass the distinctions between villages. One notices also that they are considered as providing cultivated and uncultivated vegetable food. With their role as meat providers during the first great sacrifice, this means that the original *nitu* are conceived as being providers of *all* sorts of food, whereas the *nitu* of the recently dead are only providers of meat.

The *keno* ceremony, the first funeral great sacrifice, the great platform ceremony and the annual *biloto* ceremony thus give us decisive indications concerning (i) the relations between the two categories of *nitu*, the original *nitu* and the *nitu* of the recently dead, and (ii) their relative status.

The Mono-Alu Socio-Cosmic System

This paper is composed of several interrelated themes, which I would now like to bring together. It is primarily through the detailed consideration of the form of social action we call rituals that, in Mono-Alu, we can grasp the 'framework of concepts and relations which treat the universe or cosmos as an ordered system', a system which here clearly includes persons, their components and society in its overarching treatment of the universe. But the words 'order' and 'framework' should not suggest a more or less static arrangement. I wish to show that the ultimate, most encompassing level of the Mono-Alu socio-cosmic system is associated with the original *nitu* and their dynamic potentials.

Generally speaking, the *nitu* are beings whose domain ignores and encompasses the spatial limits set to the contrasted and more limited domains of the living and of the beings called 'grandfathers' and 'grandmothers'. The *nitu* of the recently dead and the original *nitu* have no spatial limits, but they have different temporal extensions.[20] The distinction between the *nitu* of the recently dead and the original *nitu* can be understood through the dynamic relationship of the transformation of the former into the latter. During funerals, through the first great sacrifice, the original *nitu* give the initial impetus to the series of rituals which transform the image of the person into a *nitu*. Wave-like, the unceasing movement of death, funeral rites and cult, with the death of the officiant pushing the named *nitu* of the recently dead into the collective realm of the original *nitu*, delineates the rhythmic, dynamic distinction between these two fundamental aspects of the notion of *nitu*. Hence the cult of the *nitu* of the recently dead is both initiated and drawn into oblivion, and thus temporally encompassed by the cult of the original *nitu* into which it merges.

Thus, although the notion of original *nitu* usually refers to a category with which kinship relations with the living are no longer relevant, it is the original *nitu* which activate the movement of generations. The movement of successive generations following and replacing one another is conceived as the constantly reiterated flow and transformation of the *nitu* of the recently dead into original *nitu*. This is the basis of the process of succession of noble men to the role of village chief; but this is not the only aspect of the role of the original *nitu* as regards chiefship and nobility. The perpetuation of chiefship is based on the cult of the last dead chief of a village who has become the tutelary *nitu* of the village, whose officiant is his successor, the living chief. This is true for all chiefs of all ranks. But for great chiefs the confirmation of their high rank and that of their daughter and sons is effected in a most spectacular way during the great platform ceremony through a relationship with the original *nitu*.

The encompassing aspect of the original *nitu* has other important features. The dynamic potential of the original *nitu* is also shown during funerals by their attraction in the oriented circulation of the remains of the body. Furthermore, the original *nitu* are associated with the succession of the seasons, as marked by the maturing of the canarium nuts as well as the regular spatiotemporal cycle of the Pleiades. They also have life-giving potentialities, in that they are considered providers of *all* sorts of food, whereas the *nitu* of the recently dead only provide meat.[21] The original *nitu* refer to an era which includes the indefinite 'long ago' (*peu talu*) of the far past, the time of 'myth' (*lagalaga*); they are associated with knowledge about death and its certainty.[22] All these features show that the extension of the notion of original *nitu* goes beyond our definitions of society and simultaneously is crucial to it. In other words, we are dealing with an *episteme* informed by notions which integrate a wide spectrum of knowledge, including and relating man, society and the universe in a socio-cosmic system. It seems appropriate, as I attempted to do here, to leave aside our own preconceived and too often rigid categories and, in order to understand this system, to consider its inner workings and especially its various hierarchical levels.

The overriding aspect of the original *nitu* is manifold. It forms the ultimate encompassing level of Mono-Alu thinking and action, combining such features as maximum spatiotemporal, food-providing and relational extension, as well as references to regularity, certainty and dynamic potentials. When everyday village activity is considered, the cult of the *nitu* of the recently dead seems to be the most important aspect of the relationships between the living and the *nitu*. But appearances – the ethnographer's overwhelming quantitative evidence of the cult of the *nitu* of the recently dead – should not be taken at face value. The cult of the *nitu* of the recently dead (in the day-to-day expression of which the original *nitu* seemingly have no relevance) is at a lower level in the socio-cosmic system, and is in fact globally encompassed by the cult of the original *nitu* in a hierarchical relation.[23] Thus the unified description of the socio-cosmic system I present here implies the recognition of an overall hierarchical level, that of the original *nitu*.

One consequence of this analysis is that, at least for Mono-Alu, we are led to reassess Codrington's time-honoured formula concerning the 'clear' native Melanesian distinction 'between the existing, conscious, powerful, disembodied spirits of the dead, and other spiritual beings *that never have been men at all*' (1891: 121, my italics). Codrington himself was conscious of a difficulty, adding:

It is true that the two orders of beings *get confused* in native language and thought, ... All Melanesians, as far as my acquaintance with them extends, believe in the existence both of spirits that never were men, and of ghosts which are the disembodied souls of men deceased ... the natives of the Solomon Islands ... pay very little attention to spirits and address themselves almost wholly to ghosts. This goes with a much greater development of a sacrificial system in the west [i.e., the Solomon Islands] than in the east [the New Hebrides and Banks Islands] (ibid.: 121–2, my italics).

Codrington justly emphasizes the importance of what he calls the 'sacrificial system', the analysis of which helped us realize that for Mono-Alu there really is no *confusion* 'in native language and thought' but a relation of *transformation*. This enables us to recast his own formula into a hierarchical relation of transformation between the encompassed *nitu* of the recently dead (the 'ghosts') and the encompassing original *nitu* (the 'spirits'), the latter including both 'the existing, conscious, powerful, disembodied spirits of the dead' after the period of personalized worship is over *as well as* other 'spiritual beings that never have been men at all', to which we should add mythical heroes.

Another consequence of such an analysis is the question it raises 'how widespread is the hierarchical relation in this society?' Dumont writes that ' ... the hierarchical disposition entails that the successive distinctions possible are of rapidly decreasing global significance ...' (1986: 226). This, of course, does not make the relations pertaining to other, less global, levels of the system less interesting. On the contrary, much is to be learnt by paying close attention to their articulation. This is why I will conclude on two aspects of the articulation of the notions of 'grandmother' and 'grandfather' with that of *nitu*. First, the three dimensions (the world below, domain of the 'grandmothers'; the surface, domain of the living; and the world above, domain of the 'grandfathers') can be manipulated ritually. This was the case in the great platform ceremony. When they stood on top of the platform, the actors of this ceremony were neither above nor below the surface, they were everywhere at once. Their movements up and down the ladders even complicate this descriptive problem. As the foundation and support of the whole construction, the notion of 'grandmother' established a direct relation to the original *nitu*. Here the original *nitu* of the ceremony and their encompassing character *vis-à-vis* the three dimensions account for the manipulation of ritual space effected by the great platform ceremony and its actors' very unusual spatial positions and movements. Secondly, we saw that the notion of 'grandmother' displays a tendency to extension. In contrast, distinctive features pertain to the notion of 'grandfather'. This asymmetry between the notions of 'grandmother' and 'grandfather' is also to be related (i) to the direct association – through the circulation of the body – of the notion of 'grandmother' to the encompassing original *nitu* and (ii) to the indirect, delayed relation, through the giving and transmission of personal names used to address the *nitu* of the recently dead, of the notion of 'grandfather' to the original *nitu*. The asymmetry can thus be linked to the hierarchical relation between original *nitu* and *nitu* of the recently dead. Note that the fact that both notions are either directly or indirectly linked to the original *nitu* accounts for the fact that they cannot be conceived separately from each other. Hence, the hierarchical relation between the original *nitu* and the *nitu* of the recently dead informs, at a lower level, the relations between such notions as 'grandmother' and 'grandfather', which then appear complementary and asymmetrical rather than hierarchical.

LIST OF THE *LATU*, THEIR *TUA* AND THEIR *TETE*

latu	*tua*[24]	*tete*[25]
Hanapara	*tigeno**[26] (Mino Gracula kreffti)	*iau* (megapode) *dinai* (large fish)
Malatigeno	*kekeoaka* * (bird)	*iau* (megapode)
Simea	*popo* * (calao)	*sugi* (green lizard) *samoai* (sawfish)
Simea Pegata	*popo* * (calao) [Boch: *pausape* (stone)]	*sugi* (green lizard) *samoai* * (sawfish)
Oita	*kuru* (owl) or *pausape* (volcanic stone)	*samoai* * (sawfish)

Baumana	*baulu* (pigeon)	*habubusu* * (small bird) *bampa* (green and blue lizard)
Karoua (or Baumana Karoua)	*karo* (green parrot)	*habubusu* (small bird) *bampa* (green and blue lizard) [Boch: *toloo* (eel)]
Talapuini	*manua* * (eagle)	*umau** (crocodile) [Boch adds the megapode]
Bauahu	*anaa* (white cockatoo)	
Manaini (extinct)	*damau* (*?) (flying fox)	
Tabooti	*sabau* * (lizard) [Boch ; iguana]	*umau* * (crocodile)
Talasagi	*kopi* (bird) [Brown: heron]	*alele* (centipede) *alele masimasini* (red centipede) *peraoli masimasini* (red ant) [Boch: *kata* (fish)]
Talili	*samoai* * (sawfish) [Parkinson: *habubusu*]	*umau* * (crocodile) or no *tete*

Notes

1. I would like to thank Daniel de Coppet, André Itéanu and Cécile Barraud, the participants in the conference 'La société et l'univers: leurs relations ou leur coalescence en Mélanésie' (Azay le Féron 16–20 April 1990) and those of the CASA team in Leiden for their criticisms and suggestions on several versions of this paper. Special thanks to Carol Seymour for her help with the English text.

2. The ethnographic present is used to describe this period.
3. I shall reserve the word 'universe' to refer to all that there is, and use 'cosmos' for the organized system which describes and conceptualizes the 'universe' (see D. Furley 1987, 1989).
4. To facilitate legibility, I translated into English as many Mono-Alu terms I possibly could. These English translations first appear between quotation marks, followed by the Mono-Alu word between brackets; this is repeated if needed. Consistency of use throughout the article has been one of my aims. Naturally these translations should never be regarded as explanations in themselves. This is stressed by the repeated use of quotation marks for the expressions 'grandmother' and 'grandfather'.
5. MS refers to the unpublished manuscript of Wheeler's *Sociology* of Mono-Alu. MAF refers to his *Mono-Alu Folklore*; see bibliography.
6. It is also performed for young children. This is linked to a specific cult of infant *nitu* which reverses the oriented generational vector of the cult of the *nitu*, see below.
7. The container is lined with calico. The bone remains are put with plants – commonly used for personal decoration – which have macerated in the water of a young coconut, then they are wrapped with *kia* and *kasisi*, the two most valuable types of shell money.
8. The past tense refers to this period.
9. The word *korausi* is applied both to the fact of seeing something forbidden and the death which follows.
10. According to a myth (MAF 28: Nife, 'The snakes') a 'grandmother' created 'sea water' (*keno*) and the 'sea' (*keno*). In the myth of Soi (MAF 65: Soi) the close association of the hero to the marine and submarine world is emphasized and attributed to his 'grandmother's' knowledge.
11. In the myths women only climb trees in order to commit suicide by jumping off (MAF 13, 56), whereas both in myth and ritual, men often hide in trees to watch women they are about to seduce or marry.
12. The remains were buried, either in specific places also called and related to several *latu* or in 'places of the dead' (*saria famata nitu* or *nitua*) often related to a village or a group of villages.
13. For instance, Simea Pegata, which is considered a branch of Simea: these *latu* which share the same 'grandfather' also

share the same *name*. Interestingly, three of the 'grandfathers' of the *latu*, the *tigeno*, *karo* and *anaa* are birds that can be taught to speak.

14. By which I mean a distinction which does not depend on the enunciators' own sex. Several important terms in the Mono-Alu kinship vocabulary distinguish sex in a relative way (see Monnerie 1988, 1995).

15. Most writers on Mono-Alu translate *nunu* by 'spirit' or 'soul'.

16. In a Melanesian context, of course, it is difficult to say whether this is because the ethnographer was a man. In Mono-Alu, for men, a degree of secrecy surrounded female aspects of society, most noticeably births.

17. Revised translation from the original Mono-Alu text; MS: 509.

18. We have here another aspect of the notion of 'grandmother' (*tete*), its role as 'support'. In the myth of Soi (MAF 65) the sharks which the hero rides to safety are his 'support' (-*tete*-).

19. The word *darami* applies to cultivated vegetable food and is also used for ceremonial food and meals *which include meat*. The use of the word *sanaka* is restricted to meat, i.e. fish, turtle, pork, opossum.

20. These different temporal extensions correspond to contrasted ways of expressing the 'past' in the Mono-Alu language (see I. Bril in Monnerie 1988, 1995).

21. The descriptions we have of birth ceremonies offer striking parallels with the annual *biloto* ceremony and birth can be interpreted as implicating the original *nitu* (Monnerie 1988, 1995).

22. We saw (p. 119) that, on arrival in Bareka, it was original *nitu* who showed the way and informed the new *nitu* about its death. A mythical heroine of the long ago (MAF 62: Foifoiti), a 'grandmother' (*tete*) has to submit to the inescapability of old age and death in order to retain good relationships with her 'grandchild' (*fabiu*).

23. Here I am using for Mono-Alu a variant of the concept of hierarchical relation developed by L. Dumont (1966, 1986) as a tool for comparative analysis of the Indian and modern civilizations.

24. G. Brown (1910) 'totem'; Father Boch 'their tua' (*tuaria*) see MS: 449–50.

25. Boch says 'their *tete*' (*teteria*).

26. The (*) indicates a prohibition on eating for the people of the *latu*, according to Wheeler.

References

The edition used is in brackets.

Some Sources for Mono-Alu, The Shortlands and Southern Bougainville

Boch, M. Père. (n.d.) *A Short Alu Grammar*.

Brown, G. (1910). *Melanesians and Polynesians*. Macmillan, London.

Fagan, J. L. (1986). *A Grammatical Analysis of Mono-Alu (Bougainville Straits, Solomon Islands)*. Pacific Linguistics, Series B – NO 96, Canberra.

Festetics de Tolna, R. (1903). *Chez les Cannibales*. Plon, Paris.

Guppy, H. B. (1887). *The Solomon Islands and their Natives*. London.

Monnerie, D. (1988). Nitu, les vivants, les morts et l'univers selon la société de Mono-Alu, Iles Salomon. Thèse de troisième cycle, Paris EHESS.

—— (1995). *Nitu, les vivants, les morts et le cosmos selon la société de Mono-Alu*. Center for Non Western Studies, Leiden.

Oliver, D. L. (1955). *A Solomon Island Society. Kinship and Leadership among the Siuai of Bougainville*. Harvard University Press, Cambridge, Mass.

—— (1973). *Bougainville: A Personal History*. Hawaii.

—— (1989). *Oceania. The Native Cultures of Australia and the Pacific Islands*, 2 vols University of Hawaii Press, Honolulu.

—— (1968). Southern Bougainville. *Anthropological Forum*, 2 (2), 158–79.

—— (1949). *Studies in the Anthropology of Bougainville*. Harvard University Press, Cambridge, Mass.

Parkinson, R. (1907). *Dreissig Jahre in der Südsee*. Stuttgart.

—— (1899). Zur Ethnographie der Nordwestlichen Saalomoninseln. *Abhandlungen und Berichte des Königlichen Zoologischen und Anthropologisch-Ethnographischen Museums zu Dresden*.

Ribbe, C. (1903). *Zwei jahre unter der Kannibalen der Salomon Inseln*. Dresden. Elbgau-Buchdruckerei, Hermann Beyer.

Terrell, J. (1978). Archaeology and the Origins of Social Stratification in Southern Bougainville. In: *Rank and Status in Polynesia and Melanesia*, Publications de la Société des Océanistes, N°39. Musée de l'Homme, Paris.

—— (1986). *Prehistory in the Pacific Islands*. Cambridge University Press, Cambridge.

Thurnwald, H. (1937). *Menschen der Südsee*. Stuttgart.

—— (1934). Woman's Status in Buin Society. *Oceania*, 5, 142–70.

Thurnwald, R. (1912). *Forschungen auf die Salomo-Insel*. Berlin.

—— (1951). Historical Sequences on Bougainville. *American Anthropologist*, 53, 137–9.

—— (1934). Pigs and Currency in Buin. *Oceania*, 5, 2.

—— (1936). *Profane Literature of Buin*, Yale University Publications in Anthropology, VIII. Yale University Press, New Haven, Conn.

Wheeler, G. C. (1913). A Text in Mono Speech. *Anthropos*, VIII.

—— (1914). An Account of the Death Rites and Eschatology of the People of the Bougainville Straits (Western Solomon Islands). *Archiv für Religionswissenschaft*, 17, 64–112. (Leipzig–Berlin).

—— (1926). *Mono Alu Folklore (Bougainville Straits, W. Solomon Islands)*. Routledge, London. (Referred to as MAF).

—— (1928). On Some Pottery from Alu, Bougainville Straits, Solomon Islands. *Man*, 28, 38–40.

—— (1912). Sketch of the Totemism and Religion of the People of the Islands in the Bougainville Straits (Western Solomon Islands). *Archiv für Religionwissenschaft*, 15, 24–58, 321–58. (Leipzig–Berlin).

—— (n.d.). Untitled manuscript: 1092 pp., plus glossary 87 pp. (announced in Wheeler 1926 under the title of *Sociology*; for pagination see Monnerie 1988, 1995). School of Oriental and African Studies Library, London. (Referred to as MS, glossary referred to as GL, MS.)

—— (n.d.). Untitled, list of objects given to several British museums. Museum of Mankind, London.

Woodford, C. M. (1890). *A Naturalist Among the Head Hunters. An Account of Three Visits to the Solomon Islands in the Years 1886, 1887, 1888* (2nd edn.). George Philip, London.

General Bibliography

Codrigton, R. H. (1891). *The Melanesians*. Oxford, Clarendon Press.

Coppet, D. de (1976). Jardins de vie, jardins de mort en Mélanésie. *Traverses*, 5/6, 166–77.

—— (1981). The Life-Giving Death. In: S. C. Humphreys and H. King (eds), *Mortality and Immortality: the Anthropology and Archaeology of Death*. Academic Press, London.

Dumont, L. (1986). *Essays on Individualism*. University of Chicago Press, Chicago.

—— (1966). *Homo Hierarchicus*. Gallimard, Paris.

Furley, D. (1989). *Cosmic Problems. Essays on Greek and Roman Philosophy of Nature.* Cambridge University Press, Cambridge.

—— (1987). *The Greek Cosmologists*, Vol 1. Cambridge University Press, Cambridge.

Lévi-Strauss, C. (1974 [1962]). *Le Totémisme aujourd'hui.* PUF, Paris.

Mosko, M. (1985). *Quadripartite Structures. Categories, Relations, and Homologies in Bush Mekeo Culture.* Cambridge University Press, Cambridge.

Rivers, W. H. R. (1914). *The History of the Melanesian Society*, 2 vols. Cambridge University Press, Cambridge.

Tambiah, S. J. (1985). *Culture, Thought and Social Action.* Harvard University Press, Cambridge, Mass.

Chapter 5

Rituals and Ancestors

André Iteanu

To the late Samson Aroha who always sought his *ahihi* in mirrors and now dwells in the bush.

In what he has left behind him of the project of a book which would have been called *Sin and expiation in primitive societies*[1] R. Hertz wrote:

> When Jesus, to the indignation of the Pharisees there present, forgives the paralytic's sins before he tells him 'Stand up and walk', he well knows that these two achievements, the remission of sins and the curing of the sick, are both as difficult and miraculous tasks which require the intervention of the Son of Man; this does not escape the witnesses: in a state of ecstasy, they glorify God (Hertz 1988: 21).

M. Mauss, who posthumously edited the Hertz manuscript, further commented on this passage in a note:

> What is obvious in this passage is that for Jesus, just as for the Pharisees, the forgiveness of the sins necessitates divine power. It is a miraculous intervention which upsets the natural unfolding of things and which Jesus considers as situated at exactly the same level as the magical curing of the sick man, the only difference being that one is visible while the other is not (M. Mauss, in Hertz 1988: 22).

These remarks shed light on an essential dimension of our Western conception of the supernatural. In conformity with the Christian notion of miracle, it locates transcendence in the presence of personified supernatural characters associated with the modification of the natural order. This version of the sacred cannot be directly applied to Melanesian societies, which seem to have adopted a different view. First of all, although most of these societies know of a large number of personified ancestors and spirits, these do not occupy a transcendent position similar to that of the Christian God. Secondly, the interventions of these supernatural beings within the world of the living do not produce major perturbations of an order that one could call 'natural'. Rather on the contrary, the intimacy in being and in acting, between these characters and the living is so pronounced that a majority of Melanesianists consider their distinction as almost nil. It is, therefore, not uncommon to hear them talk about an 'immanent transcendence'.

This mingling between the living and the supernatural is a commonplace today. Yet, the way in which it has been conceived has evolved through time. While earlier studies reified it, recent ones accord it a more symbolical flavour. For example, in a recent book on *Religious Imagination in New Guinea*, Herdt and Stephen attempts to qualify that blend by comparing it to the ancient Greeks, he states:

> The [Greek] notion of divine revelation and inspiration, planted directly into the minds and hearts of cultural actors, is one the Melanesian would recognize in Homer's account of Heracles, for example. The texts of Sambia and Mekeo, Nalumin, Gebusi, and Ilahita recognize the integral character of spirit and human existence, much interwoven in Greek culture (Herdt and Stephen 1989: 19).

This type of analysis, like many other current ones, hopelessly fuses the natural and the supernatural in a unified field. Tautologously, they face serious problems in distinguishing between supernatural beings and living persons. To that end, many then use categories of visible and invisible.[2] But anyone who is familiar with the region well knows that this opposition is not relevant here. More importantly, however, since this indistinctness deprives the observer of the usual Western opposition between a transcendent cosmos ruled by some ultimate supernatural beings and a subordinated society shaped by a relative human order, he or she often imprudently concludes that no value distinctions are here to be uncovered.

Fortunately enough, counterbalancing this indistinctness in

the realm of personification, most Melanesian societies display a profusion of events that we call 'rituals', which simultaneously present a quality of transcendence in relation to other actions and visible effects on the social and natural order. However, since in these rituals, extraordinary characters, in the guise of masks for example, often play an important part, one may believe that, at last, the dynamic of personification is at work here in its Melanesian form. Should we therefore say, as it is often accepted, that it is these supernatural entities which grant efficiency to the rituals? As will be shown in the present paper, since outside the ritual context these characters and their powers simply disappear, this interpretation does not hold. In fact, these beings' ontology is so unstable that it shatters our notion of a personified transcendence, and one is finally led to acknowledge that it is the rituals which bring them into being, rather than their insufflating their powers into the ritual.

The above-mentioned apparent contradictions do not reflect, I will argue, the incoherence of Melanesian societies, but the inadequacy of the notion of the supernatural which is generally applied to them. To escape this bias, one must conceptually dissociate transcendence and personification. In Melanesia, the former implies an ontologically valued ritual process which orders the cosmos as a whole, while the latter constitutes an inferior level of value, where beings and things, the living and the dead, each in turn is singled out and then mingled back again with the others in a cycle of life and death. In what follows, I will argue that the hierarchical superiority of the ritual value over the process of personification, operating in the form of a circulation of beings and things, characterizes, in a comparative framework, the contrast between these societies and ours.

My analysis will be focused on the Orokaiva, a well-known group of the Oro Province of Papua New Guinea, and develops along the lines of the relations between the three types of 'supernatural' beings that this society recognizes.

Ahihi and *onderi*, created through the mortuary ritual, are the guise in which the dead appear. Since they are ritually transformed forms of the living, I study their identity within the complete cycle of life and death. While this analysis sheds light on *ahihi*, it leaves *onderi* partially in the dark. I then focus my attention on the third type of supernatural being, *jape*, the secret characters that play the central role in the initiation ritual.

Nothing here permits comparison with the living, but the Orokaiva affirm that they are related to the second form of the ghosts *onderi*, which identity remains so far mysterious. The examination of this relation, which accords to *jape* a much bigger value than to *onderi*, shows that these two categories may only be understood in the framework of a ritual hierarchy which encompasses both supernatural beings and living persons.

In conclusion, I am forced to abandon the idea that the Orokaiva supernatural beings are all-powerful universal beings, and led to consider that, like the living and objects, they are subordinated to a superior local value, manifested in rituals. This view allows us to discover a parallel hierarchic ordering of both living persons and supernatural beings which characterizes the Orokaiva global ideology.

The Life and Death Cycle

The Orokaiva know of two distinct forms of ghost, called *ahihi* and *onderi*. The mortuary ritual, through the accomplishment of its diverse steps, successively transforms the formerly living person into the first and, later, into the second of these forms. In order to grasp their nature fully, these ghosts must thus be examined in the context of a complete life cycle, where their identity may be understood together with that of the living. This endeavour, however, does not need to start from zero, since in a former study I have analyzed the identity of the living Orokaiva person, and I may briefly summarize my conclusions here.

The Social Person

The problem then faced was that, among Orokaiva, the various dimensions (subject/object of exchange, group affiliation, status) of each person's identity were fluctuating throughout his or her lifetime, and that, at each moment of this fluctuation, they could not be defined independently from the rituals that this person had taken part in (Iteanu 1990). Analysis showed that it was possible to grasp the meaning of these fluctuations by following the transformations imposed by the rituals that mark the different life stages of a person upon the *hamo*, a notion which for the Orokaiva broadly refers to the living person.

One may summarize this movement as follows. When an Orokaiva child is born, he is said to be an image, *ahihi*. 'He does not,' people say, 'have a *hamo*, but he will later gradually make it' (Iteanu 1983a: 31 and Schwimmer 1973: 92). Thus, although a child does not come to life as a *hamo*, the latter is thereafter constituted for him by his elders through the performance of numerous childhood rituals like adoption, naming, attribution of the first taro, and so forth. The child's *hamo*, thus constructed, is composed of the various social relations created for him through the rituals and of the 'physical' marks, like scars, body size, special decorations, names, emblems, familial affiliation and so forth, associated to these relations. This process does not come to end when all the childhood rituals have been completed, but continues throughout a person's life. Each time he or she participates in a ritual his or her *hamo* is said to 'grow' by being caught up in a set of new or transformed relations. One may thus say that an Orokaiva living person is not conceived as a completed whole, but as an ever-unfinished combination perpetually modified by the rituals. However, at each moment in time, for each specific living person, the nature of the relations which composes him or her and their specific combination establish him or her in a particular status and in a number of various affiliations to some of the distinct family groups which constitute the village society (Iteanu 1983b). Ritually created relations therefore simultaneously determine the existence, the status and the particular familial affiliations of an Orokaiva living person. Since these three dimensions, which anthropology normally distinguishes, may not here be discriminated, one may say, that, while alive, an Orokaiva social person is only the worth of the ritually created relations that he or she is taking part in.

This view compels us to realize that the Orokaiva do not conceive of the empirical subject, as Westerners do, that is as an entity called individual, characterized by its universal physical and moral qualities.[3] In contrast, for them, each living person is constructed in terms of relations to other similar persons which partake in the definition of his or her very existence, but which, from our point of view, are outside of him or her (Leenhardt 1971; Read 1955). I have called 'social person' the outcome of this relational construction of the empirical subject's identity.

The above conclusions led me to abandon the search for a static individual form of identity, and compelled me to focus my study on the transformations induced by the rituals. In order to describe these transformations, which in fact operate in a single movement, I had to separate them in two different stages. The first of these deals with the discrimination of encompassing categories. It arises from the fact that all the transformations brought about by the diverse rituals performed in Orokaiva society are not heterogeneous, but constitute together a general unified movement which alternates an indistinctness of (what we distinguish as) men and pigs with a momentarily separation, in rituals, of two categories, that of objects and subjects of exchange (Iteanu 1983a). The nature of these two fundamental categories thus appears not to be ontologically defined, but rather over-determined by the position that each of them occupies in the ritual (Iteanu 1990). The second step is logically dependent on the first one, and deals with the identity of the social persons involved in the ritual. Indeed, once objects and subjects of exchange have been distinguished by ritual action, the former are used in exchanges to build up the status and the various social affiliations of each participant.

In Orokaiva ideology, then, both the definition of the broad categories of subjects and objects of exchange and the position of specific social persons within the village society are constituted by a set of relations established through the accomplishment of the diverse rituals. Furthermore, a twofold hierarchy, which matches the two above-mentioned ritual steps, characterizes these relations. At a first level, the unfolding of rituals demonstrates that the subjects of exchange are superior to their objects (essentially pigs and foodstuff), since the latter are 'killed' and ingested in order to construct the former's identity. At a second level, the position of each specific social person within society cannot be conceived independently from a statutory valuation, since every one of them (*hamo*) is said to 'grow' and thus 'become bigger' each time he or she participates in a ritual.[4] However, since comparative considerations are not part of this valuation, this latter notion of size does not create a unified scale of status which would classify all members of the society. As a matter of fact, even to compare occasionally the relative growth of any two persons is not part of the accepted representations. Growth in fact only measures each social person's relative involvement in rituals.

Thus, from the point of view I have adopted here, all the elements which constitute society – the existence of the distinction between subjects and objects of exchange, each social persons' ritual status and his or her social affiliation – do not appear as ontologically defined, but as the outcome of an encompassing conception embedded in the rituals. Since rituals were thus shown to occupy a dominant value position in the Orokaiva ideology, I have called this system a 'ritual system'.

The Dead

For any social person, life thus amounts to an accumulation of relations moved about by the rituals. However, after death, this process is reversed in the unfolding of the mourning ritual. To begin with, death is not considered as a 'natural' event, but results from an act of witchcraft confirmed by the first stage of the mourning ritual. Thus, a person is only considered as dead for good after he has been buried (*pehari kovari*) (Iteanu 1990). Then, in a second stage, the funeral ritual extinguishes, one by one, each of the relations that had a part in the constitution of *the* social person of the deceased. It only comes to an end when no social person (*hamo*) is left. Two distinct terms designate the deceased during these two successive stages: during the mortuary ritual it is called *ahihi*, and thereafter, *onderi*.

The funeral ritual goes as follows (Williams 1930: 210–30 and Iteanu 1983a: 121–80). Immediately after the person has ceased to move, all those who maintained relations with him or her gather for a night-long wail. The transformation which is then acknowledged is most strikingly marked by the fact that the defunct may no longer be called by his or her personal name, but is refereed to in terms of either his or her particular plant emblem or by the name of the families he or she was attached to. If at sunrise, he or she has not returned to life, the corpse is buried. Thereafter, each mourner may choose a number of prohibitions on anything which reminds him or her of the dead person (*hajire*). Mortuary prohibitions can thus, in principle, be of any sort, but, in fact, for most of them, may broadly be grouped into two categories: firstly, not eating or not using some kind of objects, and secondly, refraining from certain activities like washing, dancing and so forth. One must add to these two types, the prohibition which falls on the deceased personal name, which is more general than the former types, but does not apply homogeneously.[5]

Those who have assumed prohibitions say that they will respect them for as long as the memory of the dead person remains vivid to them. Consequently, the closer the relation between the dead person and the mourner, the wider and longer-lasting the prohibitions. Thus, for example, the extreme case of the widow, or the widower, who generally assumes a sort of total prohibition by entering a long period of seclusion. However, once they have forgotten the dead, all the mourners, no matter how closely related to the deceased, proceed with a ceremony (*tepukerari*) that permits the prohibitions to be lifted. In the usual case, this ceremony assembles a great number of mourners in a larger and prestigious event. But one who has had enough of mourning and does not care for waiting for the others or one who still feels sorrow beyond the time of the large ceremony does not have to comply with this collective event, and may stage his or her own limited prohibition-lifting ritual.

In both cases, each mourner must have a ritual partner. The latter gives each forbidden object to the former, who breaks it, throws it away, or spits it out, if it is food, in order to cleanse it of its relation to the deceased. Then, he gives him or her again a similar object which he or she may now use. Through this action the relation between the mourner and the dead person is severed (Iteanu 1983a: 126ff.). In conclusion, food prestations are exchanged between the two partners.[6] The prestations (*pondo*) thus given are meant to honour the ritual work done by the mourner in the burial process, but also to reciprocate any standing debt towards the mourner that the deceased may have left behind.[7] Similarly, in every prohibition-lifting ceremony, each prestation given to a ritual partner terminates the relation between that person and the deceased, and eventually closes a ritual debt of the later with regard to the former. Thus, after all the prohibitions have been lifted, the deceased is considered as totally even in the exchange system, and all the relations that linked him to other persons are closed.

As has been shown, the mortuary ritual is centred on operations that deal with prohibitions. To start with, these prohibitions may be understood as a sort of temporary mutilation of the social persons of the mourners in what appears to us as their two complementary aspects: relational and physical. Abstention from washing for up to several months is the most striking of such examples. After a few days, the mourner's body degrades and starts to give off a particularly unpleasant odour, resembling that of a corpse. For reasons of modesty, this effluvium obliges him to sit alone far away from anyone else for as long as the prohibition lasts. He is thus both diminished physically and deprived of normal social relations. One may even venture to say that, through this process, the ill fate which has struck the deceased is shared out among all the mourners, who momentarily assume some part of it. The dead is thus scattered along the lines of his former social relations.

At the end of the funeral period, however, the social persons of the mourners recover their full 'dimension' during the ceremony in which they discard their prohibitions and start again to exchange food prestations with others. When all the prohibited objects are thus cleansed of the relation that they had with the dead person, all his or her relations are closed and all his or her debts paid for. All recollections of him or her as a social person are thus erased. Thereafter, no further commemorative feast is held in his or her honour. He or she is then no longer an *ahihi*, but becomes part of a collective category called *onderi*.

Detached from the specific dead person, two elements of his or her former identity survive. The first one is his or her name, formerly borne by a series of now dead people, which was only lent to him or her for the time of his or her life – for names can only apply to living social persons. This name has either already been or soon will be attributed to a new living child. The second element is eventually a number of stories referring to his or her most memorable feats. Just as he or she has become anonymous now, these stories do not refer to his or her personal identity, since the name under which he or she will appear is rapidly transformed into that of an object or a place (Iteanu 1983b). These two elements are (in the case of the name) or become (in the case of the stories) assets of the families to which he or she was related. Since these elements are part of the identity of a social group rather than that of a single person, at death they are retrieved, and thus resist the nullification produced by the mortuary ritual. They survive as detached from any specific dead person.

The three forms of the Orokaiva person, *hamo, ahihi* and *onderi*, alternate in the unfolding of the rituals that punctuate the cycle of life and death. They should not, consequently, be considered as heterogeneous entities, but as different stages in a continuous process driven by the rituals. The social person, *hamo*, is the form assumed by the person while it stands in the midst of social relations throughout the ritual cycle. *Ahihi*, image, is that assumed by the child at birth and by the deceased while in the process of escaping from human connections. It thus manifests itself each time a person is in the process of either acquiring its first social relations or of relinquishing them all. That is a state where one stands midway between relations and no relations at all.[8] Finally, *onderi* is a collective designation for all the *ahihi* who have gone through their funeral ritual to its end and have thus become anonymous, and completely detached from social life. In this process some aspects of the collective identities that were momentarily attributed to the social person are retrieved and re-used as assets of individual families. I will have to come back to this important point. However, what clearly appears so far is that *onderi* do not constitute a category of what we may call 'ancestors', since what is left of them has lost any trace of their former social identity.

Indeed, under their *onderi* form, the dead can no longer be invoked by men. However, they spontaneously make their presence felt in a number of ways. Although they never enter the villages, they are always present everywhere around them in the bush. Their most current and typical manifestation is when they attack those who venture at night alone beyond the boundary of the village. They then appear in the guise of pigs, birds, other small animals, or even skulls, but no sign of their past identity is ever available. On seeing them, the victim most often immediately faints (*pehari*). A search party then eventually finds him (or her), his body covered with scratches and spittle, more shaken than hurt, sitting on a branch near the top of a tree from which he cannot come down. More exceptionally, however, *onderi* attack entire settlements. They then assemble at the edge of the village and throw diverse objects at the inhabitants. The latter cannot see their assailants, but defend themselves by throwing back whatever they can get hold of. Although very little protection is available against these attacks of the dead against individuals or groups,[9] they are not considered as very serious.

The Orokaiva say that the social persons of the living are never affected by them, and that no one ever dies for good from them, but that 'only the skin (ando) is scratched'.

Ahihi, on the contrary, do not display such an independence. Because the relations they maintained with the living have not been terminated yet, they may be called upon by them during the prohibition period that separates the first and second funeral ceremony. Thus anyone who respects a prohibition may use the prohibited object (hajire), which bears his or her relation to the deceased, to invoke the ahihi. After he or she has been called up by using the appropriate kinship term, and after the prohibited object has been displayed, the ahihi is supposed to have come in the vicinity. Then, straight away, orders are given to it either as to what game to push towards the hunter or as to what object, belonging to the mourner or to someone else, to guard against thievery or destruction by men and as to what kind of sickness to inflict on the aggressor. Thereafter, when a feast is held with the pigs which were provided by an ahihi or with the foodstuff which was protected by it, a couple of betel-nuts or some cooked potatoes are left for it in the bush.

The relation between ahihi and the living comes however to an end after the second funeral ceremony, which severs the tie between the prohibited object and the dead person. Invocations can then no longer be made. After a certain period of time, the dead thus normally escape the reach of the living. This loss, however, is not accepted by everyone. Indeed, in order to benefit more consistently from their relation to the deceased, some mourners, then considered as apprentice sorcerers, keep hold of certain prohibited objects without submitting them to ritual treatment for an abnormally long period of time. More or less everyone in a village knows who these people are, and they slightly fear them. But this attitude, which can be profitable for a while, may not be prolonged for ever. In the long run, a mourning period which is not brought to an end is very likely to threaten the health – that is the social person – of the mourner and that of the persons composing his close family.

As we have seen, each relation that a living person maintains with an ahihi is always mediated by a prohibited object (hajire). When this object is severed from its relation to the deceased, the relation between the mourner and the dead comes to an end. Ahihi thus appear to be more attached to the objects on which the prohibitions fall (*hajire*) than to the persons, former friends or kin, who have assumed these prohibitions. It is so much so, that a person who sets a spell to protect a garden, a tree or anything else, may become the victim of the very *ahihi* he has himself invoked, be it very close kin, if he does not stay away from the protected item. In the same way, a sorcerer who refuses to end a prohibition is himself threatened in the long run by the *ahihi* that he continues to honour. One is then led to the conclusion that, for *ahihi*, relations to objects are superior to relations to people.

So far the entire Cosmos has been apprehended as a set of contrasted relations, which may be summarized as follows. While the identity of the living is constituted by social relations, the funeral ritual gradually transforms social persons into anonymous relationless images, *onderi*, through prohibition procedures. During the intermediate period covered by the funeral ritual, the observance of these prohibitions establishes a specific mode of relation between the living and the images in formation of the dead, *ahihi*. However, the dead are throughout this period rather roughly treated by the living, as though they were in a state of absolute weakness. This is particularly true in two distinct ways. Firstly, *ahihi* seem to have no alternative but to blindly obey the orders given to them by the living as to looking after their objects or providing them with game. They are thus in a state of obedience (*agi embo*) that is most systematically despised in Orokaiva society. Secondly, the position that *ahihi* occupy prevents them both from possessing a clearly marked identity – since a dead person may not be invoked by its personal name – and from recognizing that of former kin and friends. This degradation of the notion of identity characterizes the sharp contrast which opposes relations among the living to relations between the living and *ahihi*. Among the living, as we have shown, relations build up social persons' identities and their affiliation into family groups. Identity is thus created or transformed through exchanges which deal with standardized types of objects of exchange like pigs, taro and diverse vegetable foodstuffs. On the contrary, in the relations between the living and the dead, the partner's identity is erased and the mediating objects (*hajire*), souvenirs, are individualized to the point that they become unique of their kind. *Ahihi* thus appear as rather insensitive to relations with social persons, but tightly compelled by their tie with the prohibited objects.

After the funeral ritual has been completed and the dead have become *onderi*, these characteristics are reinforced still further. The impact of *onderi* in the universe of the living is even weaker than that of *ahihi*, since unlike the latter they do no even cause sickness, but 'only scratch the skin'. This characteristic is very clearly marked by the following ambiguity. Young unmarried girls normally date boys at night in the bush, not far from the village. Tradition however holds that, on arriving there, the boy is attacked by the girl, who scratches him, bites him and tears his cloth down as much as she can. The boy himself does not need to stay put, as he is supposed to return the compliment. After they have thus convened, they return separately to the village, generally presenting a most ragged appearance. When asked what has happened to them, they affirm that they were attacked by *onderi*. Although it is agreed that this assertion may sometimes be true, a rather sceptical humorous attitude in fact awaits anyone who thus justifies scratches. This rather ambiguous response is entirely congruent with the devaluation of *onderi* that emerges from the rest of the material.

In *onderi*, the personal identity of the deceased completely disappears and becomes part of an indistinct mass that has no relations left with the living, while the elements which represented the social affiliation of the dead person to a number of particular family groups are preserved. This state of affairs may not be understood in terms of the social persons' life cycle, but escapes it somehow. Since, curiously, the Orokaiva sometimes relate the most powerless *onderi* to the strong *jape* ritual characters, the study of the latter may provide us with new insights into the question.

Jape

The Orokaiva consider initiation as the most important of all their rituals. It consists of two parts, separated by a long period of seclusion of the candidates. Its declared objective is to 'make the children grow'. It is not obligatory,[10] but almost all Orokaiva are initiated. Boys and girls undergo the ritual together, and both men and women act as initiators during each of its phases. Here, I will mainly confine my description to the first part, where the supernatural characters called *jape* directly intervene (Chinnery and Beaver 1915; Iteanu 1983a: 45–120; Williams 1930: 180–250).

Initiation is inaugurated by the parents of the candidates, who place their children in seclusion for a short period of time. Then, they start preparing the necessary, items for the actual ceremony called *jape*. Whatever concerns this ceremony is secret, and non-initiates are believed to run grave risks of physical deformity if they see or hear anything about it. A few days before the actual ceremony begins, all non-initiates, including the candidates, are taken out of the village into the bush. The following nights, groups of people from neighbouring and even distant places come together secretly in the village where the initiation is to take place in order to train for the performance. During this preparation phase, the initiated actors are believed to be threatened by supernatural danger, which they avoid by submitting to a number of protective procedures, like passing under the arms or the legs of elderly people.

On the day of the *jape* rite, the candidates are brought back into the village some time before dawn. They are then immediately set upon by the initiates, who attack them violently, while a flimsy hedge of elderly men and women do their best to protect them. If a candidate is killed, he receives no funeral and is immediately buried secretly in the bush. The initiates do not just attack the children, however, but destroy everything that represents society, burning houses, killing domesticated animals, and uprooting palm trees. They set brother against brother, and sometimes have sexual intercourse with married women. Yet no revenge may be taken for any of these actions.

In the early hours of the afternoon, the attacks cease, and the elderly people show and explain to the candidates the secret instruments played, the attitudes assumed and the noises heard during the ceremony. Then they announce to them the prohibitions that they will have to respect during their three- to seven-year-long seclusion. These prohibitions affect certain categories of foodstuffs (large shrimp, crabs, grubs, certain species of bananas, large round fruits like coconuts or breadfruit) and certain activities (sexual relations, washing, loud talking or noise making . . .). If they were to violate these or other similar rules, the candidates would immediately be put to death. Finally, the candidates are led to their seclusion houses, while prestations (*ji be torari*) are given to all the initiates' groups. The *jape* ceremony then ends, and everyone returns to his or her own village.

As I showed elsewhere (Iteanu 1983a), after the *jape* ceremony ends the village where it has taken place remains in complete disarray. It is left, as people say, 'without any reason', *siosa*. Everything that constituted its social life, internal relations between kin and villagers, external relations with other villages and things (houses, trees, etc.), has been devastated. Then gradually, in isolation from other villages, the inhabitants simultaneously reconstruct their village as they concentrate their efforts on the preparation of the ceremony that will mark a few years later the candidates' reappearance. On this occasion, the novices are adorned to celebrate the end of the initiation cycle. Thereafter, the prohibitions that they have respected during their seclusion are lifted in a number of ceremonies organized by the elderly people. Finally, a large exchange feast is performed, which re-establishes all suspended relations, creates some new ones, and cements society as a whole.

The *jape* ceremony may briefly be analysed as follows. It begins with the preparation stages and continues with the stage in which the initiates personify a number of terrifying *jape* characters. Throughout the ritual, everyone including the initiates, is subjected to an immediate and gradually increasing danger, which is only controlled through the protective procedures used (such as passing under the arms of the elderly people or calling out one's family name) and the prohibitions respected (such as refraining from scratching one's head or smoking). The danger reaches its peak when the *jape* characters attack the candidates, and destroy the village and all the objects and relations which compose it. From this broad point of view, the *jape* ceremony seems to establish a bipolar confrontation between whatever represents society and the *jape* characters. This is also the way in which *jape* ceremony is vaguely described to the non-initiates.

Nonetheless, the anthropologist, just like any other novice who witnesses this ceremony for the first time, discovers that finer distinctions are actually here affirmed. Indeed, the *jape* characters who 'burst out' (*pejari*) during the ceremony do not make up an undifferentiated mass. On the contrary, the men of each family group enact a specific, named character whose role they alone may assume. Each such character is distinguished by particular sorts of behaviour and special body decoration. However, these characters do not resemble what we normally call ancestors. They are neither linked by kinship to the families who own them, nor are they identified with these families, but they are invented items whose story each family recalls. For example Gamboresusu, I have been told, was created by a 'grandfather' of the Ombisisire family, who imagined it on seeing the red seeds of the cane named *hoe* swinging in the wind. When he appears in initiation, he is said to recall that cane, since he wears a tall bunch of red feathers on his head and a large bark cloth covering his body down to the toes. He walks around the initiation ground undisturbed, 'as if he were actually flying', so the people say. Unlike men, who impersonate distinct characters according to the family to which they belong, all women together represent a single character, Sivoropoka, considered as particularly dangerous since it often attacks the candidates through sexually connoted actions, which may provoke them into breaking an important prohibition, that on laughing.

Although, as we have seen, the initiates tell the non-initiates that *jape* are similar to *onderi* ghosts, the secret characteristics of the former opposes them to the latter. Firstly, while *onderi* are anonymous and lack a sense of identity, the diverse *jape* characters are well distinguished from one another by their names, paraphernalia and behaviour. Two main forms of distinctions are here at stake. Firstly, the diverse *jape* characters which are enacted by men discriminate between different families. Secondly, initiated women escape this family distinction, since they enact together a single character, Sivoropoka, which stands in opposition to the different *jape* of all men. The *jape* ceremony thus manifests the potentiality of the most prominent social distinctions which are to be found elsewhere in Orokaiva society. Men are shown to belong to different family groups, while all women occupy a contrasted position in relation to these groups. However, *jape* only creates these collective identities in an ontological esoteric form, since no relations are then established. Later on only, at the end of the initiation cycle, during the adornment ceremony, the secret *jape* identities are eventually transformed into actual relations between various social groups, when marriages are concluded between the novices and food prestations given by the hosts to each family which has exhibited its distinctive *jape* character

(Iteanu 1983a and Barraud *et al.* 1984). Thereafter, until the next initiation is held, the village where the ritual has taken place is linked by these relations to all those families that were present. This ritual process, which proceeds in two distinct steps, finally appears as responsible among other things for the creation of the relation-oriented social units which compose Orokaiva society.

Firstly, *jape* characters' marked identities do not match those of living persons, but those of social units. *Jape* thus proposes some potential distinctions which will later be used in exchange to create actual social relations. Simultaneously, *jape* characters are not insensitive to people's social identity, but well distinguish between the different family groups when, for instance, they choose to kill certain children and destroy certain houses while leaving others alone, or when they let go a victim who uses a protective procedure which consist in shouting his or her family name. Secondly, while *onderi* appear as powerless, *jape* characters possess, during the ceremony, the most dreadful efficacy in killing children and destroying whatever represents society.

But this strong contrast is only a small part of what the novices learn. If, in spite of the fact that they have to defend themselves against violent attacks, they are sensitive at all to what happens, the diverse prohibitions imposed during the ritual afford them new surprises. Indeed, although the initiates normally say to the uninitiated that *jape* characters accept no limits to their destructions during the ritual, numerous prohibitions actually constitute a mean of protection for the initiates, just as for the candidates and more generally for village life itself.

But most important of all, the prohibitions – the detail of which we have previously mentioned – are not equally respected by all the participants. The elderly people (*tamo jape*) respect none of them. The younger initiates (*eha sarika*) observe some of them only, while the candidates must scrupulously comply with all of them, including those respected by the younger initiates. Finally, one must not forget to include in this gradation the secrecy cast over the whole ritual, a prohibition which possesses the widest scope of them all, since it opposes all those who have been initiated, including the candidates, to those who have not. The entire set of prohibitions established by initiation then covers the whole society, which it divides into distinct hierarchically ordered classes. These classes may not be considered as independent from one another, since each one of them must fulfil the position attributed to it so that the ritual may be performed. Thus, within the initiation context, these classes are complementary to each other, and constitute together a ritual representation of the society as a whole. Surprisingly enough, however, outside this context, even among initiates only, no particular status is accorded to the members of any initiation class, and no mention is even ever made of them.

The prohibitions respected in initiation thus render manifest society as an internally organized whole in the form of a status gradation which orders the participants, and furthermore all the Orokaiva people. Within this hierarchy, the classes are ordered in accordance with the value of familiarity with initiation. Thus, the more initiations one has taken part in, the higher the class in which one belongs. At the top of the hierarchy stands the elderly people's class. I here employ the term elderly only as an approximation, since within this hierarchy the emphasis is not set on age, in our sense of the term – which in any case the Orokaiva do not compute – but on familiarity with initiation. Thus, although most of those who belong to this class are indeed elderly, younger persons who have been particularly active in former initiations are to be found here as well. On the contrary, elderly persons who somehow have not been initiated at all or who have come to initiation at a late age[11] do not belong to this class. The superiority of this class manifests itself in numerous ways. Firstly, elderly people are consulted constantly about the organization of the ritual, and virtually nothing is done without their assent. Furthermore, whenever a more dangerous or complex activity has to be performed, they either do it themselves or must be present when it is done. Moreover, as I have already mentioned, they are the one who invent the *jape* characters which their family will thereafter perform. But above all, they are in charge of the prohibitions. They perform the protective procedures when, for example, all the younger initiates pass under their arms or legs. They announce to the novices the prohibitions that they will have to respect. If one of them breaks one of these rules, they either pronounce the punishments – like swollen testicles, a spotted nose, baldness, prominent articulation bones . . . – which he or she will have to suffer or enforce them themselves by killing the wrongdoer. Alternatively, when someone has fallen victim of one of these punishments, they may perform a small ritual in order to avert it. Finally, after the *jape* ceremony, for the benefit of the younger initiates, and after their adornment, for the novices, they organize numerous small rituals which permit the prohibitions one by one to be lifted. Generally, within this context, their familiarity with the initiation ritual afford them the utmost respect[12] and their actions and speeches are considered as either dangerous weapons or effective means of protection.

Initiation classes are thus distinguished from each other in the main by the position of their members towards prohibitions, and they are hierarchically ordered in accordance with a value represented by participation in initiation. This gradation may be compared, in its abstract form, to the one described by Dumont for the Indian castes and *Varna* (Dumont 1966: 80–1 and 94). Each of its steps actually opposes the lower element to all the other elements taken together as a single category. Thus, the secrecy opposes all the non-initiates to all the initiates, including the candidates. One step above, the candidates are opposed to all the initiates as it is firmly – but somehow wrongly – stated that only the candidates respect prohibitions. One further step above again, the initiates, who in fact respect some prohibitions, are opposed to the elderly people, who do not respect any of them and do not even impersonate any characters during the ceremony. This specific hierarchic form implies an encompassment relation between the diverse complementary classes, and not a simple piling up of categories.

Within this hierarchy, the value of participation in initiation, which normally only regulates the relations between classes, exceptionally applies internally to the initiates' class. Although initiates, it is said, are not supposed to respect prohibitions, each one of them actually respects some of them in accordance with his or her subjective perception of his or her own degree of acquaintance with initiation. Thus those who have participated in several ceremonies will normally respect very few prohibitions, while those who have seen *jape* only once, will respect almost all of them. This specific organization feature, which appears to leave room for individual dimensions, singles out the initiates' class from all the others, where prohibitions apply equally to all members.

Comparison of the prohibitions respected in mourning and in initiation rituals permits further clarification of this important contrast between individual and class-based prohibitions. Even if the objects they apply to are most of the time similar, the prohibitions enforced in initiation differ radically from those respected in the mourning ritual. In the latter, prohibitions apply only to the persons by whom they are chosen, who themselves determine their duration. Their breaking does not entail sanctions. In initiation, on the contrary, a certain degree of compliance with prohibitions characterizes whole classes of people, and not persons only. The list of prohibitions that applies to each of these classes is fixed and similar on every occasion on which the ritual is performed. The duration of prohibitions depends, not on personal factors, but on the accomplishment of the collective rite. Their respect is sanctioned, since their breaking directly affects the social person of the culprit.

This radical contrast between two types of prohibitions is not a simple binary opposition, but actually bears a hierarchic form. To start with, class-based prohibitions are enforced in the hierachically superior initiation ritual,[13] while personal prohibitions appear in the inferior mortuary ritual. Thus, with regard to the context in which they appear, the former are superior to the latter. Moreover, a similar hierarchic disposition is to be found again within the initiation context itself. As I have argued above, the initiates' class is characterized by personally selected prohibitions similar to those respected in the mortuary ritual. In the initiation context, this class is the only one to respect such individually-based prohibitions, and it is encompassed in a system of classes exclusively marked by collective prohibitions. Furthermore, within this hierarchic system, the initiates' class is subordinated to the superior class of the elderly people, who are the custodians of collective prohibitions. Thus in initiation itself personal prohibitions are encompassed in, and hierarchically subordinated to, collective prohibitions.

With this configuration in mind, it is indeed quite tempting to associate the weak and anonymous form assumed by the dead during and at the end of the mourning ritual to the individual nature of the prohibitions respected in the same ritual, while the collective, well-determined prohibitions of the initiation ritual seem to match the stronger and clearly identified image of the *jape* characters. In that sense, the Orokaiva ritual system appears to associate the apparent weakness of the dead with a social organization centred on the social persons of the mourners, while the stronger image of *jape* is associated with the organization of society as a whole, hierarchically ordered into classes such as are to be found in the initiation ritual.[14] In conclusion, some type of integration between these two apparently heterogeneous systems may be proposed.

Conclusion

The original aim of this chapter was to clarify the relation between society and Cosmos by examining the position accorded to the so-called supernatural beings in Orokaiva ideology. I therefore closely examined their different manifestations in the forms of *ahihi*, *onderi*, and *jape* characters.

From a first vantage point, that of the life cycle ritual process, *ahihi* and *onderi* have been shown to be two distinct forms in which the dead appear in two successive stages of the mortuary ritual, whose central role is to sever the relations between the dead and the living. Within the limits of this point of view, both *ahihi* and *onderi* possess similar characteristics, which are merely more intense in the case of the latter. That is, both may manifest themselves at any time, but, while *onderi* are restricted to the outside of the village, *ahihi* do not suffer such limitation; both display a diluted sense of identity, yet *ahihi* retain, in the form of objects, some degraded form of relation to social persons; both have lost their social markers (name and feats), which are re-integrated as family assets; both are not accorded much value and are weak. However, their apparent similarity conceals a fundamental analytical distinction. While the notion of *ahihi* complies, in a degraded form, to the relational logics of the life and death cycle, the notion of *onderi* lies outside it, totally excluded from the realm of relations. Its identity is thus to be sought at a different level of the society's ideology.

Jape is constituted by supernatural characters which manifests themselves only during initiation rituals. Its characteristics sharply contrast with those of *ahihi* and *onderi*. Indeed, *jape* characters are highly valued and considered as terrifying. They appear in a ceremony where the Cosmos is not seen as a network of relations but as a whole ordered in a hierarchy in accordance with the value of familiarity with the ritual. Furthermore, *jape* characters display varied distinct identities in the guise of names, particular behaviours and contrasted body decorations which refer to the crucial social distinctions between families and between men and women. As I have shown, these identities do not remain confined to the ritual context, but are transposed into a non-esoteric form, outside it, in the domain of social organization.

Onderi and *jape* thus appear to be opposed to each other in every respect. The initiates often recognize this opposition, when they affirm that there is no relation whatsoever between *onderi* and *jape* characters. Surprisingly, however, at other times, when talking to the uninitiated, they seem to contradict themselves by saying that '*jape* are just like *onderi*, only the former is a big thing while the latter is a small one'. This second affirmation is not a mere form of speech or even a simple conventional lie aimed at segregating the non-initiates from the others. Rather, our analysis suggests that it describes a reality situated on a different plane from the former, and that the seeming contradiction of the two discourses in fact manifests the encompassment of one plane by another.

Indeed, two levels of value have so far been distinguished. The first of them, a ritual level, is superior to the other: it emphasizes the valued *jape* characters, the initiates and the conception of society as a whole, internally ordered by a hierarchy of initiation classes. At this very same level, in addition to the former highly valued elements, *jape* ritual displays an esoteric representation of society as a collection of ontologically defined social units. However, as was previously demonstrated in the case of prohibition, this representation, which is borne by the initiates' class only – since neither the elderly people's class nor the novices' nor the uninitiated's impersonates *jape* characters – is encompassed within the whole constituted by the initiation classes.

The inferior-level value, which among other *loci* manifests itself in the mortuary ritual, is characterized by a relational notion of identity. This very same notion accounts for the distinction between the social persons and the dead represented in the weak forms of *ahihi*. It is specific to this level of value, since it plays no part at all during *jape* ritual, where no mention is ever made of either *ahihi* and *onderi*. At this level, this relational notion of identity, which determines the affiliation into the distinct family groups established in initiation, occupies a dominant value's position.

Conversely, the hierarchy manifested in the initiation classes during the ritual has no relevance at all at the subordinated level, since, as was previously mentioned, no one may invoke his relative position in initiation outside its context. Thus, when initiation is performed, society is seen as a hierarchy of initiation classes; when it is not, it is conceived as an ensemble of exchange relations between family groups, between affines and between the living and the dead.

Consequently, the two hierarchical levels possess also different extensions. The higher one is restricted to initiation, and within it to initiated persons only, while the lower one applies outside the ritual context to everyone in the society, since in daily life, initiates, just like non-initiates, are never confronted with *jape* characters but only with distinct families and with *onderi* and *ahihi*. The uninitiated remain permanently outside the ritual level and, since everything concerning initiation is concealed from them, they are exclusively submitted to the distinction between the living and the dead. Thus, at any time, they are only told that *jape* are identical to *onderi*. For them, the distinction of levels is blurred. Although they are in a diametrically opposed position, a similar indistinctness applies to elderly people. In everyday life, they normally remain in an almost permanent state of immobility, which manifests their retirement from life and the weakness of their social persons. Everything in their manner then refers to an almost total indistinctness between life and death, a distinction which, for everyone else, is central at this level. But when the ritual starts, just as if a bio-physical miracle had happened, they come out of their passiveness and display a wealth of physical and mental energy. Their acquaintance with initiation is so great that they belong to the highest initiation class and are the most perfect representations of *jape*. Since they solely function within that level, even when the performance is over, they somehow remain beyond the distinction between the living and the dead. Thus, although the discrimination between two hierarchic levels organizes society as a whole, certain categories of persons constantly remain at one level only. Within that level, however, their status is not affected by this restriction. At the inferior level, the uninitiated are not considered as inferior to initiates if they display a 'large' social person, while elderly people, who are not accorded much value at the inferior level, belong none the less to the highest initiation class.

The contrasted position occupied by these categories of persons at the different levels points to the fact that they are each characterized by the dominance of a different value in Dumont's sense of the term (Dumont 1986). At the level where society is seen from the point of view of rituals, ritual activity itself (*pure*) and the ideas which are associated to it are the dominant value, while at the subordinated level, it is exchange relations (*pondo*) which constitute the social person.

From a purely formal point of view, an analogy may be found between the different categories which characterize the two distinct levels:[15]

jape	onderi
tamo	ahihi
eha sarika	hamo
novices	jo
uninitiated	the wild

Formal resemblance between the two levels

But from the Orokaiva point of view, the relation between them is a hierarchical encompassment which may approximately by schematized as follows:

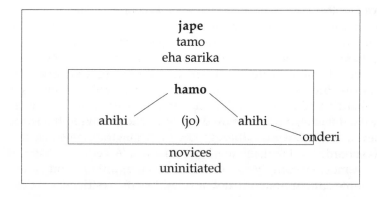

Schematic representation of the encompassment relation between the two levels

That the ritual itself is treated here as a paramount value necessitates some clarification. Indeed, in Orokaiva's conception, ritual, and especially initiation, constitutes a complex set of ideas and actions which bears value as an undissociated whole. This conception can be clarified by the notion of efficacy inherent in the initiation ritual. For example, when they explain the initiation actions to those who have just been initiated, the initiates stress the fact that although *jape* characters are played by people, the physical deformities visited on the candidates are neither to be attributed to the *jape* characters themselves, nor to the living who impersonate them, and not even to the elderly people who may name the punishments to be inflicted, but to the 'ritual action itself' (*pure*). Ritual efficacy is thus not conceived by the informants, as we may have expected it, as either an attribute of some supernatural beings, or of some living persons, but as an inherent quality of the ritual activity itself taken as a whole. Among other things, this specific feature explains why normal vindication is not enforced for the depredations committed during the initiation ceremony. Since efficacy is attributed to ritual itself only, and not to the specific persons or characters who perform the action, no one may be held responsible for what happens.

I hope that by now I have demonstrated that the study of the Orokaiva supernatural beings' identity permits the perception of two hierarchically ordered levels that order the society as a whole. *Jape* characters, which appear at the highest level, are the valued form of supernatural beings, while *ahihi* and *onderi*, which only appear at the inferior level, are lesser in value. However, the subordination of each of these forms of ghosts is established on different grounds. *Ahihi*, which is considered as a lesser social person, is subordinated to the latter. *Onderi*, on the contrary, does not bear a direct relation to social persons, but appears as a subordinated representation, at a lower level, of the otherwise valued *jape* characters. Thus, while *jape* is dominant at the ritual level, at the lower level, under the diminished guise of *onderi*, it is subordinated to the living.

A most striking image of this reversal is to be found in the complex dance from called *java*, originally only performed in the Orokaiva sub-group called Aeka. In contrast to the other dance forms, all its preparations are to be accomplished secretly, just as if it were a *jape* ritual. Lately, throughout the Orokaiva region, this dance has been performed in the context of initiation as a replacement for *jape* ritual. On the day of the ceremony, when all the guests are assembled, and before the *java* dance group performs, out of the bush appears a pair of dancers, called *onderi*.[16] They wear a costume of comedy. Instead of feathers, their heads are topped with tall leaves, their faces are painted black, and not with the beautiful red or yellow, they wear no barkcloth, but grass skirts, and their body ornamentation is made of canes of the worst kind. They dance inelegantly, and sometimes fall down to the ground or take on the wrong pace. On seeing them, the public becomes very excited and bursts into laughter. Instead of drums (*tataon*) they carry spears, with which they threaten the audience. But no one takes them seriously. When, sometime later, unexpectedly, the real dance group breaks into the village from the bush, everyone loses interest in them, to concentrate on *java*, the current equivalent of *jape*. All the dancers are decorated in a very sophisticated way, the steps they perform are quite complicated, and the choreography is almost perfect in its own right. They advance to the centre of the village, where they perform for the public. The *onderi* still continue with their comedy, but no one pays attention to them any longer, whatever their talent may be; they have been wiped out by the powerful dance, which make them look even more ridiculous still.

In Orokaiva society, therefore, the distinction between living and supernatural beings does not parallel a distinction of realm like that between society and cosmos or between profane and sacred. On the contrary, both categories appear to be full members of the same hierarchically ordered cosmos and to participate in each of its levels. This hierarchical order, however, implies that the value accorded to both social persons and supernatural beings is not the outcome of their ontological identities, but varies according to the dominant value which characterizes the level in which they are to be found. Thus, while at the highest level initiates, most perfectly represented by the elderly people, and *jape* characters are globally superior with regard to ultimate ritual value, at the lower level, dominated by the value of exchange relations, the elderly people, diminished in relations, and the *jape*, under its transposed form of *onderi*, are subordinated. Social organization, in the form of relations established in exchange between distinct families whose secret identities were set by *jape*, takes form at the confluence of the two levels.

Much effort is still required to sharpen this view of Orokaiva society in order to make it operative in a comparative study of Melanesian systems. However, a first step is here suggested. The intricate Orokaiva social form would have remained totally opaque to us if we had clung to our conventional and largely substantial conception of the supernatural which posits that the characters that intervene in ritual are but a specific manifestation of some ancestors or of some universal deities. The key to the decoding of this system is on the contrary a radical re-formulation, which states that in such a cosmomorphic society, where ritual is accorded a dominant value position, deities and ancestors may merely be devalued representations of the ritual characters that stand for the whole of society and even of the cosmos. Since the two levels are here conflated, it may look to us like an 'immanent transcendence', but when a comparative perspective is applied, it soon appears as a hierarchical configuration that probably also characterizes many other societies in Melanesia.

Notes

1. *Le péché et l'expiation dans les sociétés primitives.*
2. See also Mauss's note cited above.
3. I refer here to Dumont's distinction between the empirical subject and the individual, which is a specific modern ideological construct.
4. This feature clearly contrasts Orokaiva and modern ideologies. In the latter, the partners are defined as interchangeable elements of the universal category of human beings, while the objects specify the nature of the particular exchange. In the former, on the contrary, the objects are always the same, while the partners are clearly identified by the ritual as specific members of society.
5. In the mourning chanting the deceased's name is never mentioned, but outside this context one may very well pronounce it. This is so much so that the deceased may have already given his name to a younger namesake. The fact that this prohibition is not homogeneous sharply contrasts it with the one that falls upon the in-laws' names, which is

compulsory at all times. The latter goes as far as to forbid terms which have a phonic resemblance to the prohibited name.

6. The identity of the partners and the type of food prestations exchanged vary very widely in accordance with the identity of the dead, his or her marital status, residence, age, and so forth.

7. In the case of a secluded widow or widower, the procedure is similar in form, but is much more complex.

8. *Hamo* and *ahihi* are mutually exclusive, since the Orokaiva say that the living social person can never have or be an *ahihi*. This quality explains why *ahihi* is not comparable to our notion of soul.

9. The bark of a specific tree is said to afford some kind of protection for persons against the *onderi* attacks. It is seldom carried in the net bags by grown-up persons, but it is almost universally used to protect infants when they are taken to the gardens.

10. An uninitiated person is subject only to one limitation: he may not participate in *jape* ceremonies.

11. For example, when raised in mission stations away from the village.

12. Outside the ritual context elderly people are not particularly respected. Rather on the contrary, they often have to cope with the jokes and the insults proffered to them by youngsters.

13. The hierarchy between the diverse rituals has been establish in Iteanu (1983a).

14. This contrast is furthermore confirmed by the opposition between the ceremony which ends initiation by clearly re-constructing society as a whole, and the last mortuary ceremonies, which deal only with exchanges between persons (Iteanu 1983a).

15. The notion of *jo* has been developed in Iteanu (1990).

16. The actual Aeka name is *embahe*, and it is translated as *onderi* in Orokaiva regions.

References

Barraud, C., Coppet, D. de, Iteanu, A. and Jamous, R. (1994 [1984]). *Relations and the Dead. Four Societies Viewed from the Angle of their Exchanges.* Berg, Oxford.

Chinnery, A. W. P. and Beaver, W. N. (1915). Notes on the Initiation Ceremony of the Koko, Papua. *Journal of the Royal Anthropological Institute,* 45, 69–78.

Dumont, L. (1966). *Homo Hierarchicus.* Gallimard, Paris. (édition Tel.)

—— (1986). On Value, Modern and Non-modern. In: *Essays on Individualism. Modern Ideology in Anthropological Perspective.* Chicago University Press, Chicago.

Herdt, G. and Stephen, M. (eds) (1989). *The Religious Imagination in New Guinea.* Rutgers University Press, New Brunswick.

Hertz, R. (1988 [1972]). *Le péché et l'expiation dans les sociétés primitives.* Jean Michel Place, Paris.

Iteanu, A. (1983b). Idéologie patrilinéaire ou idéologie de l'anthropologue? *L'Homme,* 23 (2), 37–55.

—— (1983a). *La ronde des échanges.* Maison des Sciences de L'Homme–Cambridge University Press, Paris.

—— (1990). The Concept of the Person and the Ritual System. An Orokaiva View. *Man* (NS), 25, 399–418.

Leenhardt, M. (1971 [1947]). *Do Komo. La personne et le mythe dans le monde mélanésien.* Gallimard, Paris.

Read, K. E. (1955). Morality and the Concept of the Person among the Gahuku-Gama, *Oceania,* 25, 233–82.

Schwimmer, E. (1973). *Exchange in the Social Structure of the Orokaiva. Traditional and Emergent Ideologies in the Northern District of Papua.* C. Hurst and Co, London.

Williams, F. E. (1930). *Orokaiva Society.* Oxford University Press, Oxford.

Chapter 6

Revealed by Illness: Aspects of the Gnau People's World and their Perception of It

Gilbert Lewis

Illness may be accepted simply as a fact, as a natural process, as a derailment of nature. But it has often been interpreted further in religious or moral terms. From first awareness of a change or difference, a person moves through perplexity towards some interpretation of the place of that illness in his or her life. He or she feels ill and wants to know about the illness, adopts an attitude to it. The attitude will probably reflect some cultural assumptions about what sort of state illness is. The assumptions are not necessarily single or exclusive; but a doctrine of destiny, for example, is likely to instil attitudes to illness which differ from those deriving from belief in sorcery or belief in science.

An aim of understanding the personal significance of an illness is different from the aim of simply classifying it and giving it a name. Metaphysical questions are certainly not obtrusive in every illness. But in general they create attitudes to illness, and orientate the frame for the interpretation of it. The sufficiency of an explanation depends on what questions are asked and the urgency of the demand for answers.

The demands derive from various explanatory or remedial motives, and reflect what possibilities people think they have for finding out answers. People do not classify pointlessly. Bodily conditions, causes, kinds of event may all contribute to the framing of a classification of illness. But classification is not necessarily the first concern of someone during illness. The sufferer is most likely to worry about the particulars of his or her own case rather than about deciding how to place it in a scheme of classification. The possibility of illness faces everyone; it is a risk of living. Some dangers can be avoided, but the risks cannot all be calculated or predicted. Uncertainty remains. The dangers may only show in retrospect.

A study of health and sickness may therefore reveal some aspects of people's perceptions of themselves and their world. If the study is one of a Melanesian society, it will need to explore local ideas about relationships with spirits, people and the world they live in. Questions of suffering will bring up their views on human being, the body, normality, ideals and illness. It is likely to include many aspects of their religion and ideology. Illness, suffering and death have had a significant place in religious explanation; and a large place also in the ethnography of religion and ritual.

The Gnau Villages – A Bounded World

The people I shall discuss, the Gnau, live in the West Sepik Province of Papua New Guinea. The three Gnau villages lie on the southern fringes of a band of settlement along the Torricellis. The villages are situated behind Anguganak Bluff. The Bluff rises up rather unexpectedly among the hills of the southern fall of the Torricelli range, and it has been something of a barrier, isolating the villages on it or behind it from easy access. They had less contact with white people when they came. The road in the valley passes them by.

The ridges and valleys are all forested, but near the villages the bush is patched with gardens. The lower-lying hills and the flatland south of Rauit (the village where I lived) are almost uninhabited – great tracts of tall forest for hunting. The Sepik river is far south, invisible. Old people at Rauit told me they did not know about it before the Whites came (I was struck by this indication of their old small world); then pacification, new travel, and plantation work extended their horizons. Before that, they were ignorant of both the River and the Coast: they did not know how to swim or what a canoe was. Their environment was bush, garden and forest. The land they knew had narrow geographical limits, very roughly a circle round them with a radius of about ten miles. This would include 42 villages, and within this circle ten different languages were spoken.[1] They used to have little knowledge of most of the villages and places lying towards the edges of the former social horizon. The edges were known from the names of places that came into stories, or genealogies or myths.[2]

The current division of labour still in many ways reflects the general pre-colonial pattern of life. The typical pattern would include the family working at the garden, relaxed people chatting in the evening in the hamlet, the women at the sago grove, the communal men's house in the hamlet, the men on a hunt, the whole village gathered for a big celebration. In the past there had been warfare, and they used to fear surprise attack, small raiding parties, ambushes. Arranged battles were uncommon. Women at work on sago needed guards to protect them from attack. The allocation of tasks and work patterns had to take the dangers into account, and the patterns now may still remind us of them. Small groups of women from the same hamlet or family grouping like to work at the same sago grove for company. The gardens of related nuclear families often cluster within easy calling distance. When families move to another tract of bush to clear new gardens, they may reform the cluster at a new site rather than scattering individually.

Analogy in Explanation: Gnau Experience

The Gnau used ordinary experience to interpret much illness: simple observation and past events were the sources for many ideas and intuitions about possible relationships between facts. The language of description and commentary on illness contained many indicators of their thinking, especially in the verbs they used and the imagery for processes of harm that these suggested. Of course it is difficult to tell which of these verbs are dead metaphors, used merely by habit and convention, and which still have life in them. They would speak of a spirit which caused someone to be ill as 'crushing', 'holding', 'fastening round', 'tying up', 'holding tight', or 'pulling' on the person afflicted. The verbs express the sense of a patient crushed down, constrained, restricted by illness. The spirit could 'strike' or 'shoot' the patient (the idea of attack, the hurt, disease the enemy), or 'stay in' him, or 'go down into' him (the idea of unwanted presence, disease the intruder). Sometimes it seemed they took this idea of entry literally, for instance, when they sucked out 'arrow points' shot in by the spirit, or when they tied a stinking creeper round the affected part to stink out the spirit. They would sear the patient's skin with flaming coconut fronds to drive it out by heat; or startle it with blows and bangs. The son of the man with bad heart failure got hold of some gunpowder. He came up in the evening as his father slept beside a fire and dropped the gunpowder in the fire. It was to startle the spirit away. Simple verbs described how a spirit would take notice of someone: it would 'spy him out', 'put its eyes on him', 'say his name', 'call out to him', 'smell' him. Both speech and behaviour showed what they thought. Their guesses and deductions about the causes and processes of illness constituted attempts to find some order, to explain events, to predict them and control them.

'What is happening to him? What has he done to get ill? What has he eaten to get ill?' These were the questions they would ask. Food, for instance, was a common focus of attention in their diagnoses. It may seem obvious that food should be a subject of concern. Food enters the body. If illness may result from some harm inside the body, food is a vehicle for it to get inside. The idea of poisoning by food was there, but it was not the only sense or the main sense in which food was linked to cause. What also prompted their concern was the belief that spirits watch over food. They benefit the growth of particular crops, but they are also sometimes jealous and watchful of the way people use them, sometimes capricious. The person is singled out for their attention by what he or she has eaten or done. It may be because the person afflicted took what did not belong to him, or the spirit did not recognize the person's right to take it; perhaps the person showed greed or carelessness in handling the food. But the entry of the food into the victim's body singled him out and provided a reason for making the diagnosis. Sometimes it was food eaten by the mother which gave a reason for her baby's illness. Food eaten by other people could make someone sick feel worse when they came too close to him, because the spirit associated with the food would notice him. The spirit attends to those who eat food it looks after, follows them and their movements and contacts.

Their personification of spirits, based on an understanding of human behaviour, allows them to guess motives which might actuate spirits in the causing of illness. But despite the personification of spirits, they were not persons as people are. The Gnau did not know how to judge or understand their purposes and motives as well as they could those of other people. At times the spirits seemed capricious, motiveless as the wind. So the people did not assign blame and responsibility to spirits with the same moral indignation as they did to people who were thought to have caused someone's illness.

The Application of Ideas in Practice

Their general explanatory themes have to be observed in use to grasp their practical significance. Ideas of the localization of a spirit, its range of movement and attention, the danger of its adding to someone's illness, come alive when you notice the fences set up to isolate and protect someone sick from the influence of people passing by who might have eaten things dangerous to the person ill. How many paces off will make it safe? Ten paces? Twenty? Or when a spirit has a local habitation, so that the patient must move from her house, how far off must she move to get out of risk? In fact, such moves rarely involved more than two or three hundred yards' distancing, sometimes much less. How long does she need to stay away? How long to avoid that food? Answers to these questions enable us to observe what the ideas mean in realistic terms. The ideas are based on simple analogies but their consequences (how far to move? could that food have been the cause though it was eaten two weeks before the illness came on?) require people to decide what they think so as to know what to do.

Statement of theory in general terms is not enough to grasp its practical significance. In theory a particular food – sago – might be associated with a man's or woman's illness, but in practice sago was more commonly used to explain the illness of women, not because women ate it more than men, but because women had the major role in producing it, and usually they were working on their husband's land with palms his jealous ancestors watched over. The explanation for the difference seemed to me, considering it from outside, to lie in the values associated with the division of labour and rules of inheritance.

The Gnau considered the events of illness in a matter-of-fact way first, trying to deduce what might be the likely cause. They worked out possibilities by considering the timing and circumstances surrounding the illness. Their conclusions might light on certain components of a situation as significant for understanding how and why the illness had occurred. The cognitive process is similar to that which we use in trying to decide why an accident occurred. We consider what risks attach to different components of the situation (Lewis 1975: 265–6). Their diagnoses were applied to syndromes of circumstance rather than syndromes of clinical symptoms and signs.

Gnau notions about the presence of spirits, their attachments to place, their movements, their temper and interests, animate the landscape in which the people move with varied hazards. The spirits are part of the Gnau world, though neither directly visible nor quite predictable. My impression of Gnau views on the localization of spirit presence is one of fields of force which may be more or less powerful at different times, more or less concentrated. These forces can affect people who move into their field, or may follow them in their movements, and the forces may vary in response to human actions.

When people work at gardens, they are careful to observe proper behaviour, because spirits may be present, watchful, and indeed, after certain events like planting, especially activated and aware. In cutting things down, people see themselves as cutting down things in which certain spirits may have a protective interest. The sense of possessive jealous interest, of things that belong to certain spirits, goes with crops ready for harvesting. When things are taken, there is a suggestion that the spirit may be angry at the loss of what it holds dear, protects or benefits. These ideas are part of ambivalent Gnau views about spirits and their power to bring benefits as well as to harm. Spirits help crop growth and abundance, aiding people's efforts to produce their food. The power of the spirits is essential to successful gardening activities. The benefits must be sought and so the risks must be run. They are not wholly predictable and avoidable risks, even though people carefully observe proper behaviour in gardening.

The Gnau move in an environment that is variously associated with the concentration of spirit powers. Place is one of the co-ordinates of presence and danger, and so is time. For how long does an action or event carry risk? The interest of timing in diagnosis lies in the way that the interval between the occurrence of an event and recourse to it in explanation of someone's illness reveals aspects of how intense they think may be the risk involved in certain actions, and how they remember people and events – the lasting grief or sense of loss. Trivial actions may become significant only by coincidence; but some deaths, some quarrels or rites are called on to explain an illness long afterwards, and thus show how they have stayed in the mind.

The Gnau view of illness may look more like one in which illness resembles an accident or misfortune, bad luck. The risks in external things came close to appearing as natural risks for they are just there, intrinsic and hard to predict. But if risk is different from uncertainty because risks should be in principle calculable, then illness is more a matter of uncertainty. The danger may be recognizable only afterwards because it has been shown up by the illness. When harm comes so unpredictably, people cannot really be blamed for it.

These ideas make a discussion of illness between Gnau people sound highly circumstantial. They can pick out the possible relevance of events or actions for explaining the illness, but they do not need to spell out the assumptions that lie behind their deductions. The discussion sounds on the surface like a description of recent events, with a jumble of items of observation; but it can also be taken as more than a statement of plain facts. A convalescent woman visited her married daughter the week before she had a relapse. They recall the visit, but quite possibly leave unsaid that the point of recalling it is that the lineage spirits of her daughter's husband at his hamlet would have noticed her weak condition and might have struck her. A new-born baby dies: people recall that the baby's grandmother had come back to the place where the mother and baby were, straight from cutting some bamboo at a particular clump; and so on. On the surface this is simple narrative about recent events; but it is also the evidence from which they deduce the cause. And talk about recent events is shot through with potential implications to the Gnau listener who is alerted by illness.

Such narrative and conversation forms the content of Gnau 'case histories'. It answers their typical questions: What has someone done to become ill? What has he eaten to make him ill? What has struck him, or doesn't he know? Do you think it might be a spirit, or what, or is he just sick? The form of a case history stems from their assumptions, which are not the same as ours.

The external field (places, powers, activities) interacts with an internal field (the person with his or her particular strengths and vulnerabilities). The Gnau have their own ideas about human development and growth, and ideas of susceptibility to illness or harm at different stages of life (Lewis 1980: 134–85). Food and rules about food illustrate many aspects of the complex interplay between the person and the outside world.

Food Rules, the Body and the Properties of Things

For the Gnau few foods are neutral, just food and always food to all persons. Nearly all have valencies which make their use right or wrong for certain kinds of person or for persons in particular relationships or for persons in particular situations. Questions of physical maturity and social achievement affect whether some particular food is considered safe or not. Many considerations (puberty, childbirth, where the game was shot, whether someone has planted a garden on that day, etc.) might change food from being good to being a danger for the health of a particular person. The internal and external factors interact. Such views on susceptibility make one person's food another's poison.

Steiner (1967) concluded that taboo was an element of all those situations in which attitudes to values were expressed in terms of danger behaviour; it had the function of classifying and identifying the danger, narrowing it down and coping with it by institutionalized restrictions. What do Gnau rules of this sort reveal about their attitudes? Many Gnau taboos depend on age, sex, and achievement. The taboos apply to individuals, not to whole social groups such as a clan or lineage (they do not have totems or totemic taboos, the restrictions associated with hunting are not like that). For both sexes, some rules depend on physical growth, development and maturity, and some on interpersonal relations of kinship. Many also are set by achievement, first specified in terms of physical growth and development, later differentiated by sex, so that rules for women are often said to depend on their reproductive achievement and rules for men on their hunting achievement (Lewis 1980: 146–65). A man who breaks a taboo will find no game or be unable to hunt. A woman who breaks a taboo will bring illness or harm to herself or her family, or to her husband's ability to hunt. This idea can, in theory, put blame on the woman for misfortunes striking her husband or her family; it defines her position and potential in relation to him and her family; it stresses the relationship which the woman is in; but in the case of the man, even though the rule may forbid exactly the same thing, the effects of his actions fall on himself. The man is treated as more autonomous than the woman: rules for men involve their own status and action, for women they are governed more by family relationship and children. However, with many rules or taboos that apply to gardening activities, disobedience supposedly will bring harm to the crops rather than to the person involved. Despite so many rules in theory to be observed, the diagnosis of breach of taboo was rather uncommon. It was made for men rather than women. It was almost the only kind of diagnosis in which the food referred to in the explanation was animal.

Food taboos express many things. They may be set by classifications of kinds of food; or relationships between the people who give and receive; or age; or sex; or conditions of time and place, activities going on, etc. A little girl, for example, may eat a bird of paradise, but if she does, she is eating something she soon should not. Only very small children, and people whose own children are already grown up, may eat them, because they associate the birds, and eating birds of paradise, with infidelity in marriage, spouses who fly about, fickle, laughing, flirting women. As the girl begins to approach a marriageable age, she must no longer eat such birds. If those who should not, ate them, they say, their marriages would break up.

Individuals differ over the details of Gnau rules about food (Lewis 1980: 159–65). Faced with an unusual case, a bird rarely shot for instance, people may hesitate about what rule it should fall under. Individuals decide sometimes for themselves on the timing and importance of some rule which may affect them. If one has eaten mushrooms sprouted on sago pith that day, is it safe also on the same day to eat meat? Some say yes, others no. Or if you overhear someone refuse something offered, is it because of a rule you do not know, or an idiosyncrasy because of some past experience, or caution because of recent illness?

A man tells me he cannot eat mushrooms because once they

made him vomit. I believe him. A few weeks later, I am eating with his family, he asks whether mushrooms were cooked with the greens, I make some remark, and his eight-year-old daughter blurts out the truth: 'He can't eat them. He knows *minmin* (a kind of sorcery).' Or another man: he tells me he has kept to the restrictions for years, and now he thinks he will try a little to see if he can do so without harm; or perhaps he will. That is what he said; but he did not try any, at least not so far as I knew in the following few months that I was there that time.

Food as Intellectual Stimulus

People know that individuals differ in how they observe the rules. They know that the customs of other villages differ from their own; they know that in the past they adopted rules followed by other people as innovations when they learnt new rites. For instance, they did not always have the hunting taboos they have now: they learnt them from Ligawum, tried them out and found them good. Later, with colonization, men went to plantations where they tried new foods, broke rules they would have followed at home. The Aid Post Orderly tells me that in his village the rules are different: how one of his sons, out of school, defied his mother and grandparents, eating forbidden things in front of them, publicly, calling out that if the effects were so bad, then show him, let him see; and nothing happened.[3] People have to decide whether rules should apply to introduced foods like rice or pawpaws or salt. Do they hold risks? Will eating salt or European foods have bad effects on traditional crops? Should you avoid them when you plant yams and call on your ancestors?

We speak of food taboos, and may imagine a rigid system of rules. It is not like that. People keep some of their customs strictly; but the rules and prescriptions are not all equally sharply defined. There is room for interpretation, the curious, the sceptical. With the most significant foods, such as sago or yams or pork, rules about use and exchange are strict and generally followed. They have effects on their distribution and on people's nutrition even though these effects may be difficult to monitor and measure precisely. Some of the values associated with them are strong, and ideas of them permeate many activities. So when nurses or doctors ask mothers of small children to break such customary dietary rules, they may find the mothers do not follow their advice; the mothers hear the advice and wordlessly reject it. On the other hand, many rules are of less concern to them and can have scarcely any nutritional effect. How often does someone shoot a greater Papuan frogmouth or a giant Sumatran heron with a bow and arrow? Yet I have heard people discuss who should eat these after one of each happened to have been shot and they needed to work out to whom to send the gift.

On reflection, perhaps a feature of this heap of rules about food is the intellectual stimulus of an intricate play of associations and uncertainty, a sense of some sharp boundaries and of order in sequence, dangers of mixture, of possible troubles, and clever details; the implications are sometimes serious, for illness, for politeness or affront to others, for reverence and recognition of spirits or ancestors, or dead parents. To forget the gift due to this or that relative in a particular situation may lead to most bitter rifts, to a public humiliation, or possibly to some tangle of relations hard to straighten out and make smooth. The rules to do with food refine and ornament social life, they give it added interest and complexity. The rules have effects on what people eat and on food distribution, but they also make people think. The rules imply a particular understanding of the interrelationships between human beings and what they do and natural objects, creatures, and plants – a classification and an understanding of nature, its regularities and the principles and forces active in it.

Food is not there simply to be gulped down as stuff to fill one's belly. The valencies and values, associations with the land, the grower or the hunter, myth and spirit, call for discrimination and add to the significance of the food. The rules are not static and inactive. Indeed, illness is often a sharp stimulus to think about things eaten and actions. The events surrounding illness may put beliefs at stake, recall actions for questioning. The rules and taboos are meant to guide and protect people, they have a preventive or prophylactic purpose.

Problems of Belief

During an illness, the practical relevance of Gnau ideas comes
out in the detail of progress in discussion and deductions about
cause, the points at which talking stops and treatment starts. If a
treatment is tried and the patient continues ill, it might be that
they have done the wrong thing, or they have not waited long
enough for the treatment to take effect, or there might be some
other undetected cause so far untreated. In principle, only if you
have an idea of what progress to expect does it become possible
to tell whether treatment makes a difference, whether it has
succeeded or failed. Without any preconceived idea of what to
expect next, who can tell what its effect is? Ideas about the illness
set conditions for doubts to occur, and the possibilities for
scepticism. If it were thought that every untreated illness must be
dangerous, or even lethal, then almost any treatment might seem
at times to be a great success.

In terms of strategy, for a severe illness the Gnau would rather
try a number of treatments in quick succession than examine
competing, different explanations and the evidence and
reasoning that suggested them. The variety of bits and pieces of
evidence, the attention given now to one facet of the situation,
then another, permit multiple explanations for the same illness
along different lines of reasoning.

> Consistency, logical closure, uniformity and singleness of
> explanation are not prized in the face of serious illness, and the over-
> riding need to make decisions about treatment. The pressure to
> rationalise the decision would be greater if the range of possible
> explanation were confined to a more strictly limited and ordered
> scheme of knowledge, or to a single theme of explanation, or if it fell
> only to special experts in healing to give an expert diagnosis, for
> then the rightness or wrongness of their verdict would involve the
> justice of their professional claim to special knowledge and their
> authority. As many treatments may be made in one illness, as the
> prognosis and speed of action of a treatment are unspecified and
> uncertain, the conditions of proof and disproof are not set out or
> clear (Lewis 1975: 353).

Removal of concern when the patient gets better, which in theory
should show the cause because the treatment worked, combines
with the many treatments carried out almost simultaneously to

confuse a final verdict about the cause or cure of a particular illness. There is no official arbiter to announce the verdict in the end, nor is there a public forum to decide about it after a recovery. People's eventual views remain largely undisclosed, and often uncertain.

In such a situation, the appearance of a critical attitude to their own views, a general scepticism, is unlikely. Conditions for proof and disproof, for the collection and collation of evidence, are too complex and confused. The very complexity of processes in disease makes advance always difficult. Despite the early and enlightened achievements of Chinese medicine, Elvin asks what it was that kept them back from further advance:

> Why did they not pursue the relationships between ethers, flavours and pulses until problems of internal consistency and correspondence with observed phenomena made them re-think their concepts? Possibly because medicine was too complex, as compared for example with ballistics or planetary motions – typically European areas of interest which seem to have held little attraction for the Chinese. Progress would have been easier first in a simpler field (Elvin 1973: 190).

The Gnau are, I suppose, like any other people in their readiness to disbelieve in regard to the particular instance while yet continuing to believe in general. Certainly they sometimes recognized mistakes of diagnosis, or disputed the good sense of a suggestion for treatment; they thought people might feign illness or seek to trick others with promises of cure. And they supported their doubts with reasons and sometimes evidence. But the occasions came one by one, the sceptic state was temporary, with cases more or less forgotten as they passed. Doubts did not mount up to outweigh and topple the authority of consensus in established belief: they bred no attitude of general scepticism. Many of the established beliefs were by no means specialized and confined to the management of illness, they had broader social functions and their authority did not rest solely on their success in the medical sphere.

The casual rough consensus drowned individual doubts. Collective representations (common or shared beliefs) are more stable than individual ones for, while an individual is conscious even of slight changes in his environment, only events of greater gravity can succeed in catching the attention of all members in a society and move them to change their ideas. The group puts pressure on the individual to conform, as Durkheim strongly argued. Beliefs most often depend on numbers and being shared by many to have much effect.

> A man cannot retain them any length of time by a purely personal effort; it is not thus that they are born or that they are acquired; it is even doubtful if they can be kept under these conditions. In fact, a man who has a veritable faith feels an invincible need of spreading it: therefore he leaves his isolation, approaches others and seeks to convince them, and it is the ardour of the convictions which he arouses that strengthens his own. It would quickly weaken if it remained alone (Durkheim 1961 [1913]: 473).

Events must strike many to move them to doubt. Periods of radical change in ideas seem to arise from a more general ferment of the times.

The Individual's Belief

There are a number of reasons for individual variation in people's knowledge and beliefs about illness and treatment. All societies impose some patterning on experience, marking out areas of privacy, limiting access to some kinds of knowledge, or putting conditions on people's participation in some events. Particular groups or categories of people may gain authority or control by such means. There may be a regular pattern of progress through ritual, or restrictions, affecting what and how they learn. Attitudes to ideas and values change through life. These reflect people's opportunities and experience. They come to see established ideas and customs in a different light as they get older, and see them from new perspectives. Maturity inevitably must bring some experience. But the forms and possibility of social control are not the same in all sectors of experience. As individual experience of illness is uneven, ideas on treatment are likely to reflect that in their diversity.

Belief is not a matter of all-or-none commitment. Attitudes and feelings shift according to context, time and circumstance. Since illness can be so upsetting and interfere with plans and hopes, it provokes strong feelings; and sometimes strong but inconsistent beliefs. Belief in treatment, faith in a healer, or a remedy, do not have to be shared or steadfast commitments.

In practice, the outcome of illness is often uncertain. Through diagnosis, people may be able to distinguish between situations in which the need for action is urgent and others where there is less need to rush. Uncertainty and anxiety are distressing in combination. Illnesses are diverse, and the regularities of nature hard to pin down. The pace of different disease processes varies so much; with an adult there may be time to await developments, but with an infant very little. I imagine the element of experience which brings confidence is common to medical practice in any setting. People's efforts to predict the future range widely between caution and confidence. They may rest on accumulated experience or reliance on others. When people predict outcomes, they may do so precisely or vaguely, with optimism or pessimism. Thus they sometimes make it harder or easier to retain confidence in treatment by the expectations they set up.

In practice the people I lived with at Rauit were reluctant to say what they thought would happen in particular cases or to predict within what span of time an effect of treatment should be seen. One strength of saying so many illnesses will be fatal if untreated is that many people in fact get better. The value of their treatments is thus confirmed. If they had to predict outcome precisely for each case, they might find it harder to sustain belief. The gestures of prediction, like making knuckles crack or the *langit* leaf curl up, were perfunctory. No one seemed to bother much about their correctness afterwards. The main techniques of divination that I saw used were mostly done after death, or in desperate situations, to diagnose. Divination was used not to find out what would be the outcome of action, but to diagnose what had caused illness or death, or to enable them to take a decision about what to do. They did not ask too closely about the outcome, perhaps because they did not really want to risk showing themselves up as ignorant or impotent. Although in theory Gnau treatments should act as tests of hypotheses about cause, they give only fitful attention to the answers.

Individual Doubts and Dilemmas Emerging from Social and Religious Change

Medicine and religion both involve matters of belief and practice. Most people are concerned chiefly with whether treatment will be effective, not with questions of explanatory consistency or logic. If, however, medicine and religion are mixed or competing, each suggesting, for example, explanations or responses for the same situation, the mixture may pose new problems for believers. An illness may then face someone with a choice between, say, trust in God or trying something else. These were problems raised by illness for a New Guinean pastor in the case which follows. The case illustrates the complexity of moral issues which may sometimes be involved by decisions over the choice of treatment, as well as showing psychological shifts of weight in attitudes to introduced and traditional beliefs.

In this part of the Sepik, nearly all the performances of major traditional religious ritual that I saw were triggered by someone's illness. Major rituals in the past were, in some cases, originally acquired to heal someone. Perhaps that association between religion and healing gave a sharper point to the problem I shall now describe.

The nub of the problem was whether the ritual they were doing was a medical or a religious act. If it was religious, it was heathen and wrong for a Christian to take part. But if the purpose was to heal an illness, did that make it medical and excuse him? This distinction of medicine from religion would not have obtruded before the introduction of Christianity and European ideas separating the tasks and specialized responsibilities of medicine and religion.

The man concerned was a Mission Station Pastor, and thus a committed Christian prayer leader. The Mission Station is near the Gnau village where I stayed, but in a slightly different ethnic area where a different language is spoken. The pastor's home village was the same as that of the A.P.O. (the aid post orderly) who had been sent to work in the village where I lived. The A.P.O. told me the story (in Tok Pisin). It presented problems for him. He too was a Christian, and someone who owed his training to the C.M.M.L. (Christian Brethren) Mission, especially to the first missionary doctor there. The pastor Woperel[4] became ill, the

A.P.O. said, and they could not find out what was wrong with him. He went to Wewak and Lae hospitals for investigations. The doctors there could not find it out. Yet he felt ill. He kept dreaming of fish and the spirits of the dead, who said he must do the singsing. So against his will he said yes. His dreams said that he would have diarrhoea for three days after the singsing started, and this would remove the sickness from him, in the watery stools. His main trouble had been pains in his belly, and the feeling his feet were going to take off and he would fly. This, said the A.P.O., was what made the doctors at Lae concentrate on his previous motorbike accident and bangs to his head, even though he had not felt he had hurt his head at the time. So against his will, they did the singsing, and, soon after it started, he did have diarrhoea, and then he felt better. He has danced in the singsing since then, and he stays well.

The A.P.O. says that some of the people in his village, strong converts, said it was wrong to do the singsing, a sin God would see. Some of them left the village for the duration of the singsing. The A.P.O. comments that he can see that the singsing made him better; it is possible that bad spirits of the village made him ill; also the doctors at Lae could find nothing. Perhaps the accident could have harmed his brain, he finishes. Then, speaking for himself, the A.P.O. wonders what is right: he himself is a Christian, God sees everything and everywhere, the singsing is bad (*pekato*, a sin, was the word he used), yet Woperel (the pastor) is a strong Christian, he had prayed. Why hadn't God healed him? Why had he then got better with the singsing?

The A.P.O. seemed genuinely perplexed by the moral issues and the question of the nature of the illness. But I was also aware of his ambiguous position towards me, a doctor, someone who knew the missionary doctor who had trained him, and a bit about his past. Was it calculated a little by what he thought I might tell the Mission people?

Ten days later I was going through the village where the singsing was. The S.I.L. (Summer Institute of Linguistics) linguist-cum-Bible translator had come to see the pastor because he heard that Woperel was deeply upset, conscience-stricken, about allowing the singsing to be done for his illness. To the Bible-translator Woperel said he had allowed it only because of the heavy insistence of his relatives and after much anguished prayer. He said the singsing was going on too long, that he had repeatedly urged them to end it. He had prayed until he was exhausted. Then his relatives from another village turned up to dance and he could not refuse them. While the singsing is going on, Woperel said he feels that he cannot act or take part in any Christian services. He prays but he feels in the wrong.[5]

On that day, Woperel looked well, neatly dressed in white shirt, clean shorts, boots and socks, a wristwatch. He was courteous when I turned up, interrupting their conversation. I had not met him before. I left them after ten minutes, having arranged a meeting with the S.I.L. linguist.

However, Woperel seemed different when he came about three weeks later to the village where I was living. He came with some women from his village for the ceremonies to celebrate the birth of someone's first child. *Garamut* slit-gong messages to call them the night before had gone unanswered, so a relative went to fetch them at dawn next morning. As they walked in, they were greeted by Walbasu, a rugged old heathen wreathed in smiles, with loud ribald remarks on the reasons for their failure to answer the *garamut* the night before.

Woperel was wearing a blue floppy hat, his wristwatch, shirt, shorts, boots and thick socks. He sat down to chat. They offered him the mash of yams coconut and taro. He said, No, he couldn't eat that, tubers come from the ground. Then there was a lot of chat about all the things he couldn't eat because of the singsing; and a lot of reiteration and knowing agreement from his listeners. All food that has associations with the ground, ground-living birds and animals, fish, even tinned fish: he spoke about these food avoidances as a committed believer. He told me he used to have belly cramps and pains after food, feel pins and needles running about his skin, his guts twisting and turning. You could hear them making noises like sago grubs inside the trunk of a palm. He felt unsteady on his legs, but things didn't seem to turn round outside him. He had had a small high ringing sound in his ears. Both the ringing sound and dizziness had gone since the singsing. He said that he intended to keep the food avoidances for some time and then try tiny amounts of the foods, waiting in case any of his symptoms come back. His experimental attitude to trying out foods that he had been avoiding was one that many local people would follow. What struck me at the time was his cheerful and sincere conviction that the singsing had helped. In the village setting at Rauit, I would never have guessed at his perplexity, or his pangs of Christian conscience. In different situations, the relevance and intensity of different beliefs vary. Single unswerving commitment to only one set of beliefs is characteristic of monotheist religious expectations, the idea that truth is single and exclusive; local patterns did not seem to me at all like that.

Pluralism can refer to institutional arrangements, attitudes and ideas. Diversity – linguistic, social and cultural plurality – is a striking attribute of Papua New Guinea. Such pluralism implies at the least an awareness of alternatives and, more positively, implies a readiness to acknowledge or tolerate or try alternatives. As I have argued elsewhere (Frankel and Lewis 1989: 30–3), science and monotheism both have a tendency to see truth as single and exclusive. Western medicine implies that its theories about diseases and the ways to treat them are not limited in application to particular societies and cultures, but have universal relevance. Like a world religion, it has a universal message, virtue for all mankind. Believers may try to justify the sweep forward of such a religion by its truth. Those who adhere to a monotheistic religion may assert their religion is the only true one, and reject any beliefs and practices not in accord with their own. Those who believe in scientific medicine may likewise assert its exclusive truth and virtue. Yet to put scientific medicine forward as the sole way to medical knowledge and healing is to adopt something of the attitude of monotheism. The idea that Western medicine, being scientific, will supplant any alternative form perhaps feeds on the hope that truth will prevail. We may be led to think that pluralism in medicine is what is curious. On the contrary, experience shows it is the rule. Wholehearted conversion to Western medicine is the exception. Expectations of unswerving attachment troubled the conscience of Woperel, and new definitions of the boundaries between religion and healing added to his problems.

The Persuasions of Healing

It is clear that if we assess the effects of treatment in terms of the different participants' views, we find great variation. After assembling their many perspectives, we see how difficult it

might be to decide about the effectiveness of a treatment. Why do
we believe that something is the right thing to do? Why do we
think that X is the right treatment? In a lot of cases it is because
that is what everyone says; or because someone else supposed to
know says so. We may have no opportunity or means to test it.
We are used to having specialized authorities, and guarantees for
the source or status of facts. What they say, we believe.

In what circumstances, then, does treatment strengthen belief
in the explanatory theory or the ideas behind it? Treatment
involves experience, emotional and physical and social effects;
also it involves questions of meaning, cultural symbols,
communication and information. A Gnau treatment may confirm
a theory of illness by making the cause visible. It is 'make-
believe' in the sense that a spirit may be given form, made
present to sight, hearing, smell, touch; ideas are objectified;
gestures enact the extraction of illness, they throw it away. Public
representations teach the young and help to make them believe.
The excitement and interest of a performance bring the ideas
alive in everyone's mind.

'As imagination bodies forth the form of things unknown, the
poet's pen turns them to shapes, and gives to airy nothing a local
habitation and a name.' The spirit causing illness is indeed given
a name and sometimes, in treatment, form and shape. Treatments
of illness often enact a representation of the local theory about an
illness and the process of healing. In fact, much healing might be
compared for symbolic force and transparency – to see how
clearly the actions of treatment convey in gestural or other non-
verbal terms a statement or revelation of the theory of illness that
lies behind them. The expressiveness and symbolism of some
examples is dramatic and aesthetically elaborate. The treatment
includes diagnosis in the sense of defining the illness, giving it a
label and a shape. The actions make the diagnosis public, they
present what has been agreed about the nature of the illness.
They conform to theory and cultural expectations. The agent of
illness – the cause or the illness itself – is embodied or objectified.
The imagery may both inform and reinforce; it may confirm
suspicions or provide material evidence in support of an idea; it
may show to the young what the older people think. The ideas
were behind the actions of treatment and served to justify them.
In return, treatment may help in maintaining the ideas. Many of
the ideas also go beyond illness: they have broader explanatory

or religious scope. Treatment then can play some part in learning and belief. Among the Gnau illness was a spur to reflection and action, a reminder of forces present but unseen until perhaps illness triggered people into performing ritual which represented the ideas and gave them visible and public shape. Stimulation and expression may be effective in religious, symbolic and aesthetic terms, but the purpose is to heal, to treat an illness. Therefore we must ask about its effectiveness as therapy.

The value of treatment and its emotional effect can depend on the brilliance and clarity of staging. Verbal and non-verbal elements are combined. The question about efficacy needs to be answered from the points of view of both the individual who is ill and also the onlookers. The stand individuals may take as to the reality of a spirit and its image varies with their experience. Some know what the image is and how it is made; they have done it and seen it done many times before. They can remember how some of the sufferers got better, others not. There will be people present who have been through the treatment themselves personally as patient. Some of those present are close to the patient and may deeply want her to get better. In this particular performance, their emotions are deeply engaged; perhaps they watch wide-eyed with hope. But we must keep in mind the likely differences of attitude and emotional involvement. Theories of illness implied by the actions do not have to be made precise. The sense in which an image is the spirit, or only a representation of it, is open to different interpretations and does not have to be the same for all participants. Such logical differences do not need to be decided in the middle of an illness. The collective effort and conviction gives encouragement and support to the patient, and satisfaction to others. Those who have just made the spirit figure see it differently from a patient who has been pinning her hopes on the treatment, and has been alone and in some distress waiting to confront it. Then exposure to the image, the montage of sight, stings, the singing, noise, tastes of betel, ginger, herbs – an accumulation of stimuli which make a sharp contrast to her isolation and combine to heighten the shock of the spirit presence. The exposure and shock is acted out in protected space. She is surrounded by senior and experienced men, and by friends, and they are calling out on her behalf, urging the spirit to leave her, striking it, 'killing' it, taking the illness out of her and throwing it away. They show how the illness might be overcome, the process of removing it. The invocations begin as appeals to the spirit and end as commands to it to go, coupled with confident encouraging assertions that she will be well. The final act of washing is an implicit assertion that the illness is ended.

If the treatment helps, it may be for non-specific reasons to do with providing support, which people think is appropriate because it corresponds to their ideas and expectations; or with allaying the anxiety provoked by the illness; with giving encouragement and hope of improvement. Treatments in other places include examples in which the intensity, exposure, or repetition, may suggest parallels to conditioning techniques. Suggestion, persuasion, catharsis, reward and punishment, are all involved in some. Social and collective support may also be a long-term benefit of treatment, when new ties are established by it. Effects on the other participants contribute to its value in their eyes: it expresses their beliefs, confirms them by making them visible, and allows them to help.

In judgements of the relation between cause and effect, timing matters, whether from the point of view of looking forward or of looking back. In reasoning *a priori*, an idea of what to expect without treatment is needed to tell whether treatment makes a difference. If several treatments are all given almost at the same time, one cannot tell which worked. Benefits are easily mistaken. A gift for timing – close to the improvement – tempts one to link an improvement to what was done just before it, especially when considering the case *a posteriori*. Lack of a prognosis, or a wrong one, confuses the assessment of benefit. Right or wrong, prognosis can create or contribute to both favourable and unfavourable judgements. And the pacing of treatment is an art. It can be used to help to sustain hope; it may clarify or confuse the evaluation of effects.

Belief in one's ability to control the illness obviously influences response to it, and whether one attempts to treat it. Many illnesses are bearable or trivial, and do not pose those problems of meaning or cultural interpretation which have occupied much of my discussion – indeed, much of the anthropological and psychiatric discussion of healing as a whole. Much also attests to the power of illness to prompt questions from people about their deep convictions and the meaning of events. There are examples in which the introduction of a treatment – vaccination, an injection of penicillin against yaws – has removed a form of disease on which perhaps was centred some complex of belief and practice; and the effect of success in treatment was to oust belief, to destroy its point and meaning. The effects of medical treatment may sometimes have played a part in religious change and the decline of magic.

Notes

1. Gnau people are likely to know only one other language than their own (leaving Tok Pisin aside).
2. I have described elsewhere (Lewis 1980: 59–67) the great ritual songs which mark out the paths and the extent of the world which the Gnau knew, the things in it and the spirits.
3. This might almost count as a Gnau example of the experimental method.
4. I have changed the names of the people concerned.
5. The name of the singsing in Gnau, Gadugep Balwawogep, means 'Fish Landcrabs'. This singsing is not really part of the Gnau people in Rauit's repertoire of singsings, and is not performed in their language, Gnau. They explained the singsing as one to cure a man who is sick; they listed the villages that 'knew' (i.e. performed) the singsing; they linked it with the ground, with worms (*yibergep*) which are both in the ground and in wet mud and cause pains in the belly. They immediately added that worms are like germs (*mawopem jiem*), like hookworm (they have been told about hookworm), they get at you in mud, through the ground. The singsing is danced with tall light masks, it is the local form of the Fish Singsing (Marshall 1938; McGregor 1975) found around Lumi. They did not perform it in the village Rauit where I stayed, and spoke of it as a singsing for a bad spirit. They associated the ground and mud especially with the land crabs, which eject a little pile of wet mud from their holes at night. Worms had the *jiem* (germ) or agent role in this illness, but ambiguously with the spirit of the singsing.

   The idea of invisible infection corresponds to ideas they have always had about the way spirits can jump from one sick person to another, can turn their attention from one person to another if they pass too close. I am not sure if anyone bothered to sift the idea of *jiem* as material agents of disease (like dirt, worms, maggot eggs, or the germs and bacteria referred to in the talks on hygiene) from the idea of *jiem* as an invisible agent like one of their spirits (*malet, belyipeg*). Spirits can manifest themselves in material forms as stones, images, as an animal, so why should *jiem* not be the same? The idea could easily be assimilated and accommodated to previous ideas. The spread of disease by touch or contact is obvious to them in the spread of *grile* – a persistent fungal skin infection, producing scaling skin which may spread widely over the body; it is caused by the fungus *Tinea imbricata* – (for example from mother to baby at the point the baby's body touches hers), and in the spread of scabies, in the everyday observation of dirt contaminating food. Imagery for invisible spread by spirits is given by wind, smell, sound. All indicate presence without visibility.

They may understand 'germs' in medical terms or in spiritual terms, and the ambiguity helps in accommodating the new term and new ideas. People can talk to each other about the same thing while giving it different significance; it can allow them to shift according to the situation. The problems come when people are concerned to define clearly what they are doing and what it means.

References

Durkheim, E. (1961 [1913]). *The Elementary Forms of the Religious Life*. Free Press, Glencoe.

Elvin, M. (1973). *The Pattern of the Chinese Past*. Stanford University Press, Stanford.

Frankel, S. and Lewis, G. (eds) (1989). *A Continuing Trial of Treatment*. Kluwer Academic Publishers, Dordrecht.

Lewis, G. (1975). *Knowledge of Illness in a Sepik Society*. Athlone Press, London.

—— (1980). *Day of Shining Red*. Cambridge University Press, Cambridge.

Marshall, A. J. (1938). *The Men and the Birds of Paradise*. Heinemann, London.

McGregor, D. E. (1975). *The Fish and the Cross*. Privately printed, Hamilton, New Zealand.

Steiner, F. (1967). *Taboo*. Penguin, Harmondsworth.

Chapter 7

Replacing Cultural Markers: Symbolic Analysis and Political Action in Melanesia

Lisette Josephides

This is an oppositional essay, originally inspired by a critique of the following position: that the workings of Melanesian societies may be reduced to a single description, an organizing principle which is at the same time at the bottom of all ritual, cosmological understanding, and social action. This organizing principle may be located in gift exchange (where its many forms are reduced to one); in ritual (for example Barraud *et al.* 1984; Iteanu 1983); or in myths as exemplifying central social relations (for example LeRoy 1985; Weiner 1988). As a unifying analytic, it imposes a certain form on social life even as it claims to discover it there. While at one level it treats as undifferentiated all domains of social life by its implicit claim of going behind phenomenal appearances to the symbolic social patterning achieved by all human interaction (see M. Strathern 1988), this very method-ology conceptually removes the cultural markers that separate domains of social action such as ritual, politics, marriage relations and those of everyday life. Yet, as I will argue, 'cultural markers' denote the formal and implicit distinctions made locally between the various domains of social life, so that analytic attempts to remove them concurrently reduce cultural creativity to the recreation of its most spectacularly 'visible' aspects, its privileged representations. 'Privileged representations' etch themselves by their gaudy extravagance on to the ethnographer's analytic faculties. In this undifferentiating melting-pot social action assumes a circular yet undirected inevitability, like the 'selfish gene' forever reproducing itself.

'Privileged representations' could also be described as those which succeed in making their effects visible (see M. Strathern 1988). In this respect, the question arises of what sort of conditions must be in place for certain effects to be made visible, and, further, how we determine which action, or its representation, is responsible for which effect. I would like to suggest that in the very activity of making their effects visible these successful social actions simultaneously block the possibility of others' achieving visibility. What this means at the level of analysis is that the anthropologist's strategy of removing diacritical marks that denote positionality (spatiotemporal, sexual, or to do with levels of discourse) results in a claim that a particular social group can efficiently be described and understood by attention to just one discourse.[1] This discourse then becomes a master narrative, a black hole into which everything is sucked. Not only are all other voices stilled, but in addition the very voice that is heard is predicated of all social actors, since it is understood to have its source in a social core that is both the logic and the outcome of that specific form of sociality.

A similar point can be made in the case of the analytical privileging of a domain defined as 'ritual,' which becomes a prism through which to view society as a whole. Though Itéanu (this volume) recognizes different 'levels,' the very word 'level' implies hierarchy, a more crucial and somehow 'truer' description of sociality. From this follows the claim that what concerns the social whole is more 'valued' than a positional viewpoint. This assumes that 'positionality' is asocial, or that the individual is pitted against the social, and that the social whole can be viewed only from one perspective. In this particular case, the valued perspective is that of recreating social relations as they are. The acknowledgment of a 'higher value' cannot but evaluate that non-ritual sphere, 'normal life'. In accepting the 'social whole' as a higher good, one is also, it appears, accepting a specific configuration of the social whole, for it is impossible to privilege 'wholeness' in the abstract without privileging the particular, political manifestation of that wholeness that gave rise to the abstract. Further, in this act of privileging, the particular manifestation is elevated to a universal, the 'form' of wholeness whose non-reproduction threatens social life as a whole. Thus in one methodological swoop the particular is universalized and the many are made into one.

Four years between writing and almost going to press modified that oppositional stance to a more reflective one, a willingness to temper the burden of situating oneself within the discourse of a problematic developed by others with the responsibility of following the direction of one's own research findings. But the original impetus remains visible and operative and needed to be stated. The ethnographic materials that spoke to me so eloquently in favour of retaining cultural markers remain the same. They include myths, ritual songs and verses, and various actions within marriage relations. They are not all used to the same purpose, however. My discussion of Kewa myth will reveal a wider horizon of cultural possibilities and ambivalences which is locally mined for the construction of specific meanings and claims, while in a parallel operation theorists support those local constructions by analyses of myths that transform roles and persons in the narratives to underscore existing social relations. Here dominant political actors and theorists collude in their presentation of dominant social meanings. They claim, in effect, that those rich horizons are either mere metaphors for more limited mundane necessities, that is the reproduction of social reality as it is said to exist, or dire warnings of what might happen if it were not so reproduced.

I consider the verses and different genres of ritual songs from two perspectives, their symbolic constructions of marriageable partners within a domestic domain and their construction of an agnatic group in a political domain. Within the ritual/symbolic domain of their performance, women's courting songs and men's pig-killing songs appear to be engaged in a conceptual dialogue, implicitly making conflicting claims for the meaning of marriage, while men's courting verses place themselves more neutrally on the side of women's courting songs as powerful love spells. A discussion of marriage relations, expectations and behaviours is needed to clarify those meanings for each sex. Here we see that, while women may be willing to concede men's priority in the politico-ritual domain that gives rise to pig-killing songs, they contest entailments that their roles as wives are constructed in a relation to that domain. In this way they demonstrate that keeping the domains distinct affords them the possibility of participating as agents in both domains, while to characterize one as defining the other removes all agency from their grasp.

The discussion of marriage has richer ramifications than this, as the account in that section will make clear. I fully intend it to exceed the boundaries of merely providing an ethnographic example for a theoretical argument, to suggest instead a broader horizon of cultural creativity. To this end, I begin with a general, preliminary discussion of Kewa men's and women's perceptions of their cosmology and sociality.[2]

Kewa Ritual, Cosmology, and Practice

The Kewa do not have the rich spectacular ritual activity of many other Melanesian societies. Even such rituals as they have cannot be seen as serving one function in society, for example by enacting spectacular or arcane ceremonies as a normal part of rites of passage. The courting songs, verses and pig-killing songs which I propose to examine here do not detail a whole ritual cycle or a coherent cosmological view, but are partial statements of cultural and political claims, creativity, and understanding. When I add to these people's direct, unambiguous non-ritual action, we see that while it is through ritual that men and women create each other as marriageable partners, it is through ordinary everyday action that each individual marriage is realized.

A worthwhile enquiry would be one that investigates how the Kewa construct and perceive their sociality, and attempts to identify the major contrast in terms of which they express the break between their social world and what may lie beyond it (their cosmology). Kewa make one distinction quite clearly: between things that have happened and things that have not happened. Their major distinctions are not ontological, between things that exist and things that do not exist. What may exist is an open category, not a bounded one. The truth or otherwise of events is a different matter. When Kewa tell a story they start with one of two prefaces. Either they will say: 'I am retelling what was told before. This is a baseless story (does not have *re* – base, origin, reason). It has no meaning, rhyme or reason.' Or they may say, 'This is a story with a reason (*re agele*, also 'story of origin'), it truly (*ora*) happened.' *Ora* and *re* are the two notions which signal the status of the story on that particular narrative occasion. It is important to realize that this status is not an abstract attribute of the story, but rather becomes predicated to it on particular occasions. I argue that *lidi* is the larger category of myth from which specific understandings, claims, meanings are extrapolated. The argument that 'things really happened that way' becomes relevant only when someone or a group has a present stake in it. Claims to truth have an interested basis (*re*). Thus it is events rather than entities whose truth value may be contested, because *claims* can be made by reference to past events. In this connection, it is the past that is important rather than divinities and supernatural beings. What gives the past its power is the fact that it has already happened, it has been externalised in the culture (or at least it is claimed to be so) and is therefore validated by a present for which it is seen to provide a basis. For this reason it is important to see how the past has been created, and which past has received recognition. The way the past is created is through ancestors, through the recounting of past deeds and events, and past positions. For the Kewa the cosmic realm is 'the past', something activated before the present and on which the present is said to rest.

However, the claims made through the past may be contested by present actions, as when men's ancestrally-backed claims concerning the meaning or function of some social activity, institution or idiom are challenged by women's present cultural constructions, both in their actions and their songs. This is where I see a tension between 'cosmology' and 'practice'. To see that changes in cosmological understandings take place as a result of internal meanings ('sense' rather than 'reference,' as in Ricoeur's (1981) distinction), or as a result of competing cosmological understandings (as in Barth 1987) is just one side of the story. The other side is the tension between cosmology and practice (the present empowered by understandings of the past, and the present as a self-evident empowerment) as different political stands and practical strategies. Women do not claim that the past empowers them; they say 'Our mothers never did this' as frequently as men say 'Our fathers did this.' While women speak of what their mothers did or didn't do as something which restricts their own actions, men speak of being empowered by what their fathers did. Present practice, of course, follows on a direct line from past practice, so that the songs that the women sing to construct their male partners were previously sung by their mothers. But this past legitimacy is not invoked by the

women, who consider their songs to be powerful enough in the
present, in their performance, and by the empowerment that
their own bodies give them. What matters is how the songs create
the singers as objects of desire.[3]

Thus women do not appear to think that they have to ground
their claims in an amorphous and created past. Their claims are
direct, immediately creative of cultural meanings. They are not
always reactive, as they may appear in depictions of women
engaged in a tug of war with their husbands over a pig. Here
men's claims could as easily be seen as reactions to the possible
end-logic of practices, as attempts to detour those cultural
meanings created there. That is to say, the meaning created in
marriage contains no entailment that domestic pigs should be
given by the husband to his exchange partners. Men attempt to
create this entailment by linking physical reproduction to a
specific form of social reproduction.

Myth[4]

I argued above that an important axis along which Kewa contrast
their cosmological beliefs with the practice of their everyday
lives stretches from the past to the present. In the cosmological
past of events claimed to have taken place, pig-killing songs
occupy a prominent place. It is on this tension wire of the rhetoric
of the past and the claimed self-evidence of present practice
that the most poignant exchanges are stretched out. A good
illustration is the idioms used in men's and women's
disagreements over pig disposal. Whereas men cite the fact that
the pig in question has been nurtured on their agnatic land,
women will counter that they are the ones who fed it on the
sweet potatoes that they planted.

In their broadest definition, Kewa myths (*lidi*) crosscut this
axis of differentiation. They are not related to ritual, do not deal
with cults and are not tied to particular activities or groups. The
individual spirits, ogres, and sprites that appear in them do not
belong to any total scheme. People are seen in their daily
activities, where miraculous events may nevertheless occur.
Sitting round the fire of an evening, the narrator will usually
begin the story thus: 'I am retelling a story as I heard it from my

father. It has no basis (*re*).' But mentioning its pedigree gives it, of course, some 'base'. Although the men who tell them are people who have perspectives, and some aspects of their form conform to a 'master narrative', the tales as a whole do not have a tight form that attaches them to a position. They enable many positions and therefore contain many meanings. Though they are told within a context of present conditions (the status quo), they give us glimpses of other possibilities, maybe not represented in that status quo. Thus the structure of these tales is untidy and ambling. They do not seem to go anywhere purposely, because they are not telling one story but many. Convention, the taken-for-granted *doxa*, is presented as threatening, indicating that even within a homogeneous group convention is not quite taken for granted: parents become ogres, nurturing abilities are transformed into cannibalistic ones. Not only is the tension between achieved and ascribed statuses explored, but the very necessity of those ascribed statuses is put to the test. In short, their conventionality is exposed.

According to LeRoy (1985), who also worked among the Kewa, *lidi*, while not thought to be true as stories, in fact recount 'essential truths'. Myths of origin (*rapani* or *reagele*) on the other hand, though presented as 'true' stories, contain only contingent truths that link specific groups to specific names, a particular piece of land, and so on. Yet it may be short-sighted to see *reagele* in this way. They do of course claim to make these links. But their claims can acquire force only by reference to a larger one that is always implicit: that agnatic groups owe their power to some fiat that goes beyond the contingent, tying them to the ancestors, to the deities, to tradition. These are the real 'essential truths'. Specific groups of people are able to make claims by using these myths of origin. What empowers the claims is their reference to antiquity and to tradition. By contrast, *lidi*'s truths are not at all essential, despite LeRoy's argument. It is hard even to see them as 'truths'. *Lidi* provide vistas of recognized possibilities from which *reagele* as stories of origin are extrapolated in order to make specific claims. Must we then say that *lidi* contain scenarios of only possible worlds, which need to be interpreted to reveal the face of the actual world in a creative inversion? While I do not propose a return to Malinowski's 'surface meanings', I do feel let down when sophisticated, symbolic analyses of myths return us, by a more circuitous route, to a restatement of social structures, practices and powerful local ideologies. I will elaborate on my meaning here through a discussion of one mythic theme.

In many *lidi* wives appear as magical sources of wealth in the form of pigs, shells and so on. They provide for their husbands' prestige until the husband breaks a promise by a single crass act of disobedience, which results in wife and wealth disappearing. In this patrilineal society brothers rely heavily on their sisters' bridewealth for their own marriage. They also depend on their married sisters for gifts of piglets and other items which enable them finally to raise bridewealth. For these reasons, a cultural idiom frequently on men's lips is that 'all wealth comes from sisters'. This is not women's idiom, since from their perspective it is as wives that their work assumes its social character. LeRoy (1985) analyses a number of myths with the story line just summarized. Mindful of the idiom that sisters bring wealth to their brothers, he assumes that the myths must refer to sisters, even though they talk of wives. Thus in his analysis wives become transformations of sisters.

However, what he overlooks is that it is through wives that men receive most of the wealth for exchanges, and *lidi* show exactly that: women producing wealth but being betrayed by their husbands and withdrawing their powers. In real life we could see this betrayal in men's refusal completely to acknowledge the source of the wealth by not allowing wives to help direct exchanges. The myths stress this contribution of wives that is played down at pig-kills. The wealth that sisters bring comes from exchange, portrayed as men exchanging wealth against women; the wealth that wives bring comes from production, women's own work. Thus one definition of wealth stresses men's exchanges, while the other stresses women's productive activities. In proclaiming that wealth comes from sisters, real-life ideologies privilege men's exchanges over women's production as sources of wealth. (Following M. Strathern, it may be more accurate to say that they 'eclipse' the domain of production in favour of the domain of transaction, since men also are producers.) In analysing the tales the way he does LeRoy performs a similar operation. He 'transforms' the tale to fit in with a powerful local ideology, thus losing sight of the other social reality this idiom eclipses. If we foregrounded this other reality, the tale could be understood as saying the following: Women are producers of wealth, and if men do not acknowledge their powers and contributions and pay them due respect as persons by allowing them full participation they may withdraw their contributions, thus bringing about the collapse of sociality as experienced. This is just as plausible a reading of the tale, especially as it explains more of the detail. Whereas LeRoy's analysis at this level is purely formal, taking into account only the 'frame'. In searching for a single meaning in the tale it not only reiterates dominant idioms but actually reinforces them by discovering them in yet another domain. This statement becomes even stronger when LeRoy claims that *lidi* really contain 'essential' truths for the people. His rich symbolic analysis has returned us to a restatement of social structures, practices, and powerful local ideologies.

It should not be understood that these other possible social descriptions exist only within the realm of non-actualized potentialities. They exist at the level of social action, but are made visible in a particular way and within a discourse that distances them from their cause. This brings me back to an earlier point, where I questioned whether the match between causes and effects is automatic and whether we can always *see* what caused an effect. In M. Strathern's argument, women's production is seen as being caused by men, their husbands (M. Strathern 1988). It is altrocentric action. (Men also claim this, though they give different reasons: that their wives produce on *their* land. Strathern does give this as an additional reason.) If women's actions are 'made visible' as caused by men, then clearly (and if Strathern's analysis of the local social logic is correct) the idioms that describe the products of women's actions (or work) will not trace them back to women. Thus there is a 'reality' described in one way that the *lidi* suggest could be described in another: that women own their powers, and can withdraw them if they are not accorded the respect and recognition they require.

Ritual Songs and Verses

I have suggested that Kewa ritual does not have the single coherent function of constituting the group as a whole. Rather, different rituals are set against each other, and their contextualization and recontextualization make opposing claims.

In the case of courting songs and pig-killing songs, each contests the claims of the other not by arguing *against* but by talking *across* each other.

Women have their own courting songs, while men have verses. Men must purchase these verses, called *rome*, which are considered to contain such powerful magic in their very form that their recitation alone would enflame the chosen girl, 'setting her liver on fire'. Power here has to do with the ability to affect feeling, and through feeling, actions. Thus the verses' power resides in their ability to persuade the listener that the scenario they describe is indeed a desirable one. Men insist that what really attracts women is the power of the words they use; thus they see a woman's falling in love with them as something they have caused. The scenario depicted in *rome* verses is invariably the sexual union between the singer and his listener, which is described as part of the natural world:

> I look at your face
> and it is as if I am looking
> at a parrot or a *yariti* bird.
> The stars shake my ground at Yone
> I must go, farewell.

> I tell this *rome* to you and you listen
> By the fence the sugar cane ripens quickly
> We have ripened like the sugar cane
> What shall we do?

> The banana tree by the house
> has borne fruit which we bind
> What shall we do?

> Up there by the bank in the glade
> the river Yaro makes a lapping noise
> Your head my head we put together as one
> Now what shall we do?

> I tell this *rome* to you and you listen
> Many *wano* trees with teeth like little birds
> are close to the house
> the Kewa child comes close to the house

sugar cane and pitpit
are almost at the house.

(Josephides 1982b: 50)

Here men want to stress the power of their *rome* as something they have willed and which is important to their description as men. In other contexts, however, when they want to describe women as emotional and illogical and their own sexual attractiveness as immanent and unwilled, their story will be different. They will say that nobody knows a woman's mind, she will take a fancy to a man and just come and sit at his mother's house and allow nothing to shift her. Thus men often present themselves as the innocent sufferers of women's unfathomable, uncaused and unlooked-for passions.

Wena yaisia, women's courting songs (*wena* means 'woman,' *yaisia* means 'song'), also have power, but it derives from a different source. These songs constantly juxtapose dearth and plenty, barrenness and fertility. The message is clear: bachelorhood is barren and marriage fertile, not only in terms of procreation but also in terms of production, which is a sexually complementary activity.[5]

In our gardens at Yamu
cordyline leaves abounded
But when we plant them in the mud
They will not take.[6]

The special cooking leaves are ready
but where are you?
Where has my netbag gone?
You've gone somewhere they say
where have you gone?

In our gardens at Yamu
Cordyline leaves grew in profusion
But now they have been replanted
by the water at the coast.[7]

As among the casuarinas
so among the many men of Wata

Their great shadows obscure the place
Yet Rame still stands out among them
oil pours down his body.

Where many casuarinas cast shadows
it becomes dark.
Though you are a man, I cannot call you so
for at Yamu the areca palms are few.
Answer me![8]

At Yamu a new banana
will always replace the plucked one
So just look, and go.[9]

Red sugar cane at Yokere, if I cut you
it will be with a heavy heart
So let the wind break you off
and lay you down before me.[10]

(Josephides 1982b: 52–3)

In these songs it is not so much the words that have the power to move as the women and their bodies. For this reason the women's decorations and performance are important. Whereas in *rome* a man knelt behind a woman and whispered passionately in her ear while she kept her eyes lowered (both were ashamed, I was told), in *wena yaisia* women must be looked at and their dancing admired. Its power coerced men to make gifts to them. Often on these occasions women extolled the physical attributes of one man, whose physical description was given in idioms that fused pig-killing with sexual or marital activities. In these songs women 'completed' men by a description of what would make them desirable as marriage partners to women. Thus a man's sexual attractiveness was inseparable from those activities which define men.

The songs also constructed women as desirable persons. When girls formed a singing group and performed their dusk serenades, their intentions were not so much to attract or marry any particular man as to extract gifts from all the men who listened to them. The gifts were doubly prized as signs that the girls were desired and valued. Singers who receive no gifts are greatly shamed, so girls ascertain in advance that gifts will be forthcoming.

Both *rome* and *wena yaisia* can be seen as forms of action with specific short-term effects in mind. But in the long term they also affirm the recursive continuity of their effects. Men propagate an image of themselves as persons with *rome* power that resides in strong words which, in describing a possible social outcome, also achieve it. Women complete this image by fusing and reaffirming men's various social, cultural, and reproductive roles. But while the idiom that evokes marriage is men's cultural role of giving bridewealth (see last verse, above), women do not thereby suggest that it is men who create social relations. In their own courting songs women propagate an image of themselves as persons whose bodies and performance, in describing the sexual attractiveness and life history of one man, attract other men, who see them as valuable persons to be compensated with wealth. Though metaphoric exchange takes place – men give women shells, women seize men's axes – the ultimate intention is for a metonymic exchange, the unmediated exchange of marital relations. Thus we see that both *rome* and *wena yaisia* involve the individual persons in the re-creation of conditions that will lead to relationships where they can creatively propagate themselves. Though it is convention that men and women will marry, in each individual case they must create those conditions in which their personal marriages will be realized. They must make themselves attractive so that someone will desire them as a marriage partner, and in the end this is the individual's responsibility, though she or he may enjoy varying support. Attractiveness is no small matter in ensuring the stability of marriage. Kewa consider it essential that women especially should desire their husbands, otherwise they will not stay with them. Though these conventionalized performing art forms allow for a degree of innovation as a result of uncertainty (individuals may fail to establish an enduring marriage), their repeated success also affirms a sociality based on the constant re-creation of the difference between men and women, whose creativity is marriage. But it does not imply that the agnatic group manages these affairs, as men claim in their pig-killing songs.

Let us move on to these pig-killing songs. The *au yaisia* ('[war] decoration songs') are completely impersonal, abstracted from particular personal histories. They do not tell a story at all, but are statements or claims of the clan's strength. They are usually sung the day before the pig-kill, when presentations are made to former war allies. I describe one event which I observed in 1980 in the village of Wakiapanda.

While it was still light, men of the host group put on black warpaint and danced four abreast around a little house on a hill about 500 yards from the men's house. They swung axes and some carried shields (*kaga*). They were interspersed with rows of very young girls with bodies and faces painted red. The songs recalled old traditions, with the hosts congratulating themselves on fulfilling their obligations. Meanwhile the allies, also in black war decorations, arrived stealthily at the last moment, gathering and crouching at the bottom of the hill. At a certain stage the hosts went down the hill and danced around the men's house two or three times, then went back up again. This was the signal for the guests to charge, which they did with fearful war cries (*uuuuuuuu, eeeeekopkop*) and swinging of axes. They ran up the hill and down again, in the direction of the men's house, and proceeded to dance around that. Then the hosts grouped themselves at the top of the hill, where they had lined up singed pigs and wealth (pearlshells, bank notes) displayed on bamboo sticks (*kepa*). The hosts' spokesman called out the name of the group which was to receive pigs. The group thus summoned charged up the hill uttering war cries and brandishing spears and axes. Then one of two things happened. Either the host holding the pig charged through the guests, breaking their ranks, to deposit the pig by the men's house and run up again. Or one of the guests grabbed the proffered pig and threw it over his shoulder and the whole group ran down again to the men's house. Without further formalities the guests then proceeded on their way home. (Adapted from Josephides 1982b: 46–78).

Au yaisia verses display the achievements of the celebrants by playing them down, expressing debt to their fathers and allies. Here is the text of some of the versus sung on that occasion.

> HOSTS: We are small quail
>   sitting in abundant grass.
>
>   Orphan boy, as many men
>   as there is wild cane in the bush
>   come to see you.[11]

ALLIES: Orphan boy, I planted you
          and you grew.[12]

HOSTS: I follow in my father's footsteps
          and compensate with cassowaries.

          We are just ten men
          yet we have made a fence
          and cultivate gardens.[13]

          Strong armlets of those long buried
          this now I will do.[14]

          Brother, fetch the leaf of the *arimuka*
          We shall cook something.

          The longhouse pig-killing
          I have learnt from my father (refrain)

          (Josephides 1982b: 84–5)

Only fathers, sons, men, appear here. Nothing but agnatic relations; all others have been eclipsed. There is no room for any manoeuvring, for meanings to be interpreted any other way than repetitively. The songs have become proclamations of just one point of view, and other meanings the pig-kill may have are totally eclipsed. The message is that the agnatic group of males manages these matters and the affective, emotional matters of the kin group and domestic unit have no place here.

Different kinds of persons are created in these ritualized songs. While women's courting songs subordinate the pig-killer to the marriageable partner and are unconcerned with the creation of bigmen except from the aesthetic point of view (for instance, see verse 10), *au yaisia*, by contrast, define men as pig-killers, sons of their fathers. Whereas in everyday life married men are referred to by their teknonyms (as are women), patronyms are invariably used in men's ritual singing, where ancestry rather than progeny is stressed – that is, the past rather than the present or future. Courting songs create men as husbands, potential fathers. Fertility, as opposed to barrenness, is stressed. In *au yaisia* men use the past to empower their claims;

n *wena yaisia* women use the present as self-evident empowerment. In their *rome* courting songs men use magic, an external and purchased form of power, to attract women; in theirs, women expect their performance and their charms to draw men. Therefore their powers are their own and innate.[15]

Au yaisia do not create women as persons except negatively, as persons that do not reproduce sociality. In *wena yaisia* references to pig-kills are oblique, incidental to descriptions of beautiful men. (There are also references to gardening, which are metaphors for pig-killing.) The concern here is with individuals falling in love and marrying. This may appear to support a Dumontian hierarchical analysis that subordinates courting rituals to pig-killing rituals, on the grounds that the latter claim to affect society as a whole by reproducing the group. Yet the pig-kill is exactly the ritual arena where we witness counter-contestations by women, in both ritual and non-ritual form. While men sing *au yaisia* in the afternoon, and in the evening sing other metaphorical songs called *tupale*,[16] another activity takes place concurrently. In a small low house not far from the men's house, courting sessions continue into the night, with men and women sitting in a circle, singing their love songs and making assignations in the nearby bush. As we saw, marriage is not linked with pig-killing in the imagery of these courting songs, where the concern is to create marriageable partners.

In a non-ritual response we witness how, the following day when pigs are killed and pork is distributed, women become locked in physical combat with their husbands, who attempt to give pork against their wishes. These demonstrations are not ritualized, and the result is by no means a foregone conclusion. A man may overpower his wife, give the pork where he wants, then make himself scarce until she gets over her fury. But often he will bend to her wishes; and these are the occasions when the struggle will not be so visible. Here women are constructing for the pig-kill other functions that their husbands are eclipsing. They challenge their husbands' definitions of this activity as creating only certain kinds of relations connected with male prestige, and posit instead other relations which it is also creating, wider kin relations and personal exchange relations that enable them to make a stand as persons and agents, as women that will not be sucked into an oppressive definition of the group that disempowers them by neutralizing gender as an interest group. For in a world where one gender has political ascendence, to neutralize the political importance of gender can easily appear as acceding to that status quo.

Marriage

The foregoing discussion has already suggested that women and men have different claims and expectations of marriage. For instance, women resist the notion that pig-killing concerns should order their domestic activities or kinship obligations. These different perceptions can be observed even more clearly when a man attempts to take a co-wife. I turn to a consideration of polygyny with some trepidation, as I realize that to look at it at all critically is liable to be labelled ethnocentric. Yet in real life the trauma sustained by a Kewa woman when her husband takes another wife is so great that it often results in the rupture of one of the two relationships, at least for a time. It is the only occasion I know of when women use knives, which they go out to buy especially. It is not unusual for all three spouses to end up in hospital. Though monogamous couples also fight, women do not normally attack their husbands with knives without this sexual element. It is clearly a context where women see their social and personal positions threatened.

The story of Lapame and Rombola is instructive. Lapame and Rombola had been married for about fifteen years when I met them. Rombola had married a second wife some years before my arrival, but there were constant fights. Eventually Lapame, after being released from hospital following a particularly violent encounter, bought a knife and attacked the other woman. This landed all three in hospital, and soon after Rombola terminated his second marriage and the woman returned home.[17] Lapame subsequently told me that Rombola could marry again if he wanted, but she would leave him if he did. He did marry again in 1982, while I was absent from the field. According to Lapame, he had been carrying on with the woman for some time, when she caught them in the house one day 'holding each other tight'. Her behaviour at this time seemed ambivalent. She clearly did not want him to marry, yet almost dared him to. On the one hand, she said to him that it was inappropriate for a man in his position ('not young', which means 'already married') to be hiding in darkened doors in order to embrace a woman who was herself 'no longer young'. The right thing would be for them to marry, and Lapame herself 'put the woman's hand in his'. On the other hand, she upbraided him in the following words: 'If you look at my work and think it not good, if I had given you no children (by this time she was expecting her fifth child), then you could marry another woman.' In other words, Lapame considered his additional marriage an action that showed lack of appreciation for her. This statement also indicates what women consider justifiable reasons for polygyny (though no woman I knew ever thought it justified in her own case).

In spite of her proud retort that a man should marry instead of engaging in surreptitious love affairs, Lapame did not want to help Rombola when he attempted to collect the brideprice. She withheld the pigs he requested, which earned her the predictable response: 'All these pigs and gardens and wealth, did you bring them from your home? They belong to *my* ground!' She gave way when he wept and threatened in turn, especially when he said that he would go away and she would never see him again. She felt she had no choice when faced with his determination to have this woman. She did try to hide one little pig, but eventually this too was found and given in brideprice. During the exchanges Lapame looked on unhappily. Immediately afterwards she took her children to the garden and cut down all the sugar cane, giving it to everyone to eat. She told me that this was their custom; other women may vent their fury by killing pigs or even pulling down houses. (Sugar cane, pigs, and houses are 'male.') Following this, they all slept under the same roof for one night.

The next day Wata (the second wife) told Rombola she didn't like this arrangement, as he looked at his first wife rather too much. So while Lapame was at church he divided up all their possessions, took the 'best things' for himself and his second wife, and partitioned the house. He also divided up all the gardens and asked Lapame which half she preferred. But she would not speak to either of them by this time. Though half the gardens she had planted were taken over by another woman, 'everyone' told her that she shouldn't complain because gardens, pigs and shells belong to men. Rombola ate only at Wata's at this time and would not take Lapame's food. Two months later Lapame gave birth to her fifth child, a boy. Rombola then suggested that she take half the children and go back to her natal group, to which she responded that since their lives and goods were separated in any case, why throw her out too?

Rombola told a different story. He had not wanted her to go but was simply angry with her for being so difficult. He claimed that she had refused him food, telling him to go to his new wife for it. He complained that her refusal was contrary to her duties as a wife, and told me that though his new wife gave him food he still felt hungry after finishing it. Since food stands for sexual intercourse, Lapame was telling Rombola to go and eat where he copulated. Rombola's insatiable hunger may have been of both varieties, though it is unlikely that he would have pressed sexual demands on a wife whose pregnancy was almost at full term. In the end (Rombola said) it was she herself who insisted on going, and he fetched her back immediately, even managing to get to her natal clan before her. To make doubly sure of getting her back he filed a complaint with the police that she was endangering the life of an infant by taking it on a perilous journey. Peace was not completely restored until Wata finally returned to her natal clan. (This followed on a delict with Rombola's classificatory younger brother, but that's another story. Rombola gave out that the reason for her dismissal was laziness.)

The foregoing story indicates that women consider their husbands' remarriage a repudiation, a lack of appreciation for themselves and their labour. In this case it was an unjust repudiation, and Lapame echoes many women in her enumeration of what might be considered good reasons for repudiation. Yet men will not say that a second marriage implies a repudiation or even a criticism of the first wife. When they are faced with their wife's protest, however, they usually try to accuse her of something. Since a divorce or a lengthy separation may ensue, they try to pin some of the blame on her in order to mitigate the compensation they might have to pay to get her back.

Given these problems, why do men take second wives? Most women say they do it for sexual reasons, but men claim that their motive is to augment household production, which would in turn expand their exchange networks and add to the prestige of the group by enabling them to stage spectacular pig-kills. Thus it appears that a concern with prestige and pig-killing is part of a man's marriage strategies, but not part of what women consider to define the relations that create marriage. The disagreement is over what constitutes marriage relations. When questioned about their marriage, women say that their husbands married them because they desired them. They see the payment of brideprice as indicative of how much they are desired, and even inflate it in their accounts. (Contrariwise, men often deflate it, claiming that women came to them 'for nothing.') With this perceptual background, women see their husbands' proposal to acquire another wife as a non-fulfilment or a rescinding of the promise contained in that desire. More strongly put, they see it as a betrayal.

Conclusion

While men and women jointly create social relations and each other as persons, the kinds of relations and persons that are created in the different social domains are not identical. In courting songs and verses men and women define themselves as sexually attractive marriageable partners; in pig-killing songs men arrogate to themselves exclusively the powers of social reproduction. Myths are wider vistas, containing a number of positions on the creation of sociality. Men's success in pig-kills depends on their ability to have them accepted as superior, more encompassing rituals. But women tolerate men's prominent roles here only to the extent that they can differentiate their marriage and the obligations and duties entailed there from pig-kills when defined as 'male games'. Thus women themselves put the social markers back in, refusing to acknowledge the superiority of this ritual and insisting that their marriage belongs in one domain and pig-killing in another.

My examination has placed itself between critique and reconstruction. It identified a duality of cultural creative understandings, and indicated the level at which this duality was stifled so that a single cultural description emerged. In these contexts, certain rituals claimed exclusive powers of total social description (for instance, men's claims at *au yaisia*). If these kinds of rituals that claim to refer to the 'society as a whole' are further identified by analysts as containing the 'organizing principle' of that social group, dissenting voices are effectively stifled at this superior level. While they may still be recorded by the ethnographer, they have been robbed of their power to present an authentic cultural description. The collusion between the ethnographer and the local privileged representation can thus result in a misrepresentation of how Kewa sociality is constructed and perceived by the Kewa themselves. *Therefore* we must put back the markers that identify domains of differentiation. Otherwise the only analysis we can achieve is one that shows how everything functions.

Notes

1. An example of a discourse carried on at many levels is gift exchange. When the assumption is made that Hagen *moka,* for instance, defines exchange in that society, all other domains of life become signified by *moka* (see Josephides 1982a; A. Strathern 1971). 'Exchange' then becomes a discourse made up of actions that are traced through many social domains (ritual, political, kin and domestic relations), but whose definition as *particular kinds of actions* is informed mainly by men's exchanges in *moka.*
2. For a fuller ethnography of the Kewa, see Josephides 1985.
3. Men also create themselves as objects of desire, and women create them as such objects. This is not a sexually biased action that objectifies women in a pejorative sense.
4. I refer to myth as *lidi. Lidi* define a domain of cultural creativity that is richer and broader than that of the *malangan* or the Kaluli songs discussed by Munn in this volume. This is because *lidi* contain congealed memory that is not conscious of its own selectivity. Though I describe them as containing a half-conscious awareness of the possible descriptions of social creativity, more work is needed to decide the degree of their political innocence. *Tupale* and *temali* seem to me closer to the *malangan* and Kaluli songs.
5. These songs were sung by a group of women in Yakopaita on 14 April 1980. Three single girls took the lead while two married women joined in the chorus. The women gave me the interpretations in the notes which follow some verses.

6. 'There were many men before, both young and old. But they sickened and died, and now we are without men.'
7. 'The young men of this area have all gone to work in the coastal plantations.'
8. 'Your clan is small, I can't call you a real man. You are little, so don't keep discussing, just answer.'
9. 'Another woman will always replace the one that's married.'
10. 'It would not be appropriate for me as a woman to go and collect bridewealth. But if you come and give it to me yourself, it would be most suitable.'
11. Here the hosts express pride that they have attracted such a large crowd of visitors and spectators. The actual size of the clan is irrelevant; the self-deprecating convention stresses the clan's achievement.
12. The allies respond that they were the ones who saved the hosts when the hosts were being killed by warfare.
13. 'We are only few yet manage to kill many pigs.'
14. 'The many dead ancestors are now feasted, and their offspring rejoice in building a longhouse and settling old debts'.
15. Women also use love magic, but only when their charms fail them, and usually when they have already an established relationship with an errant male. Thus they rub magical substances on his food or on their young children, put powerful leaves in his tobacco, or, more viciously, burn in bamboos mud with his footprints . . .
16. These are 'vintage threnodies', sung by teams of dancing men in the long men's house (see Josephides 1982b).
17. This was Rombola's story. It's quite possible that the woman herself decided to go, and in recounting the story Rombola took on the causal, active role. I have often noticed that in narrations people arrogate to themselves clear and decisive roles, which I have never observed while events are actually unfolding.

References

Barraud, C., Coppet, D. de, Iteanu, A. and Jamous, R. (1984). Des relations et des morts. Quatre sociétés vues sous l'angle des échanges. In: *Différences, valeurs, hiérarchies*, pp. 421–520. Editions de l'Ecole des Hautes Etudes en Sciences Sociales, Paris.

Barth, F. (1987). *Cosmologies in the Making: A Generative Approach to Cultural Variation in Inner New Guinea.* Cambridge University Press, Cambridge.

Iteanu, A.(1983). *La ronde des échanges.* Cambridge University Press and Editions de la Maison des Sciences de l'Homme, Cambridge and Paris.

Josephides, L. (1982a). *Suppressed and Overt Antagonism: A Study in Aspects of Power and Reciprocity among the Melpa.* University of Papua New Guinea, Port Moresby.

—— (1982b). *Kewa Stories and Songs.* Institute of Papua New Guinea Studies, Port Moresby.

—— (1985). *The Production of Inequality.* Tavistock, London.

LeRoy, J. (1985). *Fabricated World: An Interpretation of Kewa Tales.* British Columbia Press, Vancouver.

Ricoeur, P. (1981). Metaphor and the Central Problem of Hermeneutics. In: *Hermeneutics and the Human Sciences.* Edited and translated by J. B. Thompson. Cambridge University Press, Editions de la Maison des Sciences de l'Homme, Cambridge and Paris.

Strathern, A. (1971). *The Rope of Moka.* Cambridge University Press, Cambridge.

Strathern, M. (1988). *The Gender of the Gift: Problems with Women and Problems with Society in Melanesia.* University of California Press, Berkeley.

Weiner, J. F. (1988). *The Heart of the Pearlshell.* University of California Press, Berkeley.

Chapter 8

The 'Holding Together' of Ritual: Ancestrality and Achievement in the Papuan Highlands[1]

Eric Hirsch

My interest in the study of ritual among the Fuyuge of the Papuan highlands was prompted by the intense interest Fuyuge men and women themselves had in organizing, enacting and talking about their ritual. Fuyuge men and women conceptualized their distinctiveness – as this emerged in relation to government authorities and in relation to other cultural groups – by the compulsion they felt to perform their ritual. In trying to understand the central importance the Fuyuge ascribed to their ritual two alternative ways of thinking, talking and acting stood out.

On the one hand, Fuyuge men and women would say that in performing their ritual they were following the way of an ancestral, creator force (*tidibe*, see below). It was the human-like embodiments of this force that shaped their lands and their everyday and ritual practices. Men and women would often talk as if they were simply acting out a pattern or template laid down by this creator force. It was as if they had no personal agency in these actions, but were there to act out some socio-cosmic plan which had its origins in the ancestral past. The performance of their ritual was ultimately a necessity created by this encompassing vision of ancestral origins.

On the other hand, men and women would alternatively speak of their ritual in a manner which did not make reference to an ancestral, creator force. Rather, talk would focus on very specific actions and events; actions and events which were anticipated or had just occurred, and which required the specific movement of persons and objects. For example, and as described more fully below, men and women would often speculate as to when the next stage of a ritual would occur. Their speculations were related, in many cases, to the ability of the pig-killers to gather all of their pigs together in one locale; or of dancers to complete their head-dresses. Often the realization of these actions would be delayed owing to a death in the vicinity. Men and women would then interrupt their efforts and go and cry, mourn and kill pigs for the deceased. In this mode of description the agency of the person(s) was prominent. In general, men and women were concerned with specific acts of pig-killing and distribution, the exchange of valued objects and with the performance of dancers, all of which needed to occur in relation to specific persons. The performance of their ritual was centred on the need to make particular actions and events happen, so that others would be able to witness their efficacy.

The first mode of description focused on timelessness, where the performance of ritual was the spatial realization of an otherwise transcendent process initiated by the ancestral creator force. The second mode of description was concerned with issues of temporal sequencing and how one action and/or event anticipated another as the realization of specific social relations and achievements (for example, dancers invited to perform as an anticipation of pigs killed by their hosts). One of the arguments I pursue in this chapter is that these alternative modes of description each imply and complete the other. The first mode of description, with its focus on ancestrality, and the second, with its focus on achievement, have to be seen to come together for the ritual to succeed. The coalescence of the ancestral and of achievement is predicated on what I describe below as the alignment of directionalities.

A parallel argument I pursue in this chapter is that these alternative modes of description are encoded in two anthropological models currently employed in the study of Melanesian societies. As with the local modes of description, each model, I will suggest, implies and completes the other. The first is the socio-cosmic model of Melanesian societies developed by de Coppet and his colleagues. This model corresponds to the first mode of description, with its emphasis on an encompassing image of the social whole as derived from ancestral origins and as realized through the performance of ritual. The second is M.

Strathern's model of Melanesian sociality, with its emphasis on the revelatory nature of social practices.[2] This model corresponds to the second mode of description, with its emphasis on personal agency and achievement as realized through the sequencing of social acts.

To illustrate the relationship between these models the ethnographic argument of the chapter focuses on a series of inter-linked rituals organized in the Udabe Valley of the Fuyuge during the mid–1980s. As we shall see, concerns with directionality figure centrally in the enactment of the ritual. By directionality (cf. Parkin 1992) I refer most specifically to movement or journeys along a pathway (*enamb*). The Fuyuge notion of pathway entails both the physical path and is an idiom used for denoting social action and agency. A person is referred to as an *enamb* when s/he is the means of access to a desired object or event (Hirsch 1994: 698). Melanesian social action is a continual process of anticipating and exchanging perspectives with others, where 'people forever regard themselves as moving from one position to another' (M. Strathern 1988: 271; Mosko 1992). Such movement presupposes the physical existence of pathways: in and between villages, to gardens, into the forest, to ritual sites and so on. The everpresence of pathways, both those frequently used and pathways which only emerge into prominence periodically, lends weight to the suggestion that journeys upon them are the paradigmatic cultural act: 'spatiotemporal linkages once established can become the template . . . for future actions and relationships' (Parmentier 1987: 136). This is exemplified in the creation myths of Fuyuge cosmology.

The Fuyuge cosmos was constituted by the directed movements along a pathway of the ancestral creator force – *tidibe*. This primordial process was both an act of creation and of loss: *tidibe* disappeared as the final act of the journey (Hirsch 1994: 702–4). The Fuyuge ritual known as *gab*, which translates as 'whole' or 'unity', is the attempted recreation of this *tidibe*-like unity. Men and women attempt to hold together (unify) numerous pathways by having them converge at the site of the *gab*. The process of unification is never certain and it is only through the holding-together capacities of chiefs (*amede*) and efficacious men (*aked*) that it can be precariously achieved. Images of ancestrality can only be achieved through the aesthetically correct alignment of directionalities – pathways of persons and things – as these move across the land into the central ritual space.

Fuyuge ritual is thus a specific spatial and temporal moment of person/land relationships. Persons, things, and places on the land are 'held together' – unified – so as to generate specific anticipated outcomes (as stressed by M. Strathern 1988). This reveals the person(s) as transformed from what I refer to as a foreground actuality (concealing an inner potentiality) to a background potentiality (which becomes the revealed actuality) (cf. Hirsch 1995). The transformation occurs through the activation of social relations involving movement across the land towards an anticipated, held-together unity. The activation of the social relations that are held together in this manner replicates a mythical/cosmological pattern seen as primordially constituting both the person and the land (as stressed by de Coppet 1985).

Before turning to a description of the Fuyuge and a consideration of the specific interlinked rituals, it seems appropriate to touch first on the topic of the Melanesian gift. There is a directionality intrinsic to the gift, the understanding of which has helped to undermine preconceived ideas about the interrelations of persons, things and the land.

Persons, Things and Land

One of the important outcomes of debates about the gift in Melanesian anthropology has been that the distinction between persons and things, so important for Western observers, proved to be irrelevant for Melanesian cultural constructions. In the Melanesian context, neither persons nor things are freestanding. Rather, each is involved in a process of mutual implication, such as Munn (1986) has shown in her analysis of value transformation on Gawa. More recently, M.Strathern (1992a: 177), following Mauss, has argued that coercion is intrinsic to the way in which the Melanesian gift (i.e. the relation of debt) is created: 'an object in the regard of one actor must be made to become an object in the regard of another'. In other words, people must be persuaded to enter into the elicitory regard of another. It is through dealings with others, via the interchange of objects, that the multiple set of relations which composes the Melanesian person are made evident.

The use of persuasion, either through explicit oratory and rhetoric or by the use of secret magic, is concerned to effect a movement of persons and (personified) things into appropriate places. The coercion of the gift is only effective if actual movements occur which facilitate the aspired-towards potential (for example, pigs concentrated together in exchange for the performance of a concentrated group of dancers). As we shall see below, oratory which evokes the image of dancers or pigs, so concentrated, only has effect if the dancers or pigs move across the land in an appropriate (spatial and temporal) manner. The relationship between the actual (pigs in diverse locales) and potential (pigs concentrated) can only be achieved if persons and things are thus held together in what is perceived as the (aesthetically) correct way.

The land, as with persons and things more generally, is equally implicated in this interpenetrative relationality – through gardens planted, villages and, houses constructed and, most significantly here, the pathways traversed (cf. M. Strathern 1992b: 85). But as de Coppet has noted, Melanesian conceptualizations of the land often reveal two sets of images which to the Western observer appear incompatible or even metaphysical – like the equation of persons and things broached above. On the one hand, the land is seen as constituted by the primordial acts of ancestors and mythic figures. From this perspective the land was formed in mythic times prior to human habitation. On the other hand, the land is seen as made ancestor-like through the everyday and ritual activities of men and women. From this perspective it is through the cumulative acts of humans over time that the land is understood to become ancestral (M. Leenhardt emphasized a similar dualism in his ethnography; see Clifford 1992: 38–40).

What de Coppet has brought to the Melanesianist's attention is the contrast between a foregrounded, actual relationship with the land – actual achievements on the land – and the land imagined as a potential where the ancestral is seen to precede the humanly created. Nevertheless, the ancestral is also aspired to through actual actions and movements on the land, actions which render the person and land ancestor-like (de Coppet 1985: 89).[3] This is a process of 'holding together' perspectives each of which implies and completes the other.[4]

Among the Fuyuge, to whom we now turn, it is men conceptualized as chiefs (*amede*) who are seen to facilitate this totalizing potential: of enabling others to know themselves as 'one' (one mind, one talk, one skin); as a potential, place-centred unity.[5] These figures are referred to as chiefs because, like big men, their capacity for unification is precariously demonstrated in the face of external relations (see ; Clay 1992; M. Strathern 1991: 213–14). But unlike big men, these are figures who are conceptualized as having excellent qualities (*amede* = excellent = chief) in speech-making and in their personal conduct; excellent qualities that are seen as having been passed down ('hereditary') from a limited number of persons (cf. Hallpike 1977: 142–3). Nowadays, chiefs are conceptualized as those who hold, talk over and split betelnut. The bunches of betelnut that are today concentrated together in ritual contexts are metonymic of this holding-together capacity. It is certain varieties of betelnut, as with other desired artefacts and capacities, which are imagined to have been lost in the ancestral past when *tidibe* journeyed through the lands of the Fuyuge and then disappeared towards the coast. Fuyuge men and women are preoccupied to recover and thus to maintain a hold on these dissipated artefacts and capacities of value. Chiefs, as they manifest their powers and strength in ritual, are conceptualized as central to this re-integrative process of holding together (see Hirsch 1994).[6]

Image of the Bowerbird

The Fuyuge number around 14,000, and live concentrated in five river valleys of the Wharton Ranges, Central Province. The Fuyuge conceptualize their valleys as divided into two areas. A lowland area, known as *halai*, is where yam gardens are cultivated and where the large ritual villages known as *gab* are constructed. This is in contrast to the higher altitude forest area, known as *mawant*, where many pigs are husbanded and where the Fuyuge live in small hamlets, often nearby sweet potato gardens. The distinction between *halai* and *mawant* figures centrally in Fuyuge thought. Fuyuge will say that they do not construct their *gab* in the forest; to do so would be to dance and kill pigs in a manner not visible to others. In constructing their *gab* Fuyuge men and women say they follow in the way of the bowerbird (Hirsch 1987). The bowerbird lives in the forest and constructs a bower (dancing plaza, *gab*) out of moss constructed around the sapling of a young tree. He decorates his bower with bright objects from the forest floor – shiny burnt pieces of wood are some of the most common.

I was told by men and women that their *gab* and the manner in which they decorate it replicates the customs of the bird. Just as the bird decorates the sides of its bower with decorative objects, so the people decorate the sides of their village with all varieties of yam, sugar cane and, in the past, bones of the deceased; just as the male bird is said to send out invitations to his friends to come and dance in his bower, so men send out invitations to others for them to come and dance at their *gab* (see Majnep and Bulmer 1977: Chap. 23; A. Strathern, 1985: 119–39). In fact, a direct temporal parallel is made between the ritual life centred in the *gab* and that of the bird in his: 'when we construct a *gab*, I was told, so does the bird; when our *gab* is complete, so the bird leaves its *gab* in the forest' (Hirsch 1987: 2).

In the lowlands below, Fuyuge men and women attempt to replicate the image achieved by the bowerbird. At the same time, though, the bowerbird and its bower (*gab*), as with the surroundings and the *gab* of the Fuyuge, were laid down by *tidibe* (see Hirsch 1994; forthcoming). *Tidibe* is a life-force which took the form of creator beings said to have created the lifeworld of the Fuyuge – including the acts which constitute a *gab*; acts and movements recounted in narrative form. As a *gab* is always ultimately abandoned, leaving a mark of its previous existence, the lifeworld of the Fuyuge is already *tidibe*-like in its everyday existence. In addition, the completion of one *gab* and its abandonment is part of the process of anticipating another *gab* to be enacted at a different place in the future through gardens planted, pigs raised, money obtained through cash cropping, etc. Fuyuge social relationality is created in a *tidibe*-like lifeworld, and men and women see themselves as constituted by a series of *gab* performed in various locales across the lands of their home. The directionality from one *gab* to the next, anticipated for the particular person, is replicated in the directionality anticipated for collectivities of persons.

The process of moving towards this *tidibe*-like potential is traced below. Although the *gab* plaza (*endant*) is the place where the specific performances of the *gab* are enacted, this is only after the culmination of numerous movements from diverse locales. The images of unification revealed in the *gab* plaza (betelnut, a diversity of foods, pigs, dancers, valued objects, etc.) is the result of numerous acts of provisional holding together that are achieved on the way to this centre. The process of movement along pathways is highlighted in speeches made in each context. It is the very act of movement along the pathways, of aligning the directionalities of persons and things, which men and women seek to highlight. Power is the capacity to bring about the coalescence of ancestrality and achievement, predicated on this alignment of directionalities.

It is impossible to observe this process from the numerous places that ultimately find their alignment in the *gab* plaza. It is, however, possible to capture it from several vantage points which illustrate significant dimensions of this process. The four vantage points covered here each entail a process of increasing collective unification. But this collective unity is only achieved by making particular persons the object of collective regard. The transformations brought forth from within the person(s) provide the way the held-together perspectives of the collectivity can be directed (aligned) from one context to the next. The movement along and joining of pathways to the centre of the ritual is not incidental to the words and actions expressed in each context. In an important sense the speeches are iconic of the alignment of directionalities that men and women attempt to achieve as they move closer to the *gab* centre (cf. Parkin 1992).

As indicated above, people forever regard themselves as moving from one position to another: people reveal and draw out of each other through their reciprocal agency and action the capacities they are known to potentially possess. This is as true of the everyday capacities of gardening and pig-raising as it is of the more ritualized capacities of first entering the dance or men's house or of a first pregnancy. The difference between them is that the first are 'domestic' and involve particular relations, say between husband and wife, which are only later eclipsed when the product of their capacities are fed into collective, ritual contexts (for example, pigs fed on sweet potato and later killed in ritual). By contrast, the ritualized capacities, say of a first pregnancy, although initiated through the domestic relations of sexual procreation, are made known in a collective context of public scrutiny: here it is the person who becomes the object of collective regard. The multiple relations of which the person is composed become activated and aligned into an audience. In such a context, the person and the collective become mutually defining of each other's unified capacities: the woman as wife and as expectant mother; the collectivity of its own oneness and potential for further action (for example, for the next such collective context). Men and women, youth and the aged are continually experiencing such transitions. They either provide the basis for one 'home'[7] to initiate a *gab* in their name, or they are used as a means of constituting a unified collective in order to move towards a *gab* hosted elsewhere. Both processes are at work together in aspects of the *gab* described below.

The performance of a *gab* in each home is a unique constellation of events. At the same time a common pattern can be found throughout the Fuyuge, which includes forms of dance, ceremonial pig-killing and exchanges (cf. Williamson 1912: 125–67).[8] The events of the *gab* described here were hosted by a section of one home. The home is named Visi and the section named Ambabu. The name of the *gab* village was Uyams. Three homes were invited to dance, two of which formed one collective. The northern neighbour of Ambabu, called Evese, a section of the home Ononge, was invited. The other two homes, Kambisi and Omale, live across the Udabe Valley. The neighbour of Ambabu to the south, part of the same home, called Yago, acted as 'supporters' of the hosts, and it was with them that I was resident, living in the village of Fuda.

Vantage Points on a Process of Increasing Unification

'The next day I will go there singing on the way.'

The first vantage point is from the village of Fuda, which was the site of a recently completed *gab*. In the village plaza sit women pounding bark with stone to form the cloth decoration loincloths worn as part of the dancing costume. Women dye the loincloths yellow with ginger before they are worn by men. The sound of the pounding is the first overt sign of the anticipated movement of men and women to the *gab* as dancers. To hold together and direct the movement on this occasion a small rite, *hombolsondamlad* (literally, showing or making visible the belly) is performed for a woman experiencing her first pregnancy. The process of making her belly visible as the anticipation of her first child provides the context for making visible the relations of which she is formed; relations which themselves are anticipatory to forming a collective of dancers.

A pig is killed, and yams, taro and other vegetables are gathered together for the small rite performed on behalf of the woman. Among those witnessing the performance is one of the hosts from the *gab*. A speech is made to those gathered which is also addressed to the visiting host. Again, the words (oratory) and actions (food and pork distribution) acquire their salience because of the way they invoke figures and powers of the mythical background while at once 'pointing towards' and inscribing a spatial process.

> There are guests at your house (Gome), there are no residents. What are the women going to take tomorrow? The next day I will go there singing on the way. I will go past Hul, go to Gevo. Take this piece of pig and bring it up to the *gab* and say: 'Women get sweet potatoes, bring it and put in Koud and Vari's house. Yavi, Afi and I are going up to burn their *hadofal*.

The speech directs the audience's attention to the route of the journey they will take towards the *gab*. The speaker suggests that all the hosts are now at the *gab*; it is only people like us (guests) who are now at your house (village) – in other words, they will be stopping there on the way. In making their way to the *gab* they will sing, and one of the songs evokes the names of the streams nearby the *gab*. The speaker offers a challenge to the hosts. Here is a piece of pork. Take it as a sign of our capacity to come to the *gab*. Your wives, in turn, should bring us food to eat. Finally, he evokes the image of going up to 'burn the *hadofal*'. A *hadofal* is the abandoned home of a deceased person. By singing on their way there they will be making a lot of noise so as to clear away (i.e. burn) the spirit from the house. It is from this vantage point, then, that they will complete their head-dresses before entering the *gab*.

What has been envisioned, then, is a particular movement

across the land. A movement from the actuality of the collective as constituted in the foreground at the site Fuda, to the ancestral potential that is anticipated outside the boundary of the *gab* in the background of Fuyuge social life, as it were. The collectivity of men and women assembled through the rite performed for the woman's pregnancy is simultaneously directing itself towards the next totalized context within the *gab* itself. Although the men and women from Fuda make their way to the *gab* as supporters (*hu ban*, lit. their back) of the hosts in killing pigs, they enter the *gab* as dancers and dance together with the hosts, thus becoming and acting as 'one' with them.

Joining Together

The second vantage point to the processes described here is from the context of Dibam village. Dibam is in the home section of Evese. This village has a large plaza with several houses scattered around its perimeter. It was the site of a *gab* in the past, after which the village was largely abandoned. The village, however, is to be resurrected as the site of a future *gab*. The events now staged here are an anticipation of this future process.

The ritual enacted at Dibam takes on a different form to that described at Fuda. In the first place the men and women moving from Fuda to the *gab* went as supporters in the contribution of pigs for the large killing which completes the events of the *gab*. By contrast, the men and women gathered at Dibam have been invited/challenged to perform as dancers and bring objects in exchange for pork. The invitation/challenge (*seef*) to each dancer, announced and displayed at the *gab* (but not described here) is replicated by hosts in the village of Dibam. What is enacted at Dibam is a small-scale *gab*, known as a *gave*.

A number of men and women challenged to perform at the *gab* have yet to have their capacities as dancers revealed and made known. The hosts through their challenge to come and dance are enabling the activation of this inner potentiality of particular young men and women; potentialities which the men and women gathered at Dibam will make known while at the same time constituting the directionality of the collectivity of men and women gathered together to scrutinize them. In addition, just as the hosts attempt to increase their scale by mobilizing supporters for the pig-kill, so the dancers attempt to increase their scale by mobilizing others as their supporters – in this case the other sections of the Ononge home (Migu, Ginal and Ononge).

The *gab*-like character of the event enacted at Dibam is imagined to be held together by the presence of chiefs (see Hirsch 1994). As indicated above, the holding-together capacity of the chief is given material form in the betelnut gathered together and displayed on trees chopped down from the forest and re-planted in the plaza centre (see Hirsch 1990). The betelnut gathered together from both proximate and distant sites (for example, Port Moresby and the coast) is metonymic of the collectivities of men and women held together in this context.

When a chief holds and speaks over one or more bunches of betelnut the men and women gathered as an audience remain silent and motionless. Movement into and out of the *gab* plaza is stopped. An image of singularity is momentarily achieved, whereby the collectivity renders itself as one: one mind, one purpose, a single collectivity of dancers. The dancers have activated and made known their intention to move to the *kakal em*, a shelter in which the dancing dress is prepared. It is from this shelter that the dancers emerge before they burst on to the *gab* plaza to perform.

The speech presented below evokes the movement of men and women from their actual locations in diverse contexts of Ononge towards their potentiality as a unified collective of dancers at the *gab*. The speech was given at the beginning of events enacted at Dibam, events which were centred around making known the dancing capacities of particular young men and women.

> The betelnut from this side of the Udabe came and joined with Onongegode, came up and joined with Gamenfide, came up and joined with Ualfide and then joined with Vaine. I am splitting the *yabdu kes* so you will feel good and then we will hang the betelnuts.

The speech focuses on the betelnut that has been brought to Dibam and that hangs on the tree as indicative of the persons and things held together in this context. Four major roads or pathways are evoked. The first three are pathways which lead from the other sections of Ononge towards Dibam. Together, the men and women from these locales will eventually form one collectivity of dancers at the *gab*. The other three are acting as supporters – 'their back' – to those at Dibam. The fourth pathway is from the Auga valley, west of Dibam, where much of the betelnut displayed at Dibam and at the *gab* originates. *Yabdu kes* is an ancestral name of betelnut. It refers to the archetype of betelnut laid down by *tidibe* in this home. The bunch held by the chief is a contemporary embodiment of this archetypal form.

At Dibam is initiated the process whereby each locale that is acting as a supporter must now constitute its directionality towards the *gab*, so that all the dancers can join as one. The events at Dibam are the starting-point of a journey along a series of pathways as one collectivity joins with another. The entire process of joining together culminates at a village nearby the *gab*. After Dibam, three other *gave* are performed as the dancers-to-be consolidate their directionality and scale.

'I Am Going to Cut the Rope from Your Pig and it is Going Up.'

We have seen that the words and action of Fuyuge ritual acquire their particular prominence because of the way they at once make explicit and anticipate the directionality of persons on the land. A movement from a foreground actuality, such as became evident at Dibam, to the anticipated background potentiality soon to unfold in the *gab*. Sofel is the next place in this journey. The four sections or localities which compose the home of Ononge have each travelled along their respective pathways, and through the processes of joining and being held together along the way, formed a large-scale collectivity of dancers.

Again, as we have seen above, this final holding together, before movement to the *gab*, is performed by making the capacities of particular persons evident. In this context, as in the others, pigs are killed before the particular persons enter the plaza to have their rites performed. On this occasion, 25 pigs were killed. After the pork and food gathered for the event is distributed to the various collectivities of persons present, a speech is made directing those present to the next place.

> The people on that side, all of you gather and go inside the men's house. Everyone go inside the house. Dancers, you sit on the verandah, divide the food and give it to those on the inside of the

house. Io [a host from the *gab*], now I am going to send your dancers
to you ... Dekhalo, Muinakon, Ofange, your *gob*.[9] This is your
betelnut. Halume, Sisabode, your *gob*. This is your betelnut. Vaigode,
this is your betelnut.

    Gab u bab this is your betelnut. Bring it up, chew it and if you
want to get any guests go now or it will be too late. I am going to cut
the rope from your pig and it is going up.

The speaker has instructed all the men and women gathered
at Sofel, those who have acted as an audience and those who
have performed as dancers, to unite in and around the men's
house. He then addresses one of the hosts from the *gab*, Io, and
tells him that he is now sending the dancers. This challenge is
followed by the speaker's announcing three sets of pathways.
Each set indicates the pathways of the three localities which have
come together to form the large-scale collectivity gathered at
Sofel. After announcing each set the speaker says 'This is your
betelnut.' He is referring to the betelnut, as we saw above at
Dibam, that was held together on the tree in the village plaza and
that has now been taken down and divided with the pork and
food for each collective. In referring to the betelnut he is
simultaneously referring to the pork and food.

The speaker also refers to the *gab u bab*. This literally means the
fathers of the *gab*, the hosts. He offers a challenge to them. Do not
delay in bringing your guests to the *gab* because the dancers are
on their way and if you are slow you will miss their performance.
He concludes by making a metaphorical reference to the dancers
as pigs, for it is the pigs that the dancers will receive for their
performance. There is a bursting forth image projected in his
concluding statement, one which will be replicated when the
dancers burst on to the plaza in the anticipated future.

'So Everyone Will See it and Go Home.'

Each phase of the *gab* is scrutinized by men and women from the
diverse locales, invited/challenged to the *gab* by the hosts. As we
have seen, they are recognized and spoken of by the name
of their place or the pathways which they traversed to the *gab*.
The joining together of their place to the place of the *gab* is
envisioned as creating the conditions of strength (*kagava*) the

hosts intend to reveal. When the hosts perform a particular phase its outcome is never certain, and great anxiety and trepidation accompanies the bringing together of persons and things that is required to produce the particular aesthetic effect.

For example, after the dancers described above had performed in the *gab* plaza,[10] the hosts and their supporters gathered the pigs to be killed in the name of particular young men and women. When the pigs were killed the young people should have 'danced in their blood', but on this occasion the hosts quickly cooked the pigs and placed them on raised platforms, as darkness was approaching. This action provoked considerable anger among numerous guests/witnesses. Speeches made in the plaza that evening suggested that the hosts had not followed the ways of the ancestors (*aked inoge*): the young people should have danced in the blood; an incorrect aesthetic had been evoked. The next morning two of the chiefs gave 6 kina in compensation for their 'bad ways' (*mad ko*).

What this example highlights is that attempts to make evident the potentiality of the person are not an unproblematic matter. If an aesthetically incorrect image is displayed to those scrutinizing then the hoped-for potentiality may be seen as not properly accomplished. This anxiety is particularly evident in the final phase of the *gab*, the 'true' pig-killing that culminates the entire process. It is through its enactment that the hosts are able to demonstrate whether they have the strength and power equal to their challenge put to the dancers and other guests/witnesses. Is it 'true' that they can pull together and hold enough pigs to fulfil their debts to others?

At Uyams over 260 pigs were slaughtered during the pig-killing. It was a process lasting several hours. The hosts and their supporters entered the plaza at different times, each with different groups of pigs. As each group of pigs was brought in and killed speeches of various length were made. Towards the end of this process, one of the chiefs who had come from Fuda (see above) made the following speech:

> Fanim python was making a fence around himself. Everybody you have come together around Fanim python. Hafe python, his friend, came and stopped on the mountain. Fee python came and put his head on top. Haeyond python came and joined Fanim python. So

everyone, you will see it and go home. Before it was everyone, today it is still the same.

The speech evokes an image of the coiled python as analogous to a fenced plaza. This is the fenced plaza where the speech-giver stands at that moment and in which numerous pigs are being killed. It is an image of everyone held together to see the most anticipated spectacle of the *gab*.

The names attached to each python derive from particular locales supporting the hosts with pigs. 'Fanim' is the python of the place of the hosts. The names do not indicate actual pythons, but the archetypal pythons laid down by *tidibe* when constituting the lands and ways of the Fuyuge. The speaker is evoking an image of cosmological unification: the head of each python joined to that of Fanim; those other places joined to this place.

The truth will now be revealed – 'everyone will see it' – that the hosts and their supporters have the capacity to hold together a quantity of pigs equal to and even greater than the persons challenged to make their way to the *gab*. After the killing and distributions are completed everyone will return to their home: the word of the *gab* will spread along the myriad of pathways that led to the ritual village. Finally, the speaker alludes to the past, and how the 'oneness' achieved today has been achieved in other *gab* contexts: 'today it is still the same'.

Some weeks after the pig-killing the village was largely abandoned. Men and women returned to their small settlements to tend to their gardens and pigs. The mythical potentiality aspired to in the *gab* again receded to the background. This is a potentiality both of the person and land: a potentiality that emerges from the activation of social relations, implying the movement of persons and things across the land. Ancestrality and achievement momentarily become one, and can only do so through the successful alignment of directionalities.

Conclusion

The point of departure for this chapter was the sense of compulsion displayed by Fuyuge men and women towards the performance of their *gab* ritual. This was a compulsion expressive both of a timeless transcendence and of personal and collective acts of achievement. As I have tried to demonstrate in the description of the interlinked rituals, emphases on both timeless transcendence and on achievement each imply and complete the other. But this is of course only brought about, as we have seen, through the movement of persons and things into the correct spatial position and at the appropriate moment of time. To evoke the archetypal form of betelnut in speech-making, as we saw above, is only possible when large quantities of its contemporary form are concentrated together from near and far alike.

I have also suggested that these alternative modes of ritual description are also encoded in two anthropological models of Melanesian societies. The first is de Coppet's model of socio-cosmic encompassment as realized through the enactment of ritual. The second is M. Strathern's model of the revelatory nature of social practices, with its emphasis on the temporality of agency and achievement. The ethnography presented above described how person/land relationships are encompassed by an image of ancestrality enacted in ritual (de Coppet's model). The ethnography also showed how personhood (whether particular or collective) is an achieved condition, and its achievement is always fraught with uncertainty (M. Strathern's model). However, in de Coppet's model the encompassment by ancestrality is certain and unproblematic; M. Strathern's stress on uncertainty and revelation is implied in, and completes, de Coppet's model. By contrast, in M. Strathern's model, recurrent contingency ultimately points towards 'cosmological' encompassment: the evocation of archetypal forms[11] in the speeches constructs an imagery of achievement that are predicated on notions of ancestrality (*tidibe*-ness). The focus of de Coppet's model is implied in and completes M. Strathern's model.

As I have suggested, the aim of the ritual process is to make revelation lead to encompassment. It is this goal that provides the rationale for the emphasis on directionality that was evident in the ethnography of the ritual. The alignment of directionalities is what men and women continually strive to achieve over the uncertainty and agency of others: their minds and desires have to be brought together and held as one. In the end, then, achievement and ancestrality, revelation and encompassment may be held together (coalesce), since the ritual will only succeed if they are perceived to come together.[12]

Notes

1. An early draft of this chapter benefited from the helpful comments of Allen Abramson. Adam Kuper, Jonathan Parry, Andrew Strathern and Marilyn Strathern were kind enough to provide critical comments on a second draft. To them all I most grateful. A version of the chapter was also presented to seminar audiences in the Departments of Anthropology at the Universities of St Andrew's and Edinburgh. I would like to thank participants in both seminars for their useful comments and suggestions. Any errors in fact or interpretation that remain are those of the author. Research among the Fuyuge was supported by the Wenner-Gren Foundation, Central Research Fund of the University of London, and the London School of Economics. I would like to thank the Papua New Guinea authorities for fieldwork permission and the men, women and children of Visi for allowing me to live among them.

2. It should be noted here that M. Strathern also uses the notion of encompassment in her model but in a manner different to that of de Coppet. Her concern is less with issues of ancestral origins (cosmology). She defines encompassment as 'the encapsulation of another's viewpoint, a containment of an anticipated outcome' (M. Strathern 1988: 259; cf. Josephides 1991). Encompassment here entails a process of revealing another's viewpoint or perspective that one (as a person or a collective) ultimately contains within oneself. For example, Fuyuge pig-killing hosts in the way they think anticipate the response of the invited dancers. In the argument pursued here the perceived success or otherwise of Fuyuge ritual is dependent on the ultimate coalescence of both forms of encompassment; that of the revealed viewpoint of others *and at the same time* of a perspective derived from ancestral origins.

3. Iteanu (1990) makes a similar argument as regards the actual person (consisting of actual, everyday will and desire) and the person as a potential, aspired towards in the ritual system (cf. M. Strathern 1992b: 82).

4. It is significant that the formulation presented by de Coppet derives from a key political figure in the post-War history of

the Solomon Islands. Such a figure is seen as enabling such diverse perspectives to be held together.

5. See Hirsch 1994 for an extended discussion of these processes.

6. 'Holding together' is also a Melpa idiom for what big men do: *mumuk ropa iti*, of holding together the ropes of pigs for sacrifice and also holding together the group (A. Strathern, personal communication).

7. Within each river valley the population is divided into a number of named units based on shared ideas of territory and dialect. These are referred to as places (*bu*) or homes (*em*) (see Hirsch 1994: 693–4).

8. The pattern I observed at several *gab* in the Udabe Valley was as follows:
   a. 'Opening' of the *gab* village.
   b. 'Pulling' in the supporters.
   c. Inviting the dancers and exchange partners.
   d. Taking the invitations to the dancers, etc.
   e. Dancers making their way to the *gab* through the performance of a series of small-scale *gab* (*gave*).
   f. Performance of the dancers.
   g. Pig-killing and exchanges for the 'children' (*esa*).
   h. 'True' pig-killing and exchanges for the old and dead.

9. *Gob* (orphans) is another expression for supporters.

10. See Hirsch 1988: 209–26 for a description of these various phases.

11. In the ethnography reported here the archetypal forms summoned were related to betelnut, pythons, and the image of the bowerbird's *gab*, although numerous others exist in Fuyuge cosmology.

12. I am grateful to A. Strathern directing me to this formulation.

References

Clay, B. (1992). Other Times, Other Places: Agency and the Big Man in Central New Ireland. *Man*, 27, 719–34.

Clifford, J. (1992). *Person and Myth: Maurice Leenhardt in the Melanesian World*. Duke University Press, Durham.

Coppet, D. de (1985). ' . . . Land owns people'. In: R. Barnes, D. de Coppet and R. Parkin (eds), *Contexts and levels: Anthropological Essays on Hierarchy*, pp. 78–90. JASO, Oxford.

Hallpike, C. (1979). *Bloodshed and Vengeance in the Papuan Mountains: The Generation of Conflict in Tauade Society*. Clarendon Press, Oxford.

Hirsch, E. (1987). Dialectics of the Bowerbird: An Interpretative Account of Ritual and Symbolism in the Udabe Valley, Papua New Guinea. *Mankind*, 17, 1–14.

—— (1988). Landscapes of Exchange: Fuyuge Ritual and Society, Ph.D. thesis, London School of Economics.

—— (1990). From Bones to Betelnuts: Processes of Ritual Transformation and the Development of 'National Culture' in Papua New Guinea. *Man*, 25, 18–34.

—— (1994). Between Mission and Market: Events and Images in a Melanesian Society. *Man*, 29, 689–711.

—— (1995). Landscape: Between Place and Space. In: E. Hirsch and M. O'Hanlon (eds), *The Anthropology of Landscape: Perspectives on Place and Space*. Clarendon Press, Oxford.

—— (forthcoming). The Coercive Strategies of Aesthetics: Reflections on Wealth, Ritual and Landscape in Melanesia. In: J. Weiner (ed.), *Too Many Meanings* (special edition), *Social Analysis*.

Iteanu, A. (1990). The Concept of the Person and the Ritual System: An Orokaiva View. *Man*, 25, 35–53.

Josephides, L. (1991). Metaphors, Metathemes, and the Construction of Sociality: A Critique of the New Melanesian Ethnography. *Man*, 26(1), 145–61.

Majnep, I. and Bulmer, R. (1977). *Birds of My Kalam Country*. Auckland University Press, Auckland.

Mosko, M. (1992). Motherless Sons: 'Divine Kings' and 'Partible Persons' in Melanesia and Polynesia. *Man*, 27, 697–718.

Munn, N. (1986). *The Fame of Gawa: A Symbolic Study of Value Transformation in a Massim (PNG) Society*. Cambridge University Press, Cambridge.

Parkin, D. (1992). Ritual As Spatial Direction and Bodily Division. In: D. de Coppet (ed.), *Understanding Ritual*, pp. 11–25. Routledge, London.

Parmentier, R. (1987). *The Sacred Remains: Myth History and Polity in Belau*. University of Chicago Press, Chicago.

Strathern, A. (1985). A Line of Boys: Melpa Dance as a Sign of Maturation. In: P. Spencer (ed.), *Society and the Dance* pp. 119–39. Cambridge University Press, Cambridge.

Strathern, M. (1991). One Man and Many Men. In: M. Godelier and M. Strathern (eds), *Big Men and Great Men: Personifications of Power in Melanesia*, pp. 197–214. Cambridge University Press, Cambridge.

—— (1988). *The Gender of the Gift: Problems with Women and Problems with Society in Melanesia*. University of California Press, Berkeley.

—— (1992b). Parts and Wholes: Refiguring Relationships in a Post-plural World. In: A. Kuper (ed.), *Conceptualizing Society*, pp. 75–106. Routledge, London.

—— (1992a). Qualified Value: The Perspective of Gift Exchange. In: C. Humphrey and S. Hugh-Jones (eds), *Barter, Exchange and Value: An Anthropological Approach*, pp. 169–91. Cambridge University Press, Cambridge.

Williamson, R. (1912). *The Mafulu Mountain People of British New Guinea*. Macmillan, London.

Chapter 9

'Are'are Society: A Melanesian Socio-Cosmic Point of View. How are Bigmen the Servants of Society and Cosmos?

Daniel de Coppet

One of the aims of this paper is to answer the question, to what degree society and cosmos are in coalescence in Oceania. To this end, I will concentrate on 'Are'are society, located on the Island of Malaita in the Solomon Islands.

By the end of this paper, I hope to have identified a combination of facts, ideas and values shared by the 'Are'are: their 'global ideology'. In accordance with L. Dumont's propositions (1970 and 1986), such a global ideology is expressed by a 'hierarchy of values' that gives shape to all social activities and reaffirms a common sense of identity. From the first diaries of Mendana's adventurous companions in 1568 to the period after World War II, and then on into that of the Solomon Islands' independence in 1978, 'Are'are society has proved itself strong enough to maintain its fundamental values, while engaging in a courageous confrontation with the colonial power, but also in a necessary dialogue with Western global ideology.

By setting forth the 'Are'are configuration of values, it may be possible as well to achieve some understanding of various puzzling features of Melanesian societies, such as the social relations involved in plant cultivation and pig-raising, in the circulation of shell-money and in the intense expression of bigmanship. On this last point I will not attempt to use data collected in different societies of the region to compare general types of big men and classify them. Rather, I simply try to assess the diverse manifestations of bigmanship that may be observed in 'Are'are society, from the point of view of a society taken as a whole.

To achieve such a comprehensive view, it is necessary to take into account the whole series of undertakings that constitute the core of 'Are'are social life. In the process of studying 'Are'are society as thoroughly as possible, I will be guided by a striking social feature, the contrast between two 'characters', the 'killer' and the 'peace-master', who together make up bigmanship in 'Are'are society.

Through their ceaseless activities, peace-masters participate more intensely than others in all feasts and take more responsibility for the common task, which consists in constantly renewing the 'Are'are entity. The actions and representations here involved ultimately provide a clear indication that 'Are'are entity is a socio-cosmic configuration.

A peace-master, at the end of his life, may furthermore undertake an optional series of feasts, which reinforce the cohesion of the local community, extending it to the whole of 'Are'are society, and ultimately reintegrating the anonymous murder-victims into the socio-cosmic whole. At the same time, this supplementary endeavour to achieve a higher degree of social completeness elevates the long-lived peace-master to the second highest dignity, just below the ancestors whom he will soon join.

A detailed study of the killer/peace-master opposition leads finally to a kind of paradox: the killer seems subordinate 'in terms of value' to the peace-master, who none the less, at the same time, appears as the most obedient servant of the 'Are'are socio-cosmic whole.

I shall first present the opposition between the killer and the peace-master as manifested in 'Are'are language and in the two characters' body decorations. Other related oppositions will also be identified.

Thereafter, I will study the rules through which a series of murders may be put to an end. In passing from murders to a peace settlement, a change of value level occurs which reveals that the contrast between the two figures of bigmanship expresses a hierarchy of values. If it can also be demonstrated that a similar change of value level is found in all major 'Are'are ceremonial feasts, the way out of murder series would appear, not only as an access to a brighter style of social life, but also as typical of the structure of the 'Are'are social configuration.

Then, I wish to show how all the main activities of the society – marriage and funerals, flirtation and murder, together with all the different feasts – constitute an overall movement which *animates* different kinds of beings, such as cultivated plants, domesticated pigs, men and women, and especially shell-money. This movement can be perceived and moreover understood only if we are able to accept the fact that, although these different beings seem distinct and each an individual unit, they are living combinations of three kinds of socio-cosmic relations, which I call 'external form relations', 'breath relations' and 'representation relations'.[1] Under these conditions, a living man, although he appears to be a single unit in his dealings and in his social relations, is in fact a provisional combination of the three kinds of socio-cosmic relations. This is clearly shown after his death, when at his funeral feast three kinds of beings have to be offered and then exchanged between the two sides responsible for the feast: namely, cultivated plants, pigs and shell-money. These beings are presented in order to dispose of and to continue in another form all the socio-cosmic relations that the deceased had during his lifetime. One of the two piles exchanged between the two sides of the funeral ceremony is composed of three layers: at the bottom taros and coconuts, in the middle some grilled pieces of pork and on top a four-fathoms money unit.

We will first consider the task accomplished by marriages and funerals, and then analyse the special responsibility assumed by a few peace-masters in order to ensure that the society as a whole accomplishes its collective work of mourning for both 'the dead' – those who died of illness – and 'murder victims', by means of an optional series of pig-feasts, taro-pudding-feasts and peace-master-feasts. Parallel to this development, we can observe the growing fame of these peace-masters, who, at their own peace-master-feasts, approach the status of ancestors.

Finally, all the relations manifested in the society's various ceremonies seem to compose and intensify a socio-cosmic circulation governed by the three-dimensional principle ('external form, breath and representation'), which ensures, in its entire movement, the renewal of the 'Are'are socio-cosmic entity. Such an overall circulation implies and is implied in the 'Are'are hierarchy of values, in which the two leading characters, killer and peace-master, have their place and by which their respective statuses are defined.

The Hierarchical Oppositions

In 'Are'are, the word for killer, *namo*, also means a quantity of water held back by a small dam or contained in a pond or in a small lagoon, as well as the purification pool that is constructed for a wedding ceremony. The word for peace-master is *aaraha*, which also means to 'move the two extremes of a large fishing net slowly towards each other' as well as to 'protect someone against the sun's heat or against ill treatment'. It can moreover allude to the bower formed by yam vines at the top of the sticks around which they grow.

The killer wears the following body decorations:

1. A reed belt *hoko*, turned twice around his waist, worn during murder expeditions.
2. A rosette-shaped decoration *waroi'a*, made of dolphins' teeth attached to a wicker ring and worn in the hair.
3. A wooden ceremonial stick *hau aano rereo*, inlaid with mother of pearl. Fixed at the top of the stick is a spherical pyrite in a small basketwork bag. The killer either wears the stick hanging from his neck down his back, or holds it in his hand, especially during blood-money-feasts, *siwa*.
4. The killer's bag *ma'itaka*, literally 'the bag in bloom', is also worn suspended from his neck down his back. It has long hanging fibres and is decorated with a chain of rings made of woven reeds. The killer carries it at blood-money-feasts. The number of rings in the chain corresponds to the exact number of victims the killer has murdered so far.

All these decorations and the different meanings of the word *namo* suggest an enclosure, in the form of a closed ring or of a confined sphere, and make reference to a period of life prior to marriage, devoted to ceremonial flirtations and murders.

The peace-master's decorations, on the contrary, always take the form of an open space and recall his significant achievements and a prosperous life. They consist of:

1. A mother of pearl crescent, *tahi*.
2. A breast plate, *tahi ro'aro'a*, literally 'convex like a fruit'. Its border is overlaid with an open ring of black tar.

3. A woven pearl scarf, *wa'u*. It incorporates pearls from different shell-money currencies of the region, and has a lower fringe of human teeth taken from murder victims with, at each end, a few ancestors' teeth. The scarf resembles a fishing net, which it is said to represent with its floats and sinkers. The upper border of the scarf is composed of a series of diamond-shaped decorations called 'nuts', *nari* (*Canarium indicum*), which resemble floats. The sinkers are the teeth of the lower fringe, which recall the past murder victims. The ancestors' teeth manifest the active presence of the ancestors at the two mobile ends of the net or scarf. The different kinds of beads woven into the scarf attest to the peaceful relations of the peace-master with other societies living around the Solomon Sea.

The peace-master's decorations have an open shape: the crescent, the black open ring added on the convex breast plate, and the scarf, which like a fishing net drives towards its centre (the peace-master), not fish which live in the water, but men who live on the land. These forms and movements manifest the various social engagements of the peace-master in all social relations and his widespread protective influence over the community, similar to that of yam-vine bowers, which protect against the sun.

In contrast, the killer's activity is indicated by the belt, the closed ring, the confined pyrite and the related purification ritual, which transfers to the running river the stains of premarital life (in contrast to the movement of the fishing net, which draws together fish in the water). Thus the peace-master acts for the increased prosperity of the community in terms of men and resources and for an improved style of social life, one which can expand itself to a set of related localities and become a territorial 'canoe'. The killer, on the other hand, seems trapped, since he promotes only a mediocre way of life, that of infertility, incompleteness and lasting fear (see de Coppet 1972).

This fundamental opposition between the peace-master and the killer corresponds to two explicitly distinct categories of rituals. The first category is called *tauaahi*, and concerns the welfare and the prosperity of the community: it is constituted by offerings and prayers at certain funeral sites, offered to recent ancestors and ancestresses belonging to non-unilineal ascending genealogies. In this chapter I shall henceforth refer to these recent ancestors as 'intermediary ancestors'. The second category of rituals, *rioanimae*, concerns murder expeditions and involves ritual acts addressed to the killer's 'apical ancestor' of his agnatic line. These two categories of ritual correspond also to certain degrees of ripeness of both the coconut and the areca nut. The nuts used during murder rituals are less mature than the ones needed for the performance of prosperity rituals.

'Intermediary ancestors' are located at, control and give access to a wide range of funeral sites, and consequently to different pieces of land fit for all sorts of gardening activities, while an 'apical ancestor' connects only his agnatic male descendants to their place of origin, to various murdering skills and to the means of ablution which allow the killer's return to everyday life after a murder. Apical ancestors were neither buried nor given funerals, but simply left to rot like murder victims in the forest. They are addressed only by their male descendants in a strictly dual relationship which deals with the accomplishment of murder. Intermediary ancestors, on the contrary, are carefully buried and offered an intricate series of funerary rituals, which involve the community at large, with all its funerals, its marriages, its various monetary offerings and all its activities, especially in gardening and pig-raising.

Finally this opposition corresponds also to the two categories of deceased. Those who died of illness (always considered to be caused by their own ancestors) are called *hi'ona*, here alluded to as 'the dead'. After a proper burial and a series of funeral feasts they become intermediary ancestors. Those who suffered a violent death are left to rot in the forest. They belong to the *raramua* category, which comprises not only 'murder victims' but also persons who commit suicide, women who die in childbirth, dead fetuses and stillborn children (all persons who did not reach maturity).

Thus the opposition between the peace-master and the killer is related to a series of other oppositions which can be now summarized:

1. Among the deceased, there are those who died from sickness – that is, because of their ancestors' intervention – and who themselves become ancestors (called 'the dead'), and those who have been killed or died by accident (both called

'murder victims'), who are deprived of funerals and funeral sites.
2. Two series of rituals are distinguished, depending on their efficacy. The most valued series concerns the prosperity of the community at large, while the second series concerns murder activities and the related ablution ritual.
3. Two types of ancestors are given attention. Both male and female intermediary ancestors are offered an active cult on which the community's well-being depends. For the success of murder activities, only male apical ancestors can be addressed, and only by their male agnatic descendants.

The Three-Dimensional Principle and the Scale of Beings

Beside these different oppositions, which constitute a part of the foundations on which this society rests, and before entering into the framework of the different 'Are'are social relations, we must also briefly introduce the ultimate principle that seems to govern all 'Are'are social activities. The 'Are'are recognize that the world already existed when the primeval ancestors made their first appearance on the mountain ridges and started to establish the different tasks capable of ensuring the renewal of the 'Are'are entity. These tasks are the main ceremonies and rituals that constitute what the 'Are'are consider to be their necessary and most important work. They seem to imply an ultimate principle which stipulates that, from the primeval ancestors onwards, the society had to keep flowing *through* successive human generations and different beings like cultivated plants, pigs and shell-money – three streams of social relations: 'external form relations', 'breath relations' and 'representation relations'. These streams are sometimes separated from each other, as in funerals, and sometimes reunited in a single current of socio-cosmic relations, as in each individual during his lifetime.

The different beings are composed of these relations and are ordered on a scale in accordance with their composition. Generally, plants, stones and things are constituted of 'external form relations' only. Animals, especially fish and pigs, are constituted of a combination of 'external form and breath relations'. Humans are constituted of a combination of 'external form, breath and representation relations'. On such an ontological scale, it would initially seem that humans are the most complete living beings, although certain plants and things, and certain animals, may on special occasions be as complete as humans, with 'external form, breath and representation relations'. At death the human combination of 'external form, breath and representation relations' that constitutes the person must be dissolved through funeral feasts into the three different streams, and then each of them must be converted into shell-money. Further, in the overall circulation, shell-money is converted at marriage ceremonies into the three different streams that will later flow together into the living combination of new-born babies. Thus the renewal of the 'Are'are configuration depends on the constant flow of 'external form, breath and representation relations', which constitutes a kind of socio-cosmic whole. Accordingly, plants and animals, especially cultivated plants and domesticated pigs, depend on the same socio-cosmic whole as human social relations. On the scale of beings, we can foresee that shell-money will have the highest status, as its tangible circulation concentrates, stimulates and gives new impetus to the socio-cosmic streams, and thereby represents the three-dimensional principle.

How May Murder Series be Halted and Peace Re-established? The Change of Value Level

For 'Are'are society, human beings are therefore composed of a combination of three different streams of 'external form, breath and representation relations'. The rules concerning murder series must thus answer the following question: how must murder be dealt with in order to assure the necessary flow of 'breath relations'? Murder series are said to be governed by the need to 'cover' the victim's 'breath relations' by another set of 'breath relations' taken from a new victim. Until such a new victim is murdered, the first victim's 'breath relations' are in a sense dangerously frozen. The new victim's 'breath relations', by 'covering' the first victim's 'breath relations', allow the latter to be transferred to his or her descendants. Each victim in a series therefore requires a new one dedicated to his or her 'breath relations' stream. The different rules involved can be summarized as follows:

- Each murder must be reciprocated, so that a victim's 'breath relations' will be 'covered' by another set of 'breath relations' taken from a new victim. Unless this is done, the victim will unite its ancestors in a coalition, led by a dangerous foreign spirit, which will inflict epidemics on the whole country.
- To stop a series of murders implies, first, that an equal number of losses should be suffered by the two parties. Only then may the blood-money be offered. This monetary gesture puts an end to the murder series and secures peace between the two sides to the dispute.

The blood money may be offered following one of two different procedures:

1. A price may be put on the first killer's head, or on that of one of his close relatives, by those who are in danger of suffering the effects of the first murder. When a second killer has succeeded in providing the 'breath relations' of a new victim to 'cover' the 'breath relations' of the first one, he is offered the promised blood-money.
2. The initial killer may propose to his victim's family to kill one of his own relatives to 'cover' his victim's 'breath relations'. If his offer is accepted and carried out, the losses will thereafter (from a Western perspective) be equal on both sides. As in the case described in the last paragraph, the second killing provides the first victim's relatives with new 'breath relations', which has the effect of 'covering' (that is, of liberating) the ones frozen by the first victim's murder. When the killer's relative's corpse has been handed over to the first victim's family by the double killer, the latter is offered blood money by them.

These are the only two ways to halt a murder series. In both cases, the blood-money is offered for a special service: that of securing 'breath relations' from a new victim that will 'cover' (and liberate) the first victim's 'breath relations'. At the end of the process, the blood-money is not simply offered in return for this important service. The second murder is much more than a simple act of revenge, since it also transposes 'breath relations' into money, that is into 'representation relations'.

However, if the 'breath relations' secured by the blood-money always 'cover' the 'breath relations' of the next-to-last victim in the series, they leave 'uncovered' the last victim's 'breath relations'.

In Case No. 1, where a price has been placed on the first killer's head, after the second murder the second victim's 'breath relations' remain to be covered by another victim taken from the second killer, who answered the call for new 'breath relations'. Peace is achieved between the initial killer's family and his victim's family, but a settlement remains to be found between the families of the first and second killers.

In Case No. 2, where the initial killer in his second action kills one of his own kin and offers these new 'breath relations' to cover his first victim's 'breath relations', the blood-money restores peace between the two parties. Nobody cares about the second victim's 'breath relations', which do not need to be covered. (The second victim is selected because he or she has previously broken a *tabu* and has thus already been condemned by his or her ancestors.) The murder of a person who has offended his or her own ancestors none the less has the effect of 'covering' a former victim's 'breath relations' by new 'breath relations', and it is thus also worth the blood-money. Such murder victims, with 'uncovered' 'breath relations', count for nothing, since they can neither ask their ancestors to send epidemics, nor transmit their 'breath relations' to their descendants. Their 'breath relations' seem to remain, at this point in our analysis, cut off from the socio-cosmic streams.

In all murder series, the killer is offered the blood-money because he brought a new victim's 'breath relations', thereby allowing the stream of 'breath relations' to pass through the first victim on into their conversion into money. The consequences of the blood-money may now be summarized:

1. Peace is re-established between two parties involved in a murder series. In such a context, the money offered embodies the return to peace.
2. Whoever offers blood-money, even if previously a killer, is thereafter recognized as a peace-master. Instead of being an

antagonist in a dual relationship eager to provide, on every occasion, a new victim in exchange for new blood-money, the killer becomes a peace-master, acting in conformity with the society's superior interests. He not only brings a solution to a series of murders, re-establishing peace in his surroundings, but also puts himself in a position to help in the performance of important tasks such as funerals, marriages, pig-feasts, taro-pudding-feasts and peace-master-feasts. It is worthy of note that a recipient of blood-money is felt to be subordinate, in value terms, to him who offers the money. Such a transfer of money is subject to a hierarchy of values in which the giver of money is superior to its recipient.

3. The transposition of 'breath relations' into shell-money indicates a change of value level, not only from that of a murder series to that of a peace settlement, not only from the killer's level to the peace-master's level, but also from 'breath relations' to 'representation relations'. Money is considered by 'Are'are as testifying to the presence and to the effectiveness of 'representation relations', that is, of the highest level of the human constitution and of human deeds. Money, as 'representation relations', indicates that human relations have been elevated from the level of 'breath relations', and have reached the summit of the hierarchy of social relations. One of the consequences of such a conversion into blood-money is that it allows the transference of the 'breath relations' of the first victim (not of the second one) to his or her descendants. If we find a similar change of value level from 'breath relations' to 'representation relations' at the end of marriage ceremonies and funeral feasts, conversion into money may then be considered an essential construct of the 'Are'are socio-cosmic configuration.

In 'Are'are society, not only may peace be restored through blood-money, but a solution may also be given to a husband's death or a husband's adultery (de Coppet 1970). In the former case, a widow is murdered only if she offers to die after her husband's death, and if her dead husband's family agrees to her proposal. In that case, her own brother must kill her. Then, the husband's family has to kill one of the dead husband's sisters and offer the corpse to their brother-in-law, who must then offer blood-money to the husband's family. After the husband's death has damaged the affinal relations between the two families, the complex procedure that restores these relations converts the 'breath relations' of the widow who has been killed into 'representation relations', through the blood-money, and allows the transference of her 'breath relations' to her descendants. Thereafter, the two families may resume normal relations. However, even if the relations between the two families, which were damaged by the husband's death, have now been re-established on the value level of 'representation relations', the hierarchical positions of the two parties have changed to the advantage of the 'woman's side'. By offering the blood-money, the 'woman's side' has obtained the status of peace-master, which in the previous marriage ceremonies was normally held by the 'man's side'.

If a husband commits adultery, he must be put to death by his own kin. Thereafter, a series of events similar to the preceding one unfolds. The wife's brother must first kill the adulterous husband's wife, that is, his own non-adulterous sister. He then receives the corpse of the husband's unmarried sister, and finally must pay blood-money to his in-laws. Here again affinal relations have been damaged, this time by the husband's adultery. The correct procedure consists, after an even exchange of murders, in the conversion of 'breath relations' into 'representation relations' through blood-money. This procedure is aimed at restoring normal relations. In this case also, the 'woman's side' achieves peace-master status, which was previously held by the 'man's side'.

In both cases, the murder of the wife indicates that affinal relations have been downgraded to the inferior level of 'breath relations'. These inferior relations, through blood-money, are again transposed into 'representation relations' of the same value level as those previously created by the marriage ceremonies. Any deterioration of social relations thus leads to new murders, that is, to the inferior value level of 'breath relations'. The latter are then again transposed into 'representation relations', which express the highest level of the 'Are'are configuration, that of the whole, where further transpositions become possible.

How Are Social Relations Directed into the Streams of 'Body-, Breath- and Representation Socio-Cosmic Relations'?

If we examine now the established series of five different feasts in which most of 'Are'are social life is condensed, we are driven to the conclusion that they do not simply organize interpersonal relations, but also manifest the complex development of the three-dimensional principle, that of 'external form, breath and representation' socio-cosmic relations. The constitution of individual subjects appears to be subordinate to this three-dimensional principle, which either directs 'external form, breath and representation relations' into three separate streams or causes them to merge into a single stream. 'External form, breath and representation relations' taken together constitute the 'Are'are socio-cosmic whole.

The five different feasts are: marriages, funerals, and then pig-feasts, taro-pudding-feasts and peace-master-feasts. During marriages and funerals, the relations of newly married couples or recently deceased persons are dealt with principally in order to direct these social relations into the channels of the society's cosmic renewal. During the last three feasts in the series, a general mourning process is accomplished, which does not concern persons taken one-by-one as funerals do, but rather the two categories of the deceased, those who died from illness, *hi'ona*, 'the dead', and those who suffered violent death, *raramua*, 'the murder victims'.

Every man is a potential feast-giver for the mourning of his dead relatives, and it is only after he has completed all his funeral feasts that he may begin to engage in the preparations for the last three feasts in the series, the pig-feast, the taro-pudding-feast and the peace-master-feast. Those men who give a pig-feast are definitively recognized as peace-masters, trying to follow the path that may lead them to the greatest fame, that of a peace-master-feast-giver. Thus a peace-master who has given his own relatives' funerals is in a position to take upon himself the burden of being a feast-giver for the benefit of the whole community, that is, for the sake of the 'external form and breath relations' of all those who died from illness and of all the murder victims. In opposition to the killer, who hunts for new victims' 'breath relations' and for quick monetary rewards, a man achieves the status of, and is recognized as, a peace-master when he devotes himself to the socio-cosmic relations not only of his kin but of all the deceased in general. By organizing the three feasts and by opening them to the community at large, he is in accord with the society's general system of values and with its ongoing renewal as a whole. As will become clear, the peace-master, on the social scene, is the most obedient servant as well as the master of all socio-cosmic relations.

If we look at the various proceedings of the five different feasts that constitute the core of 'Are'are social life, two main features immediately strike us. First, the different feasts, sequences and offerings are clearly concerned not simply with the fate of individual subjects but with the three fundamental streams of 'external form, breath and representation relations'. Second, these socio-cosmic relations and their respective streams are directed and given new impetus in two complementary ways:

1. On the special occasions of marriages and funerals, the feasts establish, in the former case, the socio-cosmic relations of new couples with their future descendants and, in the latter, provide new ancestors for the living. The global circulation of 'external form, breath and representation relations' which encompasses life and death can thereby be maintained and the socio-cosmic whole reinforced.
2. The three other feasts in the series (the pig-feast, the taro-pudding-feast and the peace-master-feast) do not deal with the social relations of specified individuals, as in marriages and funerals. On the contrary, the pig-feast concerns all 'the dead' (*hi'ona*, those who died of illness), while the taro-pudding-feast concerns all the 'murder victims' (*raramua*), in each case directing their 'external form and breath relations' towards the proper socio-cosmic streams. Finally, at the peace-master-feast, the last in the series, the 'external form and breath relations' of all the 'murder victims' are transposed even into 'representation relations', thereby reintegrating into the socio-cosmic streams. One should observe that, contrary to the streams of 'breath relations' of 'murder victims', the 'representation relations' of 'the dead' are always dealt with individually at the funeral feast, in reference to a particular deceased.

The last three feasts in the series are given by only a few peace-masters, at the end of their long lives. They reach the peak of their living glory at their peace-master-feast, just before dying and being promoted to the dignity of an ancestor.

The Flowing of Socio-Cosmic Relations through Marriages and Funerals

In **marriage ceremonies**, those wishing to take part in the events must chose one of two groups, the bride's or the groom's. The marriage feast, which takes place at the bride's village, is followed two or three years later by the return marriage feast at the groom's village. Two main operations are accomplished through the various offerings observed.

First, the monetary contributions offered by the 'man's side' are lent to the 'woman's side' until the return feast, on the condition that each monetary contribution be returned only after it has been converted into one of the three different *species:*[2] living taros to be planted, living pigs to be raised, or shell-money. In this last case, money is returned for money. The single stream of money, the offering which opens the marriage feast, returns three years later in the form of the three *species*, not only offering to the 'man's side' taros for its gardens and pigs for its forest, but also directing to it three distinct streams of new, living 'external form, breath and representation' social relations. These living socio-cosmic relations come from the 'woman's side' and are thereby transferred to the 'man's side'. They link together the new couple and their descendants through a set of relations with various people, with land for gardens, with pig-raising houses in the forest and with funeral sites. By combining these different factors, the three streams of living 'external form, breath and representation relations' prepare the way for the birth of the couple's children, which, like all humans, are the living conjunction of 'external form, breath and representation relations'. Only money, offered to the 'woman's side' at the start of the marriage feast, has the capacity to convert itself into living 'external form, breath and representation relations' and make possible the flow of the three socio-cosmic streams from the 'woman's side' to the 'man's side'.

One should notice that this conversion of a single stream of money into the three living *species* (taros, pigs and shell-money) invigorates not only the young couple and its descendants but also the community at large and the animal, vegetable and mineral kingdoms. Nature and society are combined under the three-dimensional principle that directs the three different streams of socio-cosmic relations. Here again the conversion into or from money indicates that the socio-cosmic whole follows its three-dimensional principle and properly directs the streams of all socio-cosmic relations.

Second, three other monetary offerings are also offered by the 'man's side' to the 'woman's side', to validate the transfer of the latter's daughter as well as of their pigs and taros which they brought for the marriage meal. The bride's transfer from her father's family to her husband's involves the transfer of her living 'external form, breath and representation relations' to the 'man's side' of the marriage.

The first event of the marriage feast is a gift of money to the 'woman's side' in compensation for the loss of their daughter. The conversion of 'external form, breath and representation relations' into a sum of money shows that the latter is not simply a compensation in the ordinary sense of the term, but that, as 'representation relations', it encompasses both 'external form and breath relations'. From the 'woman's side's' point of view, the marriage of a daughter results *for them* in the social relations of their living daughter being transposed into 'representation relations', that is into money. They have thus, in a sense, mourned for their daughter's social relations.

Then, at the end of the return marriage feast, two further sums of money are handed over to the 'woman's side'. One is said to compensate for the taros, the other for the pigs, that the 'woman's side' brought to the return feast. The former is called *korasi piina*, literally, 'to spread out the heap of taros'. Unlike the living taros and pigs offered earlier, which will be planted or raised by the new couple, these taros and pigs are all eaten at the return marriage feast. They are the two *species* of 'external form and breath relations' which, after being brought to the feast, are converted into money – upgraded thereby into 'representation relations', that is, to the highest value level – and then offered to the 'woman's side'. At the end of the marriage ceremonies, as at the conclusion of the blood-money feast, social relations from lower value levels – here 'external form and breath relations' – are raised to the highest value level of 'representation relations' by means of money. Consequently, the 'man's side', which gives the money, seems to have peace-master status.

It is now possible to understand the difference between a bride, on the one hand, and a 'murder victim' or a deceived wife, on the other. The former consists of a living combination of 'external form, breath and representation' socio-cosmic relations, while the latter are left with only very problematic 'external form and breath relations'. One could add that the pigs the 'woman's side' brings to the marriage feast for the common meal are 'breath social relations', which may be interpreted as 'covering' the 'breath relations' brought by the 'man's side' in the form of its own pigs. At the end of the return marriage feast, the man's side's money offering to the woman's side would seem to be a kind of blood-money for the latter's slaughtered pigs, converting 'breath relations' into 'representation relations'.

The bride's transfer seems to induce the 'woman's side' to do work of mourning for the loss of its newly married daughter. At the end of a funeral feast, an offering is indeed made which seems to parallel the man's side monetary offering at the return marriage feast. The deceased's family hands over a sum of money to the grave-digger in order to compensate him for the pigs he brought to the feast and that have been eaten. This monetary gesture, an important part of the mourning process, shows that the 'external form and breath relations' of the deceased are upgraded to the value level of 'representation relations', which encompass all social relations and allow the deceased to become an ancestor. In a similar sense, a woman's marriage would thus seem to involve mourning the first half of her social relations and life and launching her new life as a wife.

Funerals consist of two commemorative feasts, first the funeral feast a year after burial and then three years later the return funeral feast. Two 'sides' are in charge of both ceremonies, the deceased's family, literally 'the side of the roots' and the grave-digger and those with him, 'the side of the work [of mourning]'. Others can enroll on either of the two sides, but usually do so on the grave-digger's. At the two funeral feasts taken together, all the social relations of the deceased are dealt with.

During the funeral feast, a number of shell-money strings are presented, one by one. These strings of shell beads are then hung from the upper bar of the funeral platform, with most of them reaching to the ground. These strings are constituted of the small contributions of shell-money offered by everyone, men, women and children, who attends the funeral, that is, by those who have enrolled on either side as well as by all other participants. At the end of the feast, the total amount of money is proclaimed. It represents the new ancestor's 'representation'. The completion of the deceased's representation is achieved when the circle of his (or her) acquaintances has converted all their relations with the deceased into these shell-money units brought to the platform. The wider his (or her) circle of social relations was, the greater the tribute paid, and the greater the ancestral representation. Thus, a new ancestor emerges from the conversion into money of all his (or her) 'external form, breath and representation relations'.

The day after the funeral feast, the money presented is shared out and lent to the members of the grave-digger's side. Three years later, the same amount of shell-money units is due back, to be hung on the platform of the return funeral feast, where the grave-digger will hand it back to all the contributors to the first funeral feast. During the three years that have elapsed since the first funeral feast, the monetary image of the deceased, that is, this sum of money, has been used in all kinds of exchanges which constitute the three streams of 'external form, breath and representation relations' of the members of the grave-digger's side. After the return funeral feast, all the deceased's social relations have been exhausted, and they are redirected through the initial contributors, in the form of money, into the three streams of the latter's own socio-cosmic relations. This overall funeral process, which mobilizes almost the entire community, and constitutes new ancestors one by one, succeeds in upgrading all past and present social relations to the highest value level of 'representation relations'. The proclamation of the amount of money contributed by all those who have created and payed tribute to a new ancestor is felt as the most moving event and the peak of 'Are'are social life.

The second operation during a funeral feast involves the large number of taros and pigs brought by the two sides in charge of the feast. A large number of these taros, some coconuts, and taro puddings with pieces of pork are presented in the form of two big piles, which are exchanged between the two sides. This exchange of piles is called *kokoruha*. A shell-money unit is placed on top of the pile offered by the deceased's family to the grave-digger's side. It represents the deceased's representation before its growth and completion on the upper bar of the platform, as described above. Thus, the pile gathered by 'the side of the roots' consists of three different layers: at the bottom, the taros, coconuts and taro puddings that result from 'external form' socio-cosmic relations; the intermediate layer, composed of pork, which represents 'breath' socio-cosmic relations; and the upper layer, composed of a single unit of money, representing the harbinger of the ancestral 'representation' of the deceased. The three layers of this pile form a true representation of the hierarchy of social relations and consequently of the human and socio-cosmic constitution, in so far as they refer to the fundamental three-dimensional principle.

This exchange of piles of taros and pork is the start of a distribution, which goes on for several hours, of all the food gathered by the two sides. The taro puddings and the pork are divided into small bits and then exchanged again and again with great excitement among all the people attending the feast. This distribution and the closing meal that follows (shared by everyone except the affines and the older relatives of the deceased) give all of these participants a share of the deceased's 'external form and breath relations', while at the same time severing them all. Affines and older relatives of the deceased cannot eat the funeral meal and share his or her 'external form and breath relations', because, having already exchanged money with the deceased, their relations with him or her are 'representation relations', that is, situated at the highest socio-cosmic value level. They cannot place themselves at an inferior value level, and thus may only contribute to the completion of the deceased's ancestral representation on the upper bar of the platform.

The funeral feast concludes with a monetary offering called 'stop quarrel', *rehomou*, which is handed over to the grave-digger – the 'side of the work [of mourning]' – by the 'side of the roots'. This offering is said to constitute a kind of compensation for all the pigs and taros the 'side of the work [of mourning]' has brought to the feast, that is, for 'external form and breath relations' they have invested in the launching of the 'side of the roots' new ancestor. The conversion by the 'side of the roots' of

these 'external form and breath relations' into money, shows that
the latter have been upgraded to 'representation relations', and
thereby mourned by the living and so exhausted.

As already noted, this final monetary offering resembles the
one offered to the 'woman's side' at the conclusion of the return
marriage feast. Here again, at the end of the funeral feast, social
relations from the two lower value levels – 'external form and
breath relations', signalled by the *species* of taros and pigs – are
raised to the highest value level of 'representation relations' by
means of a monetary prestation. Consequently, the son
responsible for the 'side of the roots' is confirmed at his father's
or mother's funeral feast as holding a peace-master's status.
When the two funeral feasts are completed, the descendants'
ceremonial duties come to an end. Thereafter, their sole task
consists in accomplishing at different funeral sites the ancestor
cult that assures the ancestor's goodwill towards and protection
for the living.

It should be noted that the making of an ancestor from a living
person, who was composed of a combination of 'external form,
breath and representation relations', involves gathering the three
species of taros, pigs and shell-money at the funeral feast. The
presentation of these three *species* results in the division of the
deceased's social relations into three different streams of
'external form, breath and representation relations'. Then these
three streams are all converted into money and directed into a
single stream of 'representation relations', with the result that the
social relations of the living person are exhausted and become
ancestral relations. Thus, not only has a new ancestor been
established by the upgrading of all the deceased's social relations
to the value level of 'representation relations', but also,
considering the fact that the three flows of 'external form, breath
and representation relations' relations have been converted into
money and therefore have merged into the single flow of
'representation relations', it may be concluded that the
community is now in a position to launch further socio-cosmic
ventures.

In conclusion, and seen from the point of view of the whole,
marriages and commemorative funerals have precisely opposite
results. At the beginning of a funeral, the 'external form, breath
and representation relations', once united in the living person,
are divided into three differents streams, embodied in the three

species of taros, pigs and shell-money, which correspond to the 'external form, breath and representation relations' of the deceased. At the conclusion of a funeral, these three streams of 'external form, breath and representation relations' have all been converted into money, that is transposed into 'representation relations' which constitute the new ancestor. It may be added that the community has thus been able to pass in review its socio-cosmic relations and to renew the highest value level of the whole, paving the way for new transpositions and developments like those of marriages.

Marriages, contrasted with but linked to funerals, start exactly where the latter leave off: with a single stream of shell-money, that is, with 'representation relations'. These 'representation relations' (or monetary units), which are brought by the 'man's side', accomplish the transference of the bride's social relations from the 'woman's side' to the 'man's side', provided that they divide into the three *species* of living taros, living pigs and shell-money and therefore into the three different streams of living 'external form, breath and representation relations'. In contrast to funerals, which end with a single stream of money, marriages conclude with the conversion of money into the three *species* of taros to be planted, pigs to be raised and shell-money, all ready to multiply under the new couple's responsibility. Funerals and marriages taken together seem to form an institution through which the socio-cosmic circulation of 'external form, breath and representation relations' is ceaselessly renewed in accordance with the three-dimensional principle.

It should be noted that all these operations are accomplished by the two 'sides' of these feasts, with the exception of the constitution of the deceased's ancestral image, which results from the monetary contributions of all the people who attend the funeral feast, that is, of the community at large. It seems clear that the entire society must contribute to this most important socio-cosmic achievement: the conversion of all the deceased, social relations into 'representation relations', thereby ensuring the renewal of the streams of socio-cosmic circulation.

On the contrary, the 'external form and breath relations' of each deceased are mourned and directed towards the single monetary stream, not by the entire community, but only by the two 'sides' of the funeral feast. This contrast is a reflection of the fact that 'external form and breath relations' are encompassed by 'representation relations'. It also reveals that the highest value level is that of the constitution of the ancestral representation, which alone concerns the 'Are'are social whole.

Socio-Cosmic Relations in the Pig- and Taro-Pudding-Feasts

Marriages and funerals provide a lasting renewal of the new couple's and of the deceased's socio-cosmic relations, as well as of life in general (human, animal and plant) and, most important, of shell-money itself. They also open the way to a series of three different feasts that concern the socio-cosmic relations of the community at large, while at the same time permitting a big man to increase his fame and 'representation' and thereby to become a 'great peace-master', *aaraha paina*. Most informants stress that 'Are'are society may achieve a higher level of completeness only if certain peace-masters are in fact able to give these three kinds of feasts.

We know that only a big man who has already given all the funeral feasts for his parents and ascendants can undertake such a new series of feasts. A big man thus has a long path before him, if he undertakes to fulfil his entire social responsibility as a peace-master and, in so doing, to raise his own fame and representation to their peak.

The new series of festive activities begins with a peace-master's giving a **pig-feast**, which is followed a year later by an *'ini'ini*-**taro-pudding-feast**. (*'Ini'ini* refers to a type of taro-pudding.) Both of these feasts are undertaken at his initiative, in his on-going capacity as 'the roots of the [last] funeral feast', in close relation with his counterpart the grave-digger, 'the side of the work [of mourning]'. These two feasts follow the same ceremonial pattern. They are explicitly meant to be relaxed and joyful events, because they exclude monetary offerings and consist only of pig, taro and taro-pudding offerings.

After the peace-master has proclaimed his intention to give a pig-feast or, thereafter, an *'ini'ini*-taro-pudding-feast, a divination ritual is held in order to fix the date. These feasts are held in the peace-master's village and both begin with his publicly proclaiming to the grave-digger: 'I have raised a pig for you.' He then presents a large pig to be raised to the grave-digger, who in turn presents a pig to be raised to the peace-master. A crowd of men gathers at the feast grounds. Each man or group of male relatives brings and offers a pig for the occasion, and the two sides of the feast also contribute other pigs. With the exception of the first two pigs, offered to be raised, all the others are then slaughtered, cut into pieces and cooked.

At the pig-feast, both 'sides' of the feast, as well as all the other men in attendance, also offer piles of taro-puddings, ten such puddings (*nama housuu*) constituting one pile. The pork and taro-puddings are then shared out among all the men present, and are finally cut up into small pieces which circulate among the participants. The feast meal, in which all the men take part, follows. At the *'ini'ini*-taro-pudding-feast a taro-pudding of a different sort is shared out in a different way, as is described in more detail below.

The main features of both pig-feasts and taro-pudding-feasts may be described as follows:

1. The two sides are clearly the same as those at the funeral feast for the peace-master's last ascendant, during which the peace-master led the 'roots of the feast'. The pig-feast starts with the two sides exchanging a large pig to be raised, as if by these offerings, and in consequence of the corresponding living 'breath relations' offered, each side were acting for the other as a 'woman's side' at a marriage feast, each providing the other with prosperity and reinserting it into day-to-day social relations, which may develop first at the lower value levels of 'external form and breath' relations.

2. Thereafter, the feast goes on with the two 'sides', as well as all the other participants, contributing pigs and taros to be eaten. Thus, most of the pigs, and all the taro-puddings, brought to the feast to be eaten are offered by the entirety of the participants, that is by the community at large, and not only by the two sides, as was the case for the pigs and the taros at the funeral feast. Any man, related or not to one of the two sides, can come to the feast, on the condition that he brings a pig. These contributions resemble the shell-money units that are brought to the platform of the funeral feast by all the participants and that give its shape to the ancestor's 'representation'. But here, the offerings of pigs and taro

puddings, although contributed by all the people attending the pig-feast, have effects which go beyond a single deceased person.

3. The pork and the taro puddings are shared out, exchanged and finally eaten. This consumption in common by the men present at the feast is not restricted, as at the funeral meal, to younger male relatives of the deceased and to unrelated men. Thus the 'external form and breath relations' that are dealt with by the men who attend the pig-feast are those not only of the deceased but of all 'the dead' recently promoted to ancestry.[3] These pigs and taros are tribute paid to the general category of 'the dead'. They mark the success of all previous mournings by initiating new and generalized 'external form and breath relations' between the living. The joyfulness of these feasts is due to the fact that the participants do not manipulate shell-money or establish 'representation relations'. They thus feel free from any ancestral constraint, remaining as they do in the less dangerous domain of 'external form and breath relations'.

There are strong indications that for the community as a whole (and not only for the two 'sides' of the previous funeral feast), these equal contributions from all the participants in the pig-feast and to the taro-pudding-feast and the joyful distribution and consumption of all the food at a common meal involve the living in the revival of new 'external form and breath relations'. As a result of these undertakings, not only is the society's whole ancestry mourned, but its 'external form and body relations' are incorporated in the living and therefore redirected towards the general streams of these two socio-cosmic relations. While at the end of the funeral feast a change of value level occurs, with the transposition of the deceased's 'external form, breath and representation relations' into 'representation relations' (in money), a similar transposition does not occur at a pig-feast or a taro-pudding-feast. There, the reintegration of 'external and breath relations' into the living community through an exchange and consumption of pork and taro-puddings, without the presentation of shell-money, implies that 'representation relations' are left aside: the community celebrates the revival of the two lower value levels of socio-cosmic relations. It seems that these two feasts, by initiating a renewal of 'external and breath relations' for the whole community, mark a turning-point – after the completion of mourning but still 'behind the mirror' – which leads the flows of these relations back to life, that is back to the living side of the 'Are'are configuration. These two feasts, initiated by a few peace-masters, are new steps in the completion of an 'Are'are dynamic configuration, a circulation which, after funerals, succeeds in returning to its life side. This renewal, for the whole community represented by its men, of 'external and breath relations' intensifies the interdependence of 'Are'are society and 'nature', and thereby fuses society and cosmos.

Although the **pig-feast** and the **taro-pudding-feast** seem to be very similar, they none the less bear different names *houraa ni poo* and *houraa ni 'ini'ini,* literally 'pig-feast' and ''*ini'ini*-taro-pudding-feast'. While, at both feasts, pigs and taro-puddings are presented and therefore 'external and breath socio-cosmic relations' are dealt with, these feasts form part of a series in which the pig-feast, whose focus is 'breath relations', precedes by a year the taro-pudding-feast, whose focus is 'external form relations'.

In the expression *houraa ni 'ini'ini* (''*ini'ini*-taro-pudding-feast'), the word for taro-pudding is *'ini'ini,* which refers to a particular kind of very large pudding presented only on this occasion and at the peace-master-feast which follows and terminates the feast series. This kind of square taro-pudding is about twenty inches on a side and may be divided into a hundred small portions of two inches on a side. *'Ini* means to pinch something between the thumb and the index-finger, in this case to pull off one such portion from the pudding. It can also mean to strangle someone. The main difference between the pig-feast and the *'ini'ini*-feast lies in the fact that while piles of ten taro-puddings, *nama housuu,* are presented at the former, huge square puddings, *'ini'ini,* are offered at the latter. These *'ini'ini*-taro-puddings are made not only for the feast which bears their name but also for the peace-master-feast, where they are explicitly meant to recall the 'external form relations' of all the 'murder victims'. If it is recalled that the 'representation relations' of each member of 'the dead' category are converted into money at his or her funeral feast and that the 'breath relations' of each 'murder victim' before the last are converted into money at the blood-money feast, one may contrast the results of the pig-feast and the *'ini'ini*-taro-pudding-feast as follows:

- At a pig-feast, the society is concerned by 'the dead' as a category and by the collective processing of their 'breath and (to a lesser degree) external form relations', which are transposed through the consumption of pork and *housuu*-taro-puddings into new such relations ready to multiply among the living members of the community.
- At an *'ini'ini*-taro-pudding-feast the society is concerned by 'murder victims' as a category and by the collective processing of their 'external form relations', which are transposed through *'ini'ini*-taro-pudding consumption into new such relations ready to develop among the living members of the community.

While the pig *species* presented at pig-feasts is meant, in a way similar to pigs at funerals, to direct the 'breath relations' of all 'the dead' through the consumption of pork, one might well ask whether the pigs presented at the *'ini'ini*-taro-pudding-feast (and not mentioned in the feast's name) do not direct the 'breath relations' of all 'murder victims'. The answer to this question is, however, negative, since murder victims' 'breath relations' have already been settled, each victim's 'breath relations' having been 'covered' by the 'breath relations' of a second victim, and then converted into money at the blood-money feast (see pp. 242–6). Indeed, in contrast with 'the dead's' 'breath relations', those of 'murder victims' cannot be represented by the pig *species*: only a new murder victim's 'breath relations' may 'cover' and properly direct a prior murder-victim's 'breath relations'. What, then, does the offering of pigs at the *'ini'ini*-taro-pudding-feast signify?

I would suggest, perhaps surprisingly, that in this case the pig *species* represents not the 'breath' but also the 'external form relations' of the 'murder victims'. These 'external form relations' have been converted into the pig *species*, not at any previous *'ini'ini*-taro-pudding-feast, but in the course of time, in the forest, where murder victims' corpses, abandoned unprotected, may be eaten by pigs (just like a human placenta). The 'Are'are know perfectly well that pigs in the forest feed on corpses, and thus bury 'the dead' seated in a sort of openwork palm-wood box which shields them from the pigs. Pigs, by eating and incorporating the corpses left in the forest, are therefore essential to the conversion of the 'external form relations' of 'murder victims' into the pig *species*. In this process, these human 'external form relations' are upgraded to the value level of new 'breath relations', ready to be incorporated into the community of the living at the *'ini'ini*-taro-pudding-feast. The fact that the pigs offered at the feast have incorporated the murder victims' 'external form relations' confirms the name of the feast which focuses on *'ini'ini*-taro-puddings, and thus on murder victims' 'external form relations', without referring to the pigs.

It is now possible to understand why the *'ini'ini*-taro-puddings, although they deal with murder victims' 'external form relations', have their source in the 'external form relations' of 'the dead', who, buried in their openwork palm-wood boxes, are essential to the prosperity of the nearby gardens, contributing to the growth and multiplication of taros. The reintegration of the 'external form relations' of the 'murder-victims' into the living at the *'ini'ini*-taro-pudding-feast depends on the gardens' fertility, which originates from the 'external form relations' of 'the dead', which, as we know already, are always buried.

One can argue, further, that after funerals, which conclude with a single stream of 'representation relations', and blood-money feasts, which conclude with the previous victim's 'breath relations' converted into blood-money, both pig-feasts and *'ini'ini*-taro-pudding-feasts initiate the renewal of 'external form and breath relations' for the whole community of the living, and not simply for 'dead' or 'murdered' single individuals. At the pig-feast these new relations represent the 'external form and breath relations' of the 'dead' as a category. At the *'ini'ini*-taro-pudding-feast, the special taro-puddings, while they represent the murder victims' 'external form relations' ready to be incorporated by the living, originate nevertheless from the 'external form relations' of 'the dead' as processed in the gardens under the authority of the funeral sites. And the pigs, while they represent new 'breath relations' ready to be incorporated by the living, originate nevertheless from the 'external form relations' of 'murder victims' as processed in the forest (that is, eaten by the pigs) and upgraded to the value-level of pig *species* and further 'breath relations'. It seems remarkable that after the mourning procedures for both 'the dead' and the 'murder victims', taken one by one, at funerals and blood-money feasts, the renewal of 'external form and breath relations' among the living at pig-feasts and *'ini'ini*-taro-pudding-feasts requires that their streams intertwine and that they intermingle 'external form relations' originating from both categories of the departed, 'the dead', *hi'ona*, and 'the murder victims', *raramua*. This is a clear indication that these different streams are interdependent and subordinated to a holistic configuration.

What Then Has Thus Far Been Achieved in the Series of Feasts, and in Which Direction Have Socio-Cosmic Relations Been Guided?

At **marriage feasts** 'external form, breath and representation relations' are renewed for the new couple and its future descendance, and the bride's relations transferred from the 'woman's' to the 'man's side'.

At **funerals**, each deceased's 'external form, breath and representation relations' are transposed into 'representation relations', that is, into the shell-money units offered by all participants in the feast, and the 'external form and breath relations' are all converted into the taros and pigs offered by the two sides and then converted into money, that is transposed into 'representation relations'. Thus the community is prepared, after these conversions of relations into a single monetary stream, for any future socio-cosmic ventures.

At **pig-feasts**, 'external form and breath relations' (not 'representation relations') of all 'the dead' are dealt with collectively by all participants. These relations are not only mourned and severed, but at the same time renewed, among the living community.

At **'ini'ini-taro-pudding-feasts**, only the 'external form relations' of all 'murder victims' are explicitly and collectively dealt with by the participants. These relations are not only mourned and severed, but at the same time renewed among the living community. Some of these relations originate from the 'external form relations' of 'the dead', through taro cultivation in the gardens. Others originate from the 'external form relations' of 'murder victims', upgraded to the value level of new 'breath relations' among the living by the pigs' eating the murder victims' corpses in the forest.

At a **blood-money-feast**, an individual murder victim's 'breath relations' are converted into blood-money by the 'covering' process.

We may now raise the question whether, in the three-feast series we have been considering – pig-feast, '*ini'ini*-taro-pudding-feast, and peace-master-feast – the last of them does not deal, collectively, precisely with these murder victims' 'breath relations'?

What Are the Final Results of Peace-Master-Feasts?

We know that 'murder victims' compose a single category of the departed, understood in opposition to the other category that includes all 'the dead' supposedly put to death by their own ancestors, who will, after their funerals, become new ancestors worshipped at their funeral sites. The category of 'murder victims' includes, also, dead fetuses, stillborn babies, women who die in childbirth and people who commit suicide. 'Murder victims' are not offered either funerals, or burial, or ancestor cult. Their corpses are left to rot in the forest, where the pigs may feed on them, as they do on afterbirths, which are also left unburied.

How does the society collectively take into account murder victims and their social relations? Are these social relations held apart, as belonging to an abnormal domain, to be forgotten as quickly as possible? In 'Are'are society, which shows itself a self-conscious whole, it seems most unlikely that murder relations, even if settled between the parties, could be considered insignificant at the socio-cosmic level of reality. Even without funerals or ancestor cult, murder victims' relations are bound soon or later to rejoin the social whole, that is, the streams of socio-cosmic circulation.[4] We know that the 'external form relations' of 'murder victims', taken collectively, are socially accounted for at the '*ini'ini*-taro-pudding-feast, where they are partly represented by the '*ini'ini*-taro-puddings and transposed into new 'external form relations' among the living, and partly by the pigs brought to the feast and thereby transposed and upgraded to the higher level of new 'breath relations' among the living community.

What, however, is the fate of the murder victims' own 'breath relations'? We have observed that, at blood-money-feasts, the 'breath relations' of the penultimate victim in a murder series are 'covered' by the new victim's 'breath relations' and also upgraded to the higher value level of 'representation relations', allowing them to be transferred to his or her descendants. The 'breath relations' of each victim in the series, one after another, are thus dealt with. Are murder victims' 'breath relations' all redirected collectively, by the community at large, at the peace-master-feast, as occurs with their 'external form relations' at the *'ini'ini* feast? Before we may answer this question, it is first necessary summarily to describe the unfolding of a peace-master-feast.

A peace-master, at the end of his life, after having first organized a pig-feast and then, a year later, an *'ini'ini*-taro-pudding-feast, is finally in a position to launch a peace-master-feast. His intention must initially be proclaimed at a previous peace-master-feast, offered by a different peace-master. Divination then indicates to him when he should begin the required series of eight ceremonial flirtation campaigns. Each such campaign lasts eighteen days, and is followed by a ten-day rest-period. The eight flirtation campaigns with their corresponding rest-periods thus extend over eight lunar months. The feast itself is held at the end of the ninth month. During each flirtation campaign, the unmarried men have as many meetings in the forest as unmarried women will grant them. Each date starts with the man offering the woman a gift, consisting of an object such as a comb, a piece of calico, a pipe or some tobacco. Before they separate, the woman always offers her partner a small string of shell-money. At the end of the eighteen days' period, all unmarried men in a local group bring all the shell-money gathered by them to the their local 'sacred house', *tau*. There, at the end of each flirtation campaign, the dangerous powers of the shell-money gifts are neutralized by a special ritual, *moraha*. In each 'sacred house', all the small strings of money collected during the eight flirtation campaigns by the local group's bachelors are stored until the opening of the peace-master-feast, where they are presented, in a single bundle set on top of a split bamboo pole and hidden in the middle of a bunch of leafy branches, by a group of musicians forming a panpipe ensemble.

At a peace-master-feast, numerous panpipe ensembles, hidden by the leafy branches they carry, enter the feast ground one after another playing panpipe music. They proceed to the ceremonial platform and raise their bundles of money up to its highest level, called the 'nest'. The unmarried women's monetary contributions to the unmarried men are then all counted out in the 'nest' and their total is proclaimed. This sum is said to represent the peace-master's 'representation' at its peak. At the end of the day, when the feast is over, the shell-money bundles are returned to the panpipe ensembles, and then to the unmarried men, who quite some time after the ceremony return the strings of money to the unmarried women.

Before the ceremony, a large stage, called the 'murder victims' stage', is erected next to the ceremonial platform. At the feast, coconuts and taros are tied to the stage's many horizontal bars. *'Ini'ini*-taro-puddings, cooked and eaten in the same way as at the *'ini'ini*-taro-pudding feast, are prepared with these taros and coconuts. The 'external form relations' of 'murder victims' are thus represented at peace-master-feasts, just as at *'ini'ini*-taro-pudding-feasts, by the *species* of taros, which all come from gardens in close relation with funeral sites, and which are consequently linked to the 'external form relations' of 'the dead' as a category.

The murder victims' category is explicitly present here on the 'murder victims' stage' erected at the feast grounds. We should, however, also attempt to understand the significance of the strings of money presented at the peace-master-feast, whose total in the 'nest' of the platform at the end of the feast finally composes the peace-master's 'representation'. Unlike the situation at a funeral feast, where the deceased's 'representation' is composed of contributions from all members of the community (men, women and children), the peace-master's 'representation' is composed only of contributions from a very special section of the community engaged in a particular activity, that is, unmarried women flirting with bachelors. And, in contrast with marriages, where money comes from the 'man's side', here it comes exclusively from unmarried women. The bundles of money, when they are raised up to the 'nest' of the platform by the panpipe ensembles, are called the 'children of the panpipe music' *tare 'au*.[5] These 'children of the panpipe music' are the very special offspring of the series of flirtations in the forest which have taken place over an obligatory nine-month gestation period preceding to the peace-master-feast.

Pigs brought to the *'ini'ini*-taro-pudding-feast, like all pigs, have fed on murder victims' corpses in the forest, leading to the conversion of murder victims' 'external form relations' into the *species* of pig, which, at the different feasts, become new 'breath relations' among the living. At the blood-money-feast, only 'breath relations' taken from a new human 'murder victim' may 'cover' the 'breath relations' of the penultimate 'murder victim' in the series. The 'breath relations' of anonymous 'murder victims' *cannot* be collected by pigs in the forest (this correlates with the absence of pork at the peace-master-feast), but only by humans keen on flirting, that is, engaged in intense 'breath relations' involving the movements of respiration, blood circulation and sexual fluids.

Before a peace-master-feast, the eight flirtation campaigns in the forest have led the unmarried men and women to complete three successive operations:

- First, there is a transposition of the different objects ('external form relations') offered to the unmarried women into flirting activities, which are 'breath relations' between unmarried men and women.
- Then, the repeated flirtation encounters, which correspond to a kind of gathering of all murder victims' 'breath relations' left in the forest (where all 'murder victims' 'have drawn their last breath', *manomano suu*, and where their corpses have been left), result in a transposition of these murder victims' 'breath relations' into new 'breath relations' between the unmarried living, which may lead to future marriages.
- And, finally, the unmarried women convert these new 'breath relations' into money offered to the bachelors, that is, into the *species* of shell-money. This last conversion consists in an upgrading of flirtation 'breath relations' to the higher value level of 'representation relations'.

At the opening of the peace-master-feast, the murder victims' 'breath relations' gathered in the forest give rise to music, played by bachelors blowing into bamboo panpipes and essential to the birth of 'the children of the panpipe music'. These 'children of music' are very peculiar offspring, composed of shell-money, as if they were already dead, mourned for and converted into monetary funeral 'representations'. They resemble anonymous dead fetuses or stillborn babies that have come into the world out of a split bamboo womb for just a few hours and that are blown into the platform's 'nest' by the polyphonic panpipes' musical breath. They remain there, forming the peace-master's 'representation' at its peak, only briefly, and are soon redivided into small strings of shell-money, later returned to the unmarried women.

In contrast with marriages, where the transposition of 'representation relations' (money) into new living 'external form, breath and representation relations' prepares the birth of the couple's children, flirtations in the forest convert living 'breath relations' into money, that is into 'representation relations', while the panpipe music at a peace-master-feast gives birth to dead fetuses, representing the category of 'murder victims', in the process of being anonymously mourned and redirected into the single stream of money and 'representation relations'.

At funerals, the monetary contributions to the deceased's ancestral 'representation' come from the entire community (men, women and children), while at a peace-master-feast the monetary contributions to the living peace-master's 'representation' come only from the unmarried women, as yet only engaged in sterile flirtations. The processes of building the deceased's 'representation' and the peace-master's image are none the less strikingly similar. The peace-master, by successively offering the **pig-**, the '*ini'ini-* and the **peace-master-feasts**, succeeds in increasing his fame to the point that he is able, while still living and before his funeral, to elevate his quasi-funeral 'representation' to the 'nest' of the ceremonial platform. Not only is he at the peak of his career and deeply honoured, but he is, also, close to a living transposition into his own ancestral figure.

It may be somewhat surprising to discover that, at the end of a peace-master-feast, the peace-master's 'representation' is composed of a collection of strings of money gathered by a sterile section of the society and originating in murder victims' 'breath relations' converted into 'representation relations' through flirting activities. The building up of the peace-master's 'representation' is thus closely connected with the category of 'murder victims' and with the fact that the latter's 'breath relations' have been redirected into the stream of 'representation relations', that is into the socio-cosmic stream of shell-money, ready to be reinvested by the living in new active 'external form, breath and representation relations'.

This process represents a great socio-cosmic achievement on

the part of the peace-master. He thereby secures the problematic return of the 'external form, breath and representation relations' of the entire category of 'murder victims' to the common streams of all socio-cosmic relations. At the *'ini'ini*-taro-pudding-feast, murder victims' 'external form relations' are converted into *'ini'ini*-taro-puddings and transposed, through the *species* of pigs, into new 'breath relations' among the living. At the peace-master-feast, murder victims' 'breath relations' are gathered in the forest, transposed into flirtation 'breath relations' and upgraded to the *species* of shell-money and to new 'representation relations' among the unmarried members of the society.

The bundles of shell-money, 'the children of the panpipe music', which constitute the peace-master's 'representation', none the less implicitly recall the victims killed by the peace-master himself when he started as a killer, or, later, by the killers to whom he paid blood-money, during the peace-master's slow ascension to the summit of his glory. This accords with the fact that the panpipe ensembles, after the close of a peace-master-feast, on their way back home, destroy the peace-master's gardens and his coconut palm trees. The morning following his feast, the peace-master, although still in his full glory, must plant his gardens and coconut orchards anew. This very replanting is, none the less, a sign that the peace-master has succeeded in renewing all the society's 'external form, breath and representation relations', that is, in returning them to their life side in the overall circulation.

From the foregoing, peace-masters and killers appear clearly as the two complementary, interdependent figures responsible for the overall circulation of the different streams of 'external form, breath and representation socio-cosmic relations'. The series of three feasts we have just discussed, which are undertaken after their relatives' funerals by only a few peace-masters, raise the latter to the highest social glory, and reveal them also to be the decisive agents for the renewal of all socio-cosmic relations, and especially for the reinsertion, despite continuing murders, of the murder victims' relations into the common socio-cosmic streams. In this sense, these few peace-masters represent, at the level of the living, the social whole of the 'Are'are configuration.

The last three feasts (the series of the pig-feast, the *'ini'ini*-taro-pudding-feast and the peace-master-feast), together with marriages, funerals and blood-money-feasts, reveal how all social relations are bound finally to rejoin the three common streams of the socio-cosmic circulation. This overall movement is that of society and cosmos together. All activities, marriages and funerals, the growing of taros in gardens and the raising of pigs in the forest, even murders and flirtations, as well as the series of the last three feasts, are necessary parts of the whole. They participate in the maintenance and renewal of a hierarchical order, that of the three streams of socio-cosmic relations. Such a hierarchical configuration expresses the whole through the intertwined socio-cosmic relations, and orders it in accordance with the three-dimensional principle of 'external form, breath and representation relations'.

Conclusion

We are now in a position to summarize the main features of bigmanship in 'Are'are society. Peace-masters, by giving a pig-feast, prepare for the conversion of 'external form and breath relations' of all 'the dead' into new relations for the living. They are thus able to direct back toward life relations which had first to be mourned for and converted into money at funerals. It further appears that, by giving the 'ini'ini-taro-pudding-feast and the peace-master-feast, a peace-master secures the reinsertion of murder victims' relations into socio-cosmic life. At the same time, his own living 'representation', which consists of the 'children of the panpipe music' in the platform's 'nest', seems finally to be composed entirely of murder victims' relations, and, in this sense, murders take part in the constitution of a peace-master. This correlates with the fact that most peace-masters were killers before becoming peace-masters. Even before actually dying and being elevated to full ancestral dignity, a peace-master, at the end of his peace-master-feast, thus becomes a figure representing bigmanship and society as a whole.

At this stage of his life and career, he has taken on responsibility not only for the socio-cosmic reinsertion of his own relatives, as every man should, but also for the renewal of the socio-cosmic relations of both categories of the departed, 'the dead' (those who died from illness) and the 'murder victims'. He encompasses, at the same time, the figure of his counterpart the killer, who nevertheless remains an unavoidable key element in the system. But if killers are able to help in 'covering' the 'breath relations' of the penultimate 'murder victim', only peace-masters can re-establish the value level of 'representation relations' by systematically paying blood-money. If a first-born son, as 'the root of the funeral feast', can secure his father's promotion to ancestral 'dignity' and therefore renew ancestry itself, only peace-masters through the pig-feast can redirect towards the living the 'external form and breath socio-cosmic relations' of all 'the dead'. Only peace-masters, by undertaking an *'ini'ini*-taro-pudding-feast, can, with the help of the pigs in the forest, redirect the 'external form socio-cosmic relations' of all 'murder victims' toward the living. Only peace-masters by undertaking a peace-master-feast can, with the help of the unmarried in the forest, redirect the 'breath socio-cosmic relations' of all the 'murder victims' and even upgrade them to the level of 'representation socio-cosmic relations', thereby reintegrating them into the common stream of money and 'representation relations'.

The two leading characters, killer and peace-master, take responsibility for this order, which in turn defines their specific and contrasted statuses. If the killer's tasks are seen complementary to and interdependent with the encompassing tasks of the peace-master, it may be argued that, in those feasts where two 'sides' combine their efforts (that is, in marriages and funerals), these two 'sides' are separated and contrasted in a manner analogous to the contrast already noted between the two sides, peace-master and killer, of the blood-money-feast.

In marriage ceremonies, 'the man's side' clearly acts like the peace-master's side at blood-money-feast, while the 'woman's side' acts like the killer's side. The former offers shell-money, the latter receives it and accepts the bride's departure, the loss of a member of their side (just as the killer accepts the loss of a member of his group).

At the end of the funeral feast, the 'root of the feast', that is, the deceased's family, offers shell-money to the grave-digger, that is, the 'side of the work [of mourning]'. The former thus acts like the peace-master's side at a blood-money-feast. The grave-digger receives the 'stop quarrel' money, as the 'killer' of the pigs he brought to the feast, which have contributed to the conversion of the deceased's 'breath relations' into money, that is, have upgraded them to the value level of the socio-cosmic stream of 'representation relations'.

Finally, the division between killer and peace-master extends itself throughout the whole of 'Are'are society's activities. They express two different life-styles and two ultimate values that induce the circulation of shell-money and the three fundamental flows of 'external form, breath and representation relations'. The opposite characters of the killer and the peace-master may be seen as a hierarchical opposition between two fundamental socio-cosmic gestures: offering shell-money as opposed to receiving it. The former gesture is hierarchically superior, for it signifies the success of the work of mourning and creates the conditions for further renewal of 'external form, breath and representation relations' between the living and for the revival of all sorts of ventures. Money means 'representation relations' and the conversion into money means the upgrading of the social relations to their highest value level, that of 'representation relations', which coincide with the dynamics of the whole. Only ancestors remain until they are forgotten at this highest degree of potentials, and just a few peace-masters may before death maintain themselves for a single day at the level of the socio-cosmic whole.

It must be recalled that the transposition of 'external form, breath and representation relations' – represented by the three *species* of taro, pig and shell-money – into money alone or into 'representation relations' exemplifies the fundamental work of the funerals. This can be said also of the peace-master-feast, where 'external form, breath and representation relations' of 'murder victims' have been converted into money. Such a conversion occurs also as a kind of finale at the end of funerals, marriages and blood-money-feasts. At the end of both funerals and marriages pigs ('breath relations') are converted into money. At the end of the blood-money-feast, the murder victim's 'breath relations' are converted into money. The way blood-money payment happens after equal losses of lives suffered by the two parties and after an equal exchange of money between them, is a clear indication that it is an extra gesture that addresses not only the two opposed parties, but the socio-cosmic whole of 'Are'are configuration. It has the effect of radically changing the situation not only from murder to peace, but also from a subordinate value level to the highest socio-cosmic value level, that which opens for

living beings (humans, pigs and garden plants) the whole range
of their specific ventures and which testifies to – and reinforces –
the validity of the three-dimensional principle of 'external form,
breath and representation relations'.

A different kind of conversion and upgrading has been
observed on the part of pigs, which, while feeding in the forest
on murder victims' corpses, incorporate the victims' 'external
form relations' and upgrade them to the higher value-level of the
'breath relations' ready to develop between the living at the
'ini'ini-feast. Another kind of conversion and upgrading has been
also observed on the part of the unmarried men and women
who, while flirting in the forest, gather the 'breath relations' of all
the 'murder victims' and upgrade them to the highest value level
of 'representation relations', ready to develop into new relations
between the unmarried living after the peace-master-feast.

These various conversions and upgrading processes are clear
indication that each of the three *species* – taro, pig and shell-
money – may convert and upgrade relations up to each of their
socio-cosmic levels. The taro *species* represents the lower level of
'external form relations', and cannot upgrade them further up on
the scale, but it secures the link through the land between the
buried corpses of 'the dead' and their 'external form relations',
which then may be incorporated by the living eating taro at various feasts. The pig *species* represents the middle level of 'breath
relations', and may convert and upgrade 'external form relations'
of 'the murder victims' to 'breath relations', which then may be
incorporated by the living eating pork at the *'ini'ini*-feasts.

Finally the shell-money *species* represents the top level of
'representation relations', which then, in the hands of the living
who thread (*uuruha*) shell beads on strings, may convert and
upgrade 'external form and breath relations' of all the departed
to 'representation relations' which are means to mourn the
departed, to establish new ancestors and further to invest in the
whole range of new socio-cosmic relations, that is into the entire
activity of the society. In fact money (or 'representation relations')
has the striking property of converting and dividing itself into
new 'external form, breath and representation relations', that is
into the three kinds of streams of socio-cosmic relations. Money
circulation seems to depend on the three-dimensional principle
and at the same time to extend its validity ever further into the
future.

In such a system all beings – objects, taros, pigs, unmarried men and women, 'the murder victims' killers, married couples, peace-masters, 'the dead', ancestors, land and shell-money – are alternately subjects and objects in the overall circulation of the socio-cosmic streams. Shell-money is set at the summit of the chain of beings, for it concentrates in itself all the potentials of 'Are'are socio-cosmic entity. One may express finally the somehow surprising statement that the 'Are'are configuration sounds its socio-cosmic note far beyond the pitch of its human individuals, who are ceaselessly divided and recomposed into the three intermingled streams of socio-cosmic relations, and ultimately led by a three-dimensional principle which rules together society and cosmos in a complex coalescence, that of its specific whole.

Notes

1. In previous publications (see de Coppet 1981, 1985, and Barraud *et al.* 1994) I referred to these relations as 'body', 'breath' and 'image' relations. But to 'body', which has a deep Christian connotation, I prefer 'external form' to translate *rape*, and to 'image' *nunu*, I prefer 'representation', to express either ancestral figure *hi'ona*, or various monetary transpositions.
2. The word *species* has been chosen to allude to the Holy Communion.
3. Henceforth, the category of those who died from illness, that is, from their ancestors' intervention, will be referred to as 'the dead', while those who died violently will be called 'murder victims'.
4. In 1968, Louis Berthe, when reading a paper of mine (see de Coppet 1969), told me that murder victims were most unlikely to disappear from the social scene without a social tribute having been paid to them. Since then I have kept myself searching for the proper 'Are'are way to mourn murder victims. Let it stand here as a tribute to his anthropological sixth sense.
5. It means also 'children of the panpipe flute' or 'children of bamboo', as *'au* means both 'bamboo' and 'panpipe music'.

Reference

Barraud, Cécile *et al.* (1994). *Of Relations and the Dead. Four Societies Viewed from the Angle of their Exchanges.* Berg, Oxford.[French edn.: Des relations et des morts. Quatre sociétés vues sous l'angle des échanges. In: J.C. Galey (ed.), *Echanges, valeurs et hiérarchie*, pp. 320–420 E.H.E.S.S., Paris, 1984.]

Coppet, Daniel de (1969). Cycles de meurtres et cycles funéraires. Esquisse de deux structures d'échanges. In: J. Pouillon and P. Maranda (eds), *Echanges et communications. Mélanges offerts à Claude Lévi-Strauss*, pp. 759–81. Mouton, The Hague.

—— (1985). '. . . Land owns People'. In: *Contexts and Levels: Anthropological Essays on Hierarchy*, ed. R. H. Barnes, Daniel de Coppet, and R. J. Parkin, pp. 78–90. JASO, Occasional Papers n°4, Oxford.

—— (1970). 1,4,8; 9,7. La monnaie: présence des morts et mesure du temps. *L'Homme*, X, (1), 17–39.

—— (1972). Premier troc, double illusion. *L'Homme*, XIII (1–2), 10–22.

—— (1981). The Life-Giving Death. In: *Mortality and Immortality: The Anthropology and Archeology of Death*, ed. S. Humphrey and H. King. Academic Press, New York.

Dumont, Louis (1986). *Essays on Individualism. Modern Ideology in Anthropological Perspective.* The University of Chicago Press, Chicago.[French edn.: *Essais sur l'individualisme. Une perspective anthropologique sur l'idéologie moderne.* Le Seuil, Paris, 1983.]

—— (1970). *Homo Hierarchicus. The Caste System and Its Implications.* The University of Chicago Press, Chicago. [French edn.: *Homo Hierarchicus. Essai sur le systéme des castes.* Gallimard, Paris, 1966.]

Chapter 10

The Sibling Incest Taboo: Polynesian Cloth and Reproduction*

Annette B. Weiner

anyone brought up among Puritans knew that sex was sin. In any previous age, sex was strength. . . . Everyone, even among Puritans, knew that neither Diana of the Ephesians nor any of the Oriental goddesses was worshipped for her beauty. She was goddess because of her force; she was the animated dynamo; she was reproduction – the greatest and most mysterious of all energies.

Henry Adams, *The Education of Henry Adams*

This cruel death in exile, far from home,
Far from your sister. And I [your sister] could not be there
To wash and dress your body for the fire
Or dutifully lift the sad remains
In loving hands.

Sophocles, *Electra*

In traditional theories of kinship, the accepted priority of the norm of reciprocity focuses kinship studies on marital exchange and human reproduction. The consequence is that reciprocity becomes the pivot around which other important kin relationships – between men – are established. Reciprocity, as traditionally defined, is not the mechanism that produces homogeneity between participants in exchange. It is the many paradoxical solutions to keeping-while-giving that result in the establishment of difference between participants and make the processes of cultural reproduction central to the development of hierarchy.

* 'The Sibling Incest Taboo: Polynesian Cloth and Reproduction' by Annette B. Weiner was first published in *Inalienable Possessions – The Paradox of Keeping-While-Giving* by University of California Press, 1992. ©University of California Press.

A child is both like and unlike its parents; but, in genetic terms, it is sexual difference that makes human reproduction possible. The work of cultural reproduction also produces difference through the exchanges that begin from a person's birth and continue even after a person dies. To draw on other social identities, to enhance one's history, and to secure the appropriate transmission of inalienable possessions for the next generation involve voluminous exchanges, elaborate strategies, and productive efforts. The initial exchanges of social identities that begin at birth fall not only on to the child's parents, but involve a brother and sister whose exchange efforts with each other and with each other's children provide the kinship counterpart of keeping-while-giving.

For over a century, the sibling incest taboo has been at the core of kinship studies, because this restriction, which prohibits sexual intercourse between brother and sister, is often conflated with the rules of exogamy, prohibiting marriage between cross-sex siblings and other close kin. Therefore, the inherent motivation that has been thought to underlie reciprocal gift exchange is extended to reciprocal marriage exchange. In these exchanges as traditionally defined, a woman's role in social life is limited to her sexual and reproductive role as wife, and in this role she is merely the sign of the exchanges between her husband and her brother. What is missing from these long-held views is that both before and after she marries, a woman is prominent as a sister. In this latter role, she is dynamically involved in a multiplicity of social and political actions that accord her a position of authority – as sister – in her own right.

As an anthropological concept, the incest taboo is encumbered with such heavily pejorative sanctions that the restriction on sexual relations is thought to extend to all other intimacies between a woman and her brother. How then do we account for the extensive data that show what a strategic role sibling intimacy has played in human history?[1] Although actual sexuality between brothers and sisters is prohibited in most societies, the cultural recognition of a brother's and sister's socially and economically charged intimacy creates a unique bond that unites them for life. Like inalienable possessions, this ritualized sibling bond remains immovable because in each generation politically salient social identities and possessions are guarded and enhanced through it. Therefore, the incest taboo and sibling ties must be reconceptualized as part of reconfiguring exchange theory.

Although, in most cases, social and economic intimacy between brother and sister is surrounded with ritual avoidance and sexual separation, these prohibitions only heighten and culturally acknowledge the essential human and cultural reproductive potentialities in sibling intimacy. In fact, the stronger the sibling incest taboo the more it reveals this reproductive power and, instead of being suppressed, it is thrown into the political domain. Sibling sexuality appears in myths, genealogies, and among gods; but its constituted power emerges from the intricacies of kinship organization, from contests over political legitimation, and from the economic and political actions of women as sisters. Although actual sibling sexuality may be culturally disavowed, it is, at the same time, inexorable. My use of sibling intimacy encompasses this broad range of culturally reproductive actions, from siblings' social and economic closeness and dependency to latent, disguised, or overt incest.

The Maori example demonstrates how inalienable social identities and possessions are infused with potent cosmological forces and ancestral connections such as the *hau* and *mana*. What the Maori material only hints at, however, is that, like the symbol of a Maori woman's tattooed lips, the reproductive potency of mana, rank, and titles is sanctioned by and through women as sisters. This authority gives sisters an autonomous source of power that men cannot match or attain, making women feared and venerated, whereas men are dependent on them for their own political endeavours. More important, such power, linked as it is to a multiplicity of sexual, reproductive, and productive domains, accords to high-ranking women as sisters political authority in their own right. Although the historical past of Polynesian societies cannot always be reconstructed with complete confidence from the many mixed messages in explorers' journals and other early archival materials, when sifted through judiciously, these firsthand documents show that sisters played important political roles in Polynesian history and that sibling intimacy was always politically vital. Although many contemporary ethnographers have called attention to the sacred power of Polynesian women as sisters,[2] formal analysis of brother–sister intimacy has not followed, in large part because of traditional beliefs in the inherent nature of the norm of reciprocity.

It is therefore important to examine how incest has been viewed historically to show the way a reciprocity model makes claims about a woman's sexuality that eliminates the power and autonomy of her reproductive actions. To show the economic and political significance of sibling intimacy even in societies where the incest taboo is rigorously upheld, I compare three societies, each of which is progressively more socially and politically complex. Although I am not necessarily proposing an evolutionary scale, there are important points of comparison, such as sibling intimacy, the reproductive prominence of sacred sisters, and cloth as an inalienable possession that have not earlier been thought about in this way.

First, I discuss the long-standing debates surrounding the incest taboo from the perspective of sibling intimacy. I then analyse the reproductively essential activities in which brothers and sisters are prominent in the Trobriand Islands, in part because of my research there, but also because Malinowski's ethnography sustained so many debates on the meaning of incest taboos.[3] I then focus on the same themes in Western Samoa, because I also have done fieldwork there, and I draw on this material as well as the work of others. Ancient Hawaii provides another appropriate case, because sister–brother sexual relations and marriage were the rule for the highest-ranking nobles. Although the Hawaiian data are meager and difficult to assess and I am by no means a Hawaiian scholar, there are certain aspects of the Hawaiian material that are essential to my argument.[4] By including the Trobriands in this comparison, where élite chiefly matrilineages are set apart to some degree from commoner lineages,[5] I emphasize an analytical gradient rather than the traditional distinct separation between Polynesia and Melanesia.[6]

After comparing the processes of cultural reproduction in these three cases and showing the kinship centrality of sibling intimacy in relation to the development of rank and hierarchy, I then compare women's cloth production in the three societies. This comparative analysis of cloth reveals the political limitations in the scope of rank and hierarchy, but also shows how, in each society, power and authority are tied to gender and, despite political limitations, give women, especially in their roles as sisters, political power and authority. In terms of political hierarchy the three societies may be ranked, with Hawaii as the most complex and the Trobriands the least. I use this tripartite scale in both directions to avoid claims that the Trobrianders' social structure is the precursor to Samoan chieftaincy or that chieftaincy is the forerunner of Hawaiian hierarchy. The examples I discuss are meant to promote a different mode of ethnographic description and explanation that reverses traditional priorities and assumptions about kinship, exchange, and gender and exposes the source of difference and hierarchy in a wide range of relatively unrelated societies.

The Sibling Incest Taboo and Reciprocity

Since the time of the ancient Greek philosophers, the act of incest has served as a parable to show the uniqueness of humans in opposition to animals and nature. Thus the universality of the incest taboo is thought to reveal that society is created in recognition of the limits to sexuality (even though the biblical account of Adam and Eve depended on sexual relations between their children for the creation of society). For the nineteenth-century social evolutionists, incest was cast as the representation of sexual anarchy (nature) that, with the imposition of its taboo (culture), established formal social regulations for men over women. Yet in eighteenth-century France, sibling incest was often portrayed as a political act, a revolutionary force that through universal endogamy would create a world of 'brothers' and 'sisters'. This 'natural law' of absolute equality prompted the Marquis de Sade to exclaim that 'incest must be the law of any government of which fraternity is the base'.[7] In Victorian England, a more traditional nature-culture view of the incest taboo prevailed, in which social origins remained the main anthropological concern. Although Edward B. Tylor never explicitly tied the origin of the incest taboo to his theory of marriage alliance, his belief that people once had to choose between 'marrying out' or being 'killed out' firmly linked reciprocity to the origin of exogamy. Malinowski and Freud transmitted to modern anthropology these nineteenth-century debates, shifting the parameters of discourse from the evolution of social order to how the incest taboo specifically regulates sexuality, marriage, and the family. Freud located the universal origin of the incest taboo in the Oedipus complex, in which a boy's sexual desire for his mother comes into conflict with his mother's tie to his father, whom he then sees as his rival. Later, fearing castration, the boy identifies with his father, 'takes over the severity of the father and perpetuates his prohibition against incest'.[8] Malinowski rejected the universality of Freud's theory by showing that a different configuration existed among the matrilineal Trobrianders. For Malinowski, the incest taboo functioned as a sociological regulator that divides 'persons of the opposite sex into lawful and unlawful' relationships, that restrains intercourse in virtue of the legal act of marriage and that 'discrim-inate[s] between certain unions in respect of their desirability'.[9]

In the kinship controversies that followed, the dual terms, sexuality and marriage, incest and exogamy, were continually conflated. Whether perceived as physical kinship or social kinship, a strong male-oriented biogenetic stance kept kinship studies narrowly focused on the reproduction of social organization or the reproduction of a life cycle.[10] From either a societal or an ego-centred perspective, marriage exchange was cast as the point of fission and fusion, the event that regulates human reproduction for the next generation. In a sense, these ideas simply continue the same nature–culture opposition in which the women's position is erroneously constructed. Quite ignored are the multiple transformations of women's sexuality and human reproduction into forms of cultural reproduction that entail production and politically vital cosmological domains and that give autonomy and a political presence to women.

Nowhere is this traditional view more substantively wedded to the incest taboo and reciprocity than in Lévi-Strauss's theory of marriage exchange. The incest taboo marks the 'fundamental stop' whereby the 'transition from nature to culture is accomplished. . . . Before it [i.e., the incest taboo], culture is still non-existent, with it, nature's sovereignty over man is ended'.[11] The incest taboo not only marks out where 'nature transcends itself', but by nature imposes alliance, so that culture need only define the rules. In this way, Lévi-Strauss moves from incest to the rules of exogamy, defining society as relations among men over women. His approach was revolutionary in its theoretical sophistication; but his synthesis never departs from the traditional biogenetic assumption that defines kinship and society as the exchange of women's biologically ordained procreative roles.

Although Malinowski's functional analysis of the incest taboo as the basis for familial social cohesion is fraught with problems discussed by others,[12] his inability to understand why Trobrianders expressed such strong interest in brother–sister incest, despite the strictest prohibitions, offers an important clue into the kinship–incest problem. Malinowski argues that Freud's account of the Oedipus complex is Eurocentrically based on a model of the patrilineal Aryan family, because the presumed universality of the Oedipus complex cannot account for the Trobriand 'matrilineal nuclear complex' in which a boy's mother's brother – not his father – is the authority figure. The Trobriand father, lacking jural authority over his children, remains loving and affectionate, and never becomes the hated rival for his mother's sexual love. So within the Trobrianders, the Oedipus complex becomes the 'repressed desire to kill the maternal uncle and marry the sister'.[13] Ernest Jones rebuts Malinowski's position on the basis that a Trobriand son does not come under his mother's brother's authority until adolescence, whereas the resolution of the Oedipus complex occurs by the age of six.[14] In all the decades of subsequent debates, however, only Anne Parsons touches on the key element in the argument: the critical relationship between a Trobriand sister and brother. In psychoanalytic terms, Parsons shows how a son develops the Oedipal desire for his mother as he is aware of the important presence of her brother in her life. Therefore, the boy's ego censures this incestuous undercurrent and his libidinal desires are transformed from this woman as his mother to his mother as his mother's brother's sister.[15]

This interpretation calls attention to the psychological proximity of a sister and brother in each other's life. Indeed, the ethnographic record is filled with examples of women's close social and economic intimacy with their brothers or their brothers' children long after they marry. Thomas Beidelman is one of the few anthropologists who has pondered extensively over this problem, exploring why the matrilineal Kaguru give such prominence to brother–sister incest in folktales, jokes, and gossip.[16] Not only in matrilineal societies, but in societies with other kinds of descent systems, sister–brother incest is a recurring theme in genealogies, myths, or rituals, and in some

cases, such as ancient Egypt or Hawaii, sibling sexual relations
became a political fact.[17] These latter cases are usually thought of
as aberrant circumstances; but examples of both the acceptance
and taboo of sibling sexuality attest to the fact that women are
not merely a counter exchanged between brothers-in-law. When
a woman marries, the full range of her reproductive powers is far
too essential to be lost to her brother and the other members of
her natal group. Whereas in most cases, a woman's biological
procreative role is established within her marriage, thereby
sexually upholding the sibling sexual relations taboo, her other
productive and reproductive roles – those usually omitted in
kinship theory – remain dearly tied to the relation between
herself and her brother. Even when the sibling taboo is rigorously
upheld, the desire for and possibilities of sibling intimacy are
present, giving women as sisters a unique kind of power.[18]

Some societies make greater claims than others on maintaining
close relationships between women and their brothers. Lévi-
Strauss acknowledges such differences by stressing that in cases
where the brother–sister tie is strong, the husband–wife tie is
weak, as does David Schneider in his classic essay on the
characteristics of matrilineal societies.[19] This opposition,
however, skims over the important shading of these differences,
the problems that matrilineal, patrilineal, or cognatically defined
societies face when people marry out, and the solutions that
emerge. Giving a sibling to a spouse is like giving an inalienable
possession to an outsider. Some way must remain open to
reclaim the sibling. In a Motu myth, a man poignantly says, 'You
can have our sister's body but you cannot have her bones.'[20] But
the reclaiming actions for keeping siblings when they marry do
not wait for death; they are ongoing and remain a formidable
part of kinship and political processes. The controls and avenues
open for sustaining the stability of siblings' culturally
reproductive roles play directly into the level of rank and
hierarchy that some societies attain. Therefore, the intimacy of
sister and brother directly affects a woman's presence in
economic, cosmological, and political affairs.

Sibling Intimacy and Kinship

The Trobriand Case

The main kinship theme in the Trobriands is of a society divided between commoner and ranked matrilineages where, in the latter, chiefs have rights to specific prerogatives and authority. But a chief's power is limited by the number of wives he is able to take,[21] and neither chiefly titles nor rank can be transmitted to members of other matrilineages. Therefore, being born into one of these ranked matrilineages provides the only access to chieftaincy, making women the primary means to one's birthright. So unifying is this claim that women are thought to conceive through the impregnation of an ancestral spirit child, maintaining the Trobriand belief that those who are members of the same matrilineage have the 'same blood'. This spirit child is believed to be regenerated from a deceased matrilineal kin. Most often, a woman is impregnated with the spirit child by another deceased kinsman, who transports the spirit child from the distant island of Tuma where, after death, all Trobrianders continue their existence.[22] Although a woman's husband is not thought to play a part in conception, he contributes to the external growth and well-being of the fetus through the contribution of his semen in repeated sexual intercourse. But even this part of a husband's supposed biological role in reproduction is often suppressed: when a child is born it is not thought to have any internal substance from its father. Yet it is always thought to resemble him because now the infant's sociological affiliation with its father is of public concern; a father provides for his child's well-being by giving possessions, such as names and chiefly decorations, from his own matrilineage, as *mapula*, what Malinowski originally described as 'pure gifts'.[23] Publicly, a child is adorned with its father's matrilineal resources, showing its father's support; but since these possessions remain inalienable to the members of the father's matrilineage, they must be reclaimed by the father's sisters at a later time.

Although much effort is made to objectify the social presence of a man as father, the prominence of the brother–sister relationship diminishes its centrality because of the need to ensure the enduring strength of the matrilineage. Sexual

intercourse or marriage with a member of one's own
matrilineage is considered an inviolate transgression of the
sister–brother incest taboo. Yet Trobriand belief demands that
conception occur within the confines of the matrilineage. The
'cosmological' intimacy between a woman and her deceased
kinsman – the purveyor of her child – provides for the tightly
controlled reproduction of matrilineal identity. The many
anthropological debates that arose over Malinowski's description
of Trobriand beliefs in reproduction were subsequently glossed
'virgin birth'.[24] Yet the enormous ritual attention that
Trobrianders give to premarital sexuality ensures that no
Trobriander is a virgin at marriage, so that the opposition
between sexuality and virginity as it has been defined in Western
mores and religion is no more the issue than is the argument over
whether or not Trobrianders are ignorant of biological parentage.
Sibling sexuality, although overtly prohibited, is fundamental to
the 'pure' reproduction of matrilineal identity.

Women's sexuality has been cast in a sexually inflammatory
way by anthropologists, and Malinowski was no exception. He is
quite emphatic about the sexual separation between a sister and
her brother, and constructs a picture of their life together which
has become a classic rendition of brother–sister avoidance, with
the drama of women as seductive sexual symbols.

> They must not even look at each other, they must never exchange
> any light remarks, never share their feelings and ideas. And as age
> advances and the other sex becomes more and more associated with
> love-making, the brother and sister taboo becomes increasingly
> stringent. *Thus, to repeat, the sister remains for her brother the centre of
> all that is sexually forbidden – its very symbol; the prototype of all unlawful
> sexual tendencies within the same generation and the foundation of
> prohibited degrees of kinship and relationship.*[25] [Emphasis mine].

Lévi-Strauss simply shows us these same views of a sister as
an allurer when he defines a woman as the sign of marriage
exchange because she is 'the object of personal desire, thus
exciting sexual and proprietorial instincts' and, 'as the subject of
desire' as well, she binds others through alliance.[26]

How then do we reconcile the fact that when a woman
marries, she assists her brother whenever she can, persuading
her husband to help her as well? Since most marriages take place

among young people living within the same or nearby villages, a woman's brother is geographically close to her; she sees him often and gives him cooked food whenever she can. Her brother is her protector and his major obligation is to make a large yam garden each year in her name. The harvest is presented to her and her husband; these yams form the economic and political core of all marriages and all brother–sister relationships[27] because the yams obligate husbands to work for their wives, ultimately strengthening the brother–sister tie.

Sibling intimacy has other far-reaching implications, because the relationship between a brother and his sister to each other's children secures possessions, relationships, and knowledge for the next generation. It is a sister who reclaims the inalienable possessions, such as personal names and lineage decorations, that her brother gives to his children. Not only is a man responsible for giving his sister's son the knowledge and information necessary for his eventual succession to a leadership position, but his sister encourages and heightens the adolescent sexual life of her brother's children, transposing into the next generation the vitality of sibling intimacy. Technically, her own daughter is the preferred marriage partner for her brother's son.[28] The time for the most important sexual liaisons that eventually lead to marriage occurs during the yam harvest season, when it is a woman's responsibility to perform beauty magic for her brother's children and even assist them with finding lovers. Sexuality is hardly suppressed, since in all these incidents a sister is directly involved in sexual matters with her brother, even though it is through his children.

In several instances, Malinowski alludes to the ambivalence that Trobrianders feel about sister–brother sexuality, pointing out the few actual cases he was told about. Clan endogamy is also considered incestuous. Still, it occurs with some regularity, and such marriages are usually attributed to love magic that is so potent it overcomes the force of the incest taboo.[29] This belief is at the heart of a famous myth, Kumilabwaga, recorded by Malinowski about sibling sexual relations and the origin of love magic. By accident, a young girl brushes her brother's coconut oil (a powerful love potion) over herself and is overcome with passionate desire for him. After the two make love, they neither eat nor drink, then die. Subsequently, a flower emerges from their bodies whose fragrance is the foundation of love magic.

Malinowski not only gives the transcription of the myth, but also gives an informant's commentary. In the latter, a change is made in the text, indicating that the sibling's shame prevented them from eating and drinking and, therefore, their remorse was the cause of their deaths.[30] This shame is what Malinowski defines as 'The Supreme Taboo'.

As a general rule, when love magic is strong, the desire it instils is so intense that the person can neither eat nor drink.[31] For example, if a young person truly desires someone as a spouse but their relatives object, the person refuses food and water. The relatives then recognize that someone has used strong love magic and they accept the marriage. It follows then that the siblings in the Kumilabwaga myth died, as the original text stated, not because of shame but because of their passion for each other. In this sense, the myth is a celebration of sibling sexuality – the origin of love magic and the more hidden origin of matrilineal reproduction.

In everyday life, the social and economic intimacy of siblings in each other's lives and to each other's children is pervasive. At the cosmological level, sister–brother sexuality itself is not totally subverted; a woman conceives through the agency of ancestral spirits who are members of her matrilineage, who are like brothers. In this way, Trobriand beliefs in conception sanction the 'supreme' purity of matrilineal identity, thereby keeping rank and chiefly status uncontested. If ancestral sibling sexual relations act as a guard against losing or diluting matrilineal autonomy, the down side to this solution is that matrilineages cannot incorporate outsiders as permanent members, and even chiefly matrilineages sometimes die out. Spouses and fathers, whose resources are essential for political power, must be repaid for their care and efforts when a husband, wife, or child dies. In actuality, the exchanges spread much wider than these central participants, to relationships between each member of the dead person's matrilineage, to members of other lineages connected to them affinally, patrilaterally, or as friends and allies. In this way, each death puts a drain on accumulating resources, and the constitution of chiefly authority never builds beyond dependency on localized, ego-centred siblings and affinal relations. Although a chief's potential for expanding his authority occurs through the success of his marriages, his authority still must be authenticated in these exchanges by his sisters.

When a man is told of his sister's marriage, he stays in his house or lives alone at the beach for several days. Is it only from shame that he hides away, or is this also a response to loss? One of the most devastating insults that any Trobriander can make is to tell a man, 'Fuck your wife!' The lack of acknowledgement to the most obvious sexuality between a husband and wife speaks directly to the political potency of sibling sexuality.[32] Trobrianders acknowledge a strong sibling incest taboo, yet their beliefs in incestuous matrilineal reproduction as well as the basic organization of descent and kin relations are dependent on the intimacy – at once social, economic, cosmological, and sexual – of a sister and brother relationship.

The Samoan Case

Whereas in the Trobriands the beliefs and practices associated with matrilineality are centred in the attempts to keep lineage identity and political authority free from the claims of others while incorporating the work and resources of those from other lineages, Samoan descent is more complex, but reveals the same prominence of sisters. In Samoa, the basic unit of descent is not a lineage but a multibranching group (*'àiga*) with genealogies traced back for ten or fifteen generations.[33] Given the enormous complexity in genealogical reckoning and the many ways that people can attach themselves to other kin groups, the core kinship relationship, like that of the Trobriands, is still a sister and brother.[34]

The founding ancestors of a descent group most usually are a woman and her brother, and in each generation they remain the foci for the two descent categories, *tamatane* and *tamafafine*, through which all major titles are traced. Titles are most often reckoned through women who stand in the *tamafafine* category to men in the *tamatane* category. In most cases, men compete to gain the highest-ranking *tamatane* titles, because such a title gives rights to chiefly authority over people, land, and other descent group resources. *Tamafafine* titles also are sought in this competitive way, as before to changes wrought by missionaries the highest titles were associated with mana and bestowed upon the eldest sister, called by Samoans the *feagaiga* or 'sacred' sister.[35] Because the original sacred sister had access to mana, subsequently all first-born women in each generation through these titles are believed to possess this ancestral power, which gives them a domain of authority and political power with which men must reckon.

Shore sums up the authority of Samoan chiefs (*matai*) when he writes, 'If asked to suggest the single most important pillar upon which their culture rested, most Samoans would probably respond without hesitation that it was their system of chiefs'.[36] Access to chiefly titles and authority for women and men is further complicated by the fact that the many branches within each descent group own rights to specific titles, and all titles vary in rank, status, and historical depth.[37] A person may simultaneously obtain titles from several branches; residence, adoption, and even marriage allow individuals to align themselves, work for, and even gain chiefly titles from different descent groups at the same time. With many possibilities to hold titles, competition is endemic.[38] Unlike Trobriand chiefs, who are for the most part *primus inter pares* and politically control villagers within a relatively small geographical area, a Samoan titleholder wields authority over widely dispersed members of the descent group as well as members of other descent groups who have attached themselves or over those in other descent groups who have given him (or her) a title. Since all titles are ranked, chiefly authority is also ranked, from titles that bestow nobility to those that bring minimal prestige.

Samoan women, much like the Maori examples, use mana autonomously in both subversive and regenerative ways.[39] On the one hand, a sacred sister has the power to cause illness or even death; on the other hand, through her own mana, she insures that chiefly titles carry the potency and force of her mana.[40] Further, in political meetings, a sacred sister has the autonomous right to veto any decision concerning the conferring of a title on someone within the descent group. She can also arbitrate disagreements within the descent group to the point where she defies her brother. A sacred sister can 'throw her weight around the *'àiga* and tell off her brother even if he has a high title,' a Samoan elder emphatically told me.[41] Even from an early age, relationships between a woman and her brother remain socially close. A young man is the protector of his sister; he should always treat her with respect. As Shore points out, a man is extremely shy and deferential to his sister, even though men are assertive and domineering in other relationships.[42] Although women should act with dignity in public, they can openly chastise their brothers for being lazy, because men are expected to channel their energies productively for their sisters.[43] And, as in the Trobriands, it is exceptionally traumatic for a man to be told that his sister is married. But in contrast to the Trobriands, it is the sister–brother incest taboo that is extended as a standard for all young people to show, in general, the wrongness of premarital sexual relations.[44]

Thus the sibling incest taboo appears to be rigidly upheld, and most writers emphasize the prominence of premarital virginity for women, in the light of Samoa's traditional marriage ritual that proves a woman is a virgin.[45] But there is another side to the emphasis on virginity that involves the political power lodged in sibling intimacy. The virginity of a sacred sister until her marriage to a person of high rank ensures that her first-born son and daughter have access to titles of high rank through their father.[46] The issue of virginity, however, involves the special relationship of a woman's oldest son and daughter to her brother. By adopting his sister's first son, historically a common practice, a brother retains claims to the important titles to which the sister's son has full rights through his father.[47] In the same way, a woman's first-born daughter, who will become the sacred sister in the next generation, is also adopted to strengthen claims for her mother's descent group to the most sacred titles to which she may gain rights through her father and his sister. By marrying out, a sister reproduces children who, in becoming her brother's children, augment the resources to high titles for her and her brother.

Here at the core of the intricate complexity of Samoan chieftaincy we see that, although sibling marriage is taboo, its precepts are cultural practice as sisters reproduce children for their brothers. On another level, actual sibling sexual relations are neither denied nor subverted. Some of the most powerful spirits (*aitu*) who still return to the living even today are thought to have come into being through the circumstances of brother–sister sexual relations.[48] Historically, sibling marriage between a sacred sister and her brother was the ultimate way to achieve a titled chiefly line that had the greatest power. The genealogies of famous women and men chiefs reveal many cases of these brother–sister marriages, because sibling sexuality was thought to produce the most intense mana.[49] Still today, these genealogies that trace ancestral cases of brother–sister sexual relations demonstrate one's authority and power. When recited in the midst of a political debate over a title, the power of this knowledge when publicly revealed conclusively proves one's legitimate right to the title.

In Samoan kinship, the sister–brother relationship is the controlling force in the midst of long, complicated, and often contested genealogies and political strategies that allow for the incorporation into the descent group of many outsiders and the ranking and proliferation of titles that intricately cross and recross descent-group boundaries. The social and political closeness between sister and brother and even the public dominance of a sacred sister over the chief are evidence of the essentialness of this core relationship. The importance of keeping a sister reproductively united with her brother is enacted through cosmological connections to ancestors and the highest *mana*, through the cultural reproduction of each other's children, through access to titles through her children's father's descent group, all of which increase the ranking and the prerogatives of power and authority from which both she and her brother benefit.

The components that constitute principles of Samoan descent differ significantly from Trobriand descent, yet in both cases, sibling sexuality, mythologized or historicized, and its transformations into other essential sister–brother culturally reproductive areas create the elementary locus and force for the cultural reproduction of kinship and the political order. In both cases, sibling sexuality guards the unity of cosmological forces as these forces are reproduced for the next generation by women as sisters. And in both cases, sisters reproduce children for their own natal group. The Samoan solutions keep these sibling connections politically intact in the face of kinship diversity and genealogical ambiguity in all other kinship relations, generating far greater political authority and control than in the Trobriands. Hawaii provides a different example. In Samoa, because of the competition to maximize claims to titles within and across descent groups, a strong commoner–chiefly opposition occurs within each descent group. But the embeddedness of titles within descent groups to which anyone outside the group potentially can gain legitimate access prohibits the full emergence of a chiefly class, organizationally segmented from commoners with chiefly authority that, following Dumont, encompasses the group. This is the level of hierarchy that developed in Hawaii.

The Hawaiian Case

In ancient Hawaii the island populations were sharply segmented into chiefly and commoner divisions, with a noble class distinguished by eleven grades of sanctity involving rigidly held privileges and taboos.[50] Unlike those of the Trobriands and Samoa, Hawaiian descent groups were not the basis for kinship alignments. According to Valeri, kinship for commoners was ego-centred without reference to ancestral connections, whereas kinship among the nobles was ancestor-centred, as individuals publicly had to verify their connections to specific ancestors to legitimize their rights to the prerogatives of noble rank.[51] Sahlins points out that, in these latter cases, it is ascent rather than descent that matters, as individuals chose 'their way upward, by a path that notably includes female ancestors, to a connection with some ancient ruling line'.[52]

Vast diversity surrounds tracing up, as affinal ties and genealogically related connections through myriad branchings and multiple genealogical interpretations allow for and prevent the attainment of ancestral legitimation. Within this genealogical maze of actual and fabricated ancestral ties, brothers and sisters form the predominant focus for reckoning ascent through sisters. According to Jocelyn Linnekin, 'lines of women descended from a sister in a [brother–sister] sibling set occur in the Hawaiian chiefly genealogies', revealing the importance of women's transmission of mana as well as the political strategies and negotiations over genealogies in which women must have been engaged.[53] Although there is only minimal information about social organization among commoners, there was great fluidity in terms of multiple liaisons, residences, and group affiliations after marriage. Here, too, even among commoner groups, the elementary kinship principle for residence and land rights is the sister–brother sibling set.[54] Brother and sister often lived together after marriage, and older sisters served as the heads of households with considerable authority.[55]

Among the élite, great care was taken to ensure the highest and purest genealogical connections, at least for the first child, whether a boy or a girl, and the mother's rank always counted above the father's.[56] High-ranking women were surrounded by rituals indicating the sacredness with which all high-ranking births were held. Within the complexity of genealogical ascendancy, the pool for marriage partners that would produce the highest-ranking royal heirs was so rigidly segregated that sibling marriage was recognized as the most appropriate act for procreation. Although both women and men were polygamous, birthright and primogeniture for women and men provided the predominant claims to chiefly successions, with a child born to a very high-ranking brother and sister accorded the highest sanctity.

Sibling intimacy among Hawaiian Islanders was not disguised; it was an overt fact of the political order at the highest level of society. Samuel Elbert reported that seventeen marriages of blood relatives of high rank were noted in the tales and chants he examined, of which 'ten were between brother and sister'.[57] Keôpûolani, the first and most sacred wife of Kamehameha I, was born with divine rank because her parents were sister and half-brother to each other and their mother was of the highest rank. In fact, the sanctity and mana that surrounded Keôpûolani were so powerful that if a man inadvertently came into contact with her or her possessions, he would be killed.[58] Valeri, however, believes that Hawaiian women were denied access to gods and mana. Therefore, he describes the Hawaiian system of nobility as one in which the hierarchy of high-ranking men was encompassed by the gods within one single order because only men had access to the mana that came directly from the gods.[59]

As the example of Keôpûolani's powerful mana makes clear, high-ranking women were the agents who conveyed the most potent mana from the gods. This potency surrounded all rituals associated with giving birth as well as women's own temples and gods. Although Valeri denies that women had access to gods, female chiefs worshipped their own gods, and certain women had so much mana that they could enter men's temple precincts.[60] Furthermore, because Keôpûolani was of the highest rank and accorded all taboos associated with extreme nobility, her husband Kamehameha I worshipped her goddess, who was descended from Maui nobility.[61] And politically, a ruler's sisters were persons of great authority who held important offices in government, even after European contact, including the position of prime minister or queen.[62]

Although the Samoans and Hawaiian Islanders differ in the organization and structure of their descent and kinship systems, in all instances sibling intimacy is fundamental to the authentication of the highest mana and rank. Sisters act as a powerful stabilizing force, standing out as a link and autonomous executor in the great labyrinths of genealogical and affinal reckoning that occur in the pursuit of political power. In Hawaii, sibling marriage segments the highest ranks of society, affirming the uncompromised connections that sisters have to divine gods and the most efficacious mana. In Samoa, the sacred sister's mana similarly conferred ancestral sanctity and power on the highest titles, with the public recognition that ancestral sibling marriage had unparalleled political advantage. Although contemporary sibling marriage is openly abhorred, exogamous marriage in which children are adopted by their mother's brother enables siblings to reproduce their own children with access to titles that potentially establishes political control in the next generation.

Setting the Trobriand example beside the Polynesian cases reveals similar political potential in sibling intimacy and the prominence of women in cultural reproduction. But Trobriand sisters' involvement is to reproduce matrilineal identity by conserving the separation between ranking and non-ranking lineages. This reproductive work not only is invested in women reproducing their own children, but extends to their culturally reproductive activities with their brothers' children. Further, sibling intimacy depends on gaining resources from fathers and then marrying out to gain additional resources from spouses; but all these exchanges keep the boundaries contained between one matrilineage and another. In both Samoa and the Trobriands, women's marriages are the means to reproduce resources for themselves and their brothers: cloth, titles, and children. In Hawaii everything of political significance is controlled through those who claim the highest *mana*; in Samoa this control can only be effected by claiming the highest titles; in the Trobriands only the claim of an ancestral conception belief allows such control. In each case, however, economic resources are essential, and it is in these actions as they authenticate cosmological controls that the political authority of women as sisters is realized.

Cloth and Inalienable Possessions

The Hawaiian Case

In ancient Hawaii, brother and sister sexual relations and marriage create a political situation of autonomous endogamy in the marked division between nobles and commoners. We also find that cloth production was organized by class. Commoner women and men produced barkcloth fabrics, expressly as 'tribute' for nobles and island rulers as well as for their own household use and exchange, although there is very little information about the ritual and economic circulation of cloth as wealth.[63] Noble women produced only special kinds of cloth, but the highest veneration surrounded these fabrics. For example, sacred skirts constructed of ten thick layers of finely made barkcloth were worn only by high-ranking women. Such skirts were replicas of those worn by goddesses, which were thought to have magical properties, and the ritual restrictions and *tapu* states of women during cloth production indicated that the presence and powers of gods or goddesses entered into the cloth itself.[64] Women remained in a *tapu* state while producing this cloth, as did their implements and even the area where the cloth was prepared.[65]

Although Hawaiian barkcloth reached an unprecedented aesthetic zenith for the Pacific, Hawaii clothmaking is best represented today by the beautiful feather cloaks collected by early explorers and displayed in museums around the world. These cloaks, along with precious ornaments decorated with feathers, such as *leis*, feathered hair combs, helmets, and *kabili*, sacred insignia of rank (often called 'fly flaps' by early writers), were the exclusive inalienable property of the highest-ranking men and women rulers.[66] Chiefs wore feather cloaks in battle, and, as with the Maori, capturing such a cloak gave the victor claims to a more prestigious genealogy, for these validated the connections to particular high-ranking genealogies. Kamehameha I, in his rise to power, captured the prized feather cloak from his higher-ranking rival, Kalani'ôp'u, and by this ownership, validated his right to rule.

Who made and owned these high-ranking inalienable possessions is a subject of debate. As Linnekin points out, the most often-cited references to the manufacture of feather cloaks are by Peter Buck, who writes that, because the cloaks were imbued with *mana*, they had to be the property of men, and as such, they only could be made by men.[67] Later writers have simply accepted Buck's biased assumptions. However, feather garments and valuable feather ornaments were owned by high-ranking women, and women did play a role in their production.[68] Louis Freycinet in 1819 describes women producing feather cloaks, and Samuel Kamakau comments on a great feast for Ka'ahumanu, a politically powerful woman, who was 'borne by the chiefs upon a litter ... spread with feather cloaks and cushions'. In preparation for the feast, impressive feather fly flaps and a great feathered *lei* were prepared. In correspondence between Charles Reed Bishop and William Brigham concerning the collection of Hawaiian featherwork for the Bishop Museum, Bishop remarks that Liliuokalani loaned her few feather cloaks for photographs in Brigham's memoir on featherwork, but Kapi'olani, 'who owned some of the finest capes known', declined permission to have them photographed.[69] Although these references pertain to nineteenth-century élite women, there are other indications that women's ownership of featherwork had a long history, as two of the earliest descriptions of women rulers recorded during Captain Cook's voyage to Hawaii indicate. David Samwell describes the visit of a woman 'chief' who came on board his ship wearing great quantities of new barkcloth, boars' tusks on her arms, the prized whale-tooth ornament around her neck, and carrying the great chiefly fly flap – each a symbol of the highest-ranking chiefs.[70] After Cook's death, when his ships were anchored off Kauai Island, Captain Charles Clerke was visited by a 'Queen' and her daughter. Dressed in chiefly regalia, both women carried the treasured fly flap made with sacred feathers attached to human bone handles.[71]

Unfortunately, data are unavailable on the actual circulation of cloaks among Hawaiians, but many were exchanged for Western goods brought by European voyagers.[72] This suggests, as we find with the Maori, that trade and payments were made in cloaks, keeping other cloaks and chiefly insignia inalienable. Just as the styles of Maori cloaks varied through time, so too did the Hawaiian styles change dramatically following the visit of Captain Cook. As Adrienne Kaeppler shows, the feather cloaks came to be more and more associated with warfare and conquest, whereas the sashes were fabricated while genealogical chants were recited over them.[73] Kaeppler, following the traditional assumptions that because only men had mana only they owned these possessions, notes that the sashes would protect 'the chief's vital parts for the perpetuation of the societal ruling lines'.[74] When we recognize that women not only had access to mana but were the reproducers of the highest mana, then these sashes may have symbolized women's 'vital parts', acting as ancestral conduits through which procreative power was transmitted. Given high-ranking women's strategic management of genealogical verifications, the accepted association of men, mana, and feather cloaks is another ethnographic muddle in which women are simply ignored.

A further source, and perhaps the most important one, leaves no doubt that women did fabricate and control cloth that was imbued with the highest mana. This cloth brought the presence of gods directly into human affairs, making these women, rather than men alone, the agents of transfer between humans and gods.[75] In Hawaii one of the most vivid recorded examples comes from the Luakina ceremony, in which the consecration of a new ruler's temple took place. In Valeri's account, the Luakina ceremony is the precise ritual moment when chiefs become divine; but we never learn from him that during the major part of the ritual the prohibition about the segregation between the sexes did not apply.[76] As the moment of consecration approached, high-ranking chiefly women entered the temple precinct carrying huge pieces of specially fabricated white barkcloth. These cloths were exactly the same kind of fabric necessary for presentations at the birth of a high-ranking child.[77] This 'life-giving' cloth sanctified the temple when the women wrapped it around the god figures. Only then did the presence of the god enter the figure. Without the cloth, the image alone had no power, and the ruler could not be sanctified.[78]

In Hawaii, however, women did not just serve male rulers, they themselves took on full political office, ruling over districts and entire islands.[79] Their daughters and sons inherited these positions of autonomous authority from them. A woman's high rank gave her equal rights with men of similar rank, and many prerogatives over men of lesser rank, including her husband if she overranked him.[80] Although women as sisters were politically vital to their brothers, women as mothers and wives also had access to political office. Even though most cloth production was done by commoners, women and men rulers guarded their most prized cloaks as inalienable possessions that were to be inherited only within the appropriate genealogical lines. Élite women not only had access to feather objects that were the highest insignia of rank, such as fly flaps and cloaks, but they themselves controlled the most prized cloth of all – the sacred barkcloth described above used at high-ranking births and chiefly inaugurations to bring forth the divine presence of gods. As ancient Hawaii reached the highest level of political stratification found in Oceania, so too, élite women achieved full political and sacred status.

Although historically this sacred barkcloth expresses the power and status of Hawaiian women, the fabric also conveys the instability of power. The ancient Hawaiian political system gave women and men at the top vast latitude in autonomy and authority. But by excluding so many below who were less socially well-connected and less endowed with ancestral and godly *mana*, the way was left open for rival successors who attempted to alter genealogical connections or marry their way into higher ranks. This Hawaiian political drama intensified during the century prior to Western contact, leaving us with evidence of increasing warfare, the rising power of priests, and the elaboration of inalienable feather cloaks more as a symbol of men's victorious battles than of a long-reigning nobility. Prohibitions levelled at women by male priests impinged on women's autonomous hold over the highest sanctity and *mana*. Women's strong political hegemony over royal birth, cosmological authentication, and sacred cloth had to be contested if those without aristocratic privileges from birth were to gain ascendancy. To usurp women's containment of *mana* was, at the same time, to erode the aristocratic powers of men born into the highest noble classes. With the rise of Kamehameha I, these dynamics were already set in motion shortly before Captain Cook anchored in Kealakekua Bay.

The many references to Hawaiian women rulers in ancient genealogies, even though fragmentary, attest to the long history of women chiefs. Despite the erosion of the hegemony of the noble class and the effects of colonial governments and missionaries throughout the eighteenth and nineteenth centuries,

women continued to exercise power and political autonomy to
an unparalleled degree, another indication of their ancient ruling
presence. In the nineteenth century, the changes that élite women
initiated or carried out were strikingly radical, a sign of their vital
political dominance, support and power. For example, in 1823,
the chieftainess Kapi'olani defied the ancient gods and the priests
by breaking with sacrificial rituals. Four years previously, the
high chieftainess Keôpûolani dissolved the traditional eating
taboos, thereby firmly establishing Christianity against rival
factions. In another later revolutionary and decidedly feminist
venture, Liliuokalani opened a bank for women, the first of its
kind. Recognizing that the bulk of Hawaiian money acquired
through the inheritance of land was owned and controlled by
Hawaiian women, she established the bank to allow women,
especially those married to non-Hawaiians, to manage their own
affairs, making it less likely that their Western husbands would
take these monies from them. These changes, including women's
claims to leadership roles, often were contested by strong rival
political factions; but women managed to hold on to a large
measure of their authority and power. Such resistance also can be
seen in cloth production, which similarly underwent drastic
changes. The missionaries who arrived in the 1820s taught a few
élite women to sew patchwork. The skills of these women
quickly evolved into the fabrication of beautifully designed
quilts that are still made today. These quilts, presented at births,
marriages, and deaths, and to visiting royalty, continue to
accumulate histories that symbolize Hawaiians' indigenous,
sacred origins, which include the political presence of women.[81]

The Samoan Case

The power of Samoan sibling intimacy is lodged in reproduction,
mana, and the relation between a chief and his sacred sister. But
political potentiality is also acclaimed in the keeping and giving
of fine mats, the wealth of women and men. These are the plaited
pandanus fine mats that Mauss alluded to in the first pages of
The Gift: 'feminine property . . . more closely bound up with the
land, the clan, the family, and the person' than things called '*oloa*,
manufactured objects and food'.[82] Even though Samoans today
have a cash economy, they still exchange hundreds of fine mats

each time someone is born, at a marriage, a death, and the inauguration of a new titleholder.[83] For each event, fine mats are given and received in over twenty named categories that define specific kin and affinal relationships. Before being given, each one is ranked in terms of age, quality, name, and history; there are as many strategies in giving and keeping as there are fine mats.[84] The splendour of these presentations, especially when someone of high rank dies, is politically essential.[85] Samoan informants say that the sacred sister 'sits opposite the chief' in her responsibility for the well-being of the descent group, and it is she who officiates at the distribution of fine mats, when a death occurs or when a title from her descent group is conferred.[86]

Samoan fine mats are the wealth of both women and men, with the highest titleholder able to draw substantially on the wealth of others. But even with the huge distributions of fine mats, chiefs have great difficulty in accumulating fine-mat treasuries. First, chiefs eventually must replace all fine mats they have taken from their supporters. Second, their sisters, especially the sacred sister, accumulate and guard the most valued fine mats. At the commencement of any fine-mat distribution, the sacred sister is presented with a special fine mat to honour her dignity.[87] Even more important, after the event is over, the sacred sister must be given the best one the chief (her brother) has gained. A chief's sons, continuing this practice, give the highest-ranking fine mats to their father's sister or to her daughter.[88] These are the exchanges between brothers and sisters and their respective children that mark vital connections to expand control over titles. These possessions are the indices of how the political process works.

Sibling sexual relations are alluded to in the circulation of fine mats, as stories of incest figure centrally in origin stories associated with the ancient names of the most revered fine mats, giving these mats, when presented or kept, enormous political advantage. Most notably, the names given to high-ranking fine mats often refer to what are thought to be actual ancestral accounts of sibling sexual relations that were prominent because they involved the powerful mana of high rank. On the occasion of a woman's marriage and again at the birth of her first daughter, her brother brings her an extremely important fine mat. When she dies, her brother brings to her funeral another high-ranking fine mat, which he calls *ie o le measà* (*measà* means sacred genitals of either sex). This presentation symbolizes sibling sexual relations and reveals the sacred sister and her brother as the conserving and reproductive forces in the complex political and economic affairs of the descent group.[89]

Fine mats given at these presentations are among the most precious that people have. Usually they are kept for decades or generations, only to be presented when the politics of a marriage or, when a death demands it. Such revered fine mats are carefully stored, guarded as inalienable possessions because, like Maori cloaks, they authenticate claims to titles and mana.[90] Traditionally, the production of fine mats was under the authority of the highest-ranking women; the work itself was considered sacred. In production, women's own mana was infused into the fine mat, bringing women's access to the highest mana into economic circulation.[91]

Because of the inviolate power of a fine mat, its circulation was limited, as demonstrated by an ancient story.[92] A woman was to be married and the members of her descent group stood before her prospective husband's relatives with only one fine mat, whereas the latter had assembled a thousand of them. But when this simple fine mat was finally presented by the bride, thunder and lightning rent the skies, proclaiming the mana that made this fine mat prized far above any others. Since even a thousand fine mats could not match its honour and power, it was returned to the bride's kin. Even today, when a person brings a highly valued fine mat to a distribution and the receivers do not have an equivalent one to exchange, it must be returned to the givers. This is how fine mats become inalienable. They are not reciprocally exchanged for 'oloa, the category of manufactured things, food, or money, as most writers assume.[93] Fine mats always are exchanged for fine mats, but underlying this overt reciprocity are two endeavours: first, to keep the best ones inalienable, and second, with each exchange to show one's rank. This latter strategy takes great finesse because, in matching the values of fine mats, the game plan, unless one decides to comment unfavourably by returning a lesser fine mat, is to select one that is only a fraction more valued than the fine mat given. This is the way one asserts difference and conserves.

When a crisis erupts, however, the only strategy is to give up the most precious fine mat to which one has access. If a murder or rape is committed, the highest titleholder in the culprit's descent group immediately sits in front of the offended chief's house covered completely with a treasured fine mat.[94] If the offended chief accepts the fine mat, then further retaliation for the crime is brought to a halt. A Samoan friend asked me why I thought Samoans attributed such significance to pandanus strips that have no practical use at all. Answering his own question he replied that 'fine mats are more important than your gold. They are protection for life.' Much like the Maori example of giving up a treasured *taonga* to an enemy to thwart an attack, the strong possibility of defeat leaves no alternative but to give over one's most cherished inalienable possession.

Although Samoan women do not completely control the distribution of fine mats, in their roles as sacred sisters they have the opportunity to obtain those of the highest rank from their brother or his sons and even to keep them inalienable. In the past, a sacred sister's mana made her brother's title strong, just as women's production and control of fine mats strengthened the economic and political foundation of the title. In these ways, women as sisters assumed a base for political authority that, although less hierarchical than in Hawaii, still accorded them extensive political power, as women could, and still can, hold the highest titles. In fact, the four highest titles in all of Samoa, traced through female ancestral connections, once came under the rule and authority of one person who was a woman. In 1500 AD Salamasina held these titles, an achievement that for the first recorded time united all major traditional political districts under one person's rule.[95] Schoeffel shows that most of the great titles of Samoa today are descendants of Salamasina; Neil Gunson traces the dates for many other famous Samoan female rulers.[96]

Even in the early 1900s, Kramer wrote:

> girls and women of rank enjoyed an almost godlike veneration. It is not only through their prestige that they have great influence over their husbands and relatives and through them, over affairs of state, but titles and offices, even the throne are open to them.[97]

What makes Samoa an important example is its illumination of how difference institutionalized into ranking through sibling intimacy and cultural reproduction supersedes gender distinctions.[98] Because women are accorded chiefly authority and power as sacred sisters, on occasion they gain the same access to chiefly authority and power as men. To be sure, today there are many more male Samoan chiefs than women chiefs, but my point is that because women play a reproductive role of fundamental importance, they do become chiefs. Even today, some women claim the privileges and prerogatives of the highest political office.

Over the past hundred years, the effects of colonialism, especially missionization, deeply disrupted women's political power. Missionaries terminated women's endowment of mana and halted polygamy and a brother's adoption of his sister's children.[99] When women's access to *mana* was decried by church teachings, the dominant role that sisters held over chiefs was undermined. It is not coincidental that the Samoan word for sacred sister (*feagaiga*) is also the term for pastor. By weakening beliefs in the notions of mana, the church effectively undercut the once awesome sacred role of women as sisters; as the belief in *mana* was discredited, reckoning rank through women diminished in importance, since titles were no longer thought to be imbued with mana.[100] Preachers and priests, even today, define marriage in terms of women's submission to their husbands' wills, undermining the freedom that women had in their roles as sisters. European administrators, too, interfered with women's roles as they systematically tried to ban fine-mat exchanges. In the early 1900s, German and New Zealand administrators were shocked that fine-mat exchanges produced disagreements and fighting over debts and repayments, as well as over chiefly ranking.[101] Arguing that these huge distributions of fine mats prevented Samoans from learning the work ethic of capitalism, administrators tried to outlaw all fine-mat distributions, especially the more competitive ones at the installations of chiefs and at deaths, thereby further eroding, but by no means destroying, the power of all women, especially in their roles as sisters.

Yet the cultural configurations surrounding fine mats and the role of the sacred sister are so deeply embedded in what it means to be Samoan that missionaries and administrators could not completely dismantle these traditions. In order for a titleholder to be politically influential today, he must keep the support of his sacred sister; her veto power within the descent group's affairs still makes her a political ally or foe.[102] Élite women today who hold high titles are accorded the utmost respect and maintain a degree of dominance despite the strong patriarchal position of men. Although fewer women plait fine mats than in the past, the

demand for mats has increased, as they now circulate inter-
nationally – an intimate part of the lives of Samoans who now live
in San Francisco, Auckland, or Honolulu, and who still recognize
the power in keeping-while-giving. Fine mats still are the most
public forum in which Samoan women negotiate their political
presence, and are as prized and politically influential as ever.

The Trobriand Case

In contrast to the Polynesian examples, where cloth is essential at
all births, marriages, deaths, and the taking of titles or rulership,
Trobriand cloth wealth-bundles of dried banana leaves and
banana fibre skirts are necessary only when a death occurs in a
matrilineage. Then a major distribution of women's cloth takes
place, in which women disperse thousands of bundles and
hundreds of skirts. Today more than ever before, trade-store
cloth and even cash are added.[103] Villagers, primarily related
affinally or patrilaterally to the dead person, are the major
recipients of these cloth possessions, and the largest distributions
go directly to the deceased's father and spouse. By repaying all
'outsiders', women as sisters reclaim for their own matrilineage
all the care that went into making the dead person more than she
or he was at conception.[104]

Women are the sole producers, as well as the controllers of
Trobriand cloth wealth, but the full circulation of skirts and
bundles involves men. Although annual yams given by a man to
his married sister provide the fulcrum around which marriages
thrive, cloth wealth is attached to this pivot in the most basic
way. Because a man receives these annual yams from his wife
and her brother, he is obligated to provide his wife with his own
wealth to help her buy more cloth whenever a death occurs in
her matrilineage. In this way, a man reduces his own resources to
support his wife and her brother. Since most deaths are assumed
to be caused by sorcery, his help makes his wife and her brother
economically and politically strong when their matrilineage is
most under attack.

The use of cloth at each death demonstrates the political
vitality of a matrilineage and shows the particular strengths of
every marriage as well as each brother–sister relationship within
the lineage. The control over cloth wealth also enables women as

sisters to participate fully in the politics brought into play at a death as one woman emerges in each distribution as the wealthiest and most important woman of her matrilineage. Overall, these distributions give women a domain of political and economic autonomy that exceeds such roles for women in other Melanesian societies. Still, ownership of cloth and control of its distribution does not allow women public participation in most other chiefly political affairs.

These limitations are revealed in the very form of the Trobriand cloth that represents these relationships. First, the most valued Trobriand cloths are new bundles and skirts that are made specifically for each distribution, not ancient ones that have been treasured for years. Skirts and bundles not only lack historical substance: neither are they associated with ancestral connections, *mana*, or chiefly powers. Unlike land, ancestral names, and decorations, cloth wealth is not inalienable, so that women's control over these economic resources must be built up and re-established at every death. Second, cloth wealth is necessary only following a death; it does not demonstrate political support and alignments at a birth, marriage, or the inauguration of a chief, as we find in Samoa or among the Maori. There, the presentation of cloaks or fine mats shows political support (or its absence) from each of the multibranching descent groups. In the Trobriands, neither marriage nor chiefly succession establishes immediate wide-ranging political networks. Such influence and patronage accrue slowly after years of building up alliances. Only death triggers an immediate need for economic and political accounting, not just to show political stability but to free the dead person's lineage from debts to members of other matrilineages for the care of the dead person during life.

Skirts and bundles symbolize the 'purity' of matrilineal identity, reproduced through the ancestral and political union of brother and sister. This is the unity that each death undermines. Like the Samoan example of giving up fine mats in seeking absolution, skirts and bundles are used to exonerate the matrilineage from any retribution that the father and spouse of the dead person and their extended kin may claim for the care and attention they gave while the deceased was alive. In this sense, like Samoan fine mats, skirts and bundles are 'protection for life'. Protecting the survival of the matrilineage in its 'purest' form proceeds without problem through marriage and birth, but by the time of death, the investments made by members of other matrilineages must be reclaimed and replaced with cloth.

Reconciling these debts is accomplished at the cost of giving up matrilineage and marital wealth and thereby limiting women's political power. Men, too, are limited politically, because death and women's needs for cloth continually usurp their own accumulations of wealth. Whereas cloth distributions provide the economic base for a degree of ranking that gives some men more authority and power over others, it ultimately checks the level of ranking and the scope of men's political engagement. Even for the few chiefs who are polygynous, each wife that a chief takes obligates him to provide her with cloth wealth each time someone in her lineage dies. A husband's wealth is levelled to build up the political presence of his wife and her brother.

In the contemporary Trobriand situation, the value of bundles and skirts is continually being inflated, as younger men now have more access to cash and women's demands for larger quantities of skirts and bundles are an increasing drain on men's resources.[105] Some men, wanting to conserve their cash for other Western benefits, tell women that bundles have no practical use, making women rethink these traditions. But such challenges have unanticipated repercussions. Women insist that if they stop making bundles, the distributions will continue with skirts and trade-store cloth, thereby placing even greater financial hardships on men.

Keeping-While-Giving: Sisters and Inalienable Possessions

The exchanges that take place throughout a person's life dramatize social difference; but when difference is institutionalized into rank, the stakes of how much is exchanged and what possessions can be kept increase. To reveal difference and rank induces images of finite monopolies over things and people; but behind these appearances, the realities of competition, loss, and death never disappear. For this reason, the privileging of one inalienable possession over another limits power as much as it creates it. The possibility of loss, what

Beidelman calls 'the pathos in things', is so paramount to an inalienable possession's uniqueness that the more the possession grows in importance, the greater is the threat of its loss. To participate in exchange is to be conscious of this possibility. The relations between persons and things negotiated in each exchange bring together the force of these paradoxical conditions where difference is most sought after at the very moment it emerges and is held back. To transcend these opposing forces requires the will to destroy, usurp, command, and possibly die. Therefore, protecting one's social identity, searching for fame, and striving for immortality are always enacted against the threats of loss, expenditure, violence, and death.

In the Polynesian societies I discussed, inalienable possessions are the markers of the difference between one ranking person or group in the face of the flux of exchange that repays debts and obligations to all those outside the group. What creates the highest-ranking inalienable possession is its sacred authentication through mana that is thought to infuse the object itself. Here mana is not only reproduced in things via women and human reproduction, but this procreative force is transmitted to the activities associated with women's cloth production, making the cloth the carrier of political legitimacy. The Maori, Samoan, and Hawaiian examples reveal that rather than the elimination of women from participation in political affairs, gender is not subsumed by the political; élite women as sisters achieve authority and power in their own right and outrank many men.

Although the societies of the Trobriands, Samoa, and Hawaii each exemplify alternatives to the problems of keeping-while-giving, each attempted solution reveals the strengths and limitations of the political system. The labour-intensive process of making Trobriand skirts and bundles indicates how much production is necessary just to discharge indebtedness. Samoan fine mats are technically more elaborate; the greater intensive labour increases the economic value of each fine mat. With a kinship system of greater intricacy, Samoan fine mats are used not only to discharge obligations, but to signify the direction of political contests in the continuous rivalry over titles. The ranking of fine mats enables some to be kept out of circulation. To obtain this goal, huge quantities that can be exchanged must be produced. In this way, replacements for the best possessions heighten the possibilities to attain an impressive level of hierarchy. And in Hawaii, the most sacred cloth, in which the power of gods was directly present, had an ultimate authority that, from the beginning, never circulated.

In each of these cases, what gives women a political presence is the cosmological authentication that they reproduce in things and people. Cosmological authentication not only is fundamental for creating possessions that are more than bits of flax threads or dried pandanus strings; such authentication is vital to kinship relations. Sibling marriage keeps the cosmological authentication of rank, mana, and gods intact. Where sibling marriage is prohibited, cultural approximations and substitutions give rise to the cultural reproduction of alliances and identities in siblings' children, constituting strong sibling connections one or several generations removed. All these solutions are in response to a basic question with profound kinship and political implications: how to keep brothers and sisters reproductively active even with exogamous marriage. Marrying out is accomplished at a cost that involves much more than a pattern of reciprocal exchanges. Even when sibling sexual relations are safely embedded in the historical or mythical past, the beliefs and the political advantages of sibling intimacy continue to affirm that, *contra* Tylor, the choice is not simply between marrying out or being killed out. When reproducing rank is at stake, marrying out results in dying out unless sibling intimacy recreates rank through the reproductive processes of keeping-while-giving.

Yet sibling intimacy can also be the source of conflict and division. The validation of rank through cosmological authentication is embedded in women's connections to and control over human and cultural reproduction. But reproduction as the locus of power for women also becomes the site of their subordination, as women's control remains vulnerable to other powers and political ideologies. The potential for growth, production, and hierarchy is, at the same time, the source for decay, death, and domination. Women's control over cloth production is no exception. It is not easy to create heirlooms, to keep possessions inalienable and to authenticate hierarchical relationships while still creating enough replacements for other exchanges. The power to do so heightens one's political presence. For this reason the work of sisters in terms of what they produce and reproduce becomes the primary target for those who seek to redefine cosmological beliefs for their own economic and political aims. Western history is full of such examples, and so is that of Oceania.

From the perspective of changing world systems, it is not simply Western colonialism and capitalism that destroys traditional modes of production, nor is it only Christianity that subverts these islanders' cosmological beliefs. Internal changes brought about by competing groups, such as chiefly rivals and the growing power of a priestly hierarchy, can change the technology or alter the meanings of inalienable possessions so that women's presence in political events is decreased and comes under the control of men. Not only do we see these changes occurring in eighteenth-century Hawaii, but they have also been documented for the Andean region, showing how the growing power of the Inca subverted the economic and political authority that local Andean women once held.[106] Throughout human history, reproduction in its biological and cultural manifestations has always been the site of great political intensity. In the United States, the current political controversies over abortion and new reproductive strategies raging at all levels of government are witness to the ancient and historical unrivalled potency and power that resides in women's strategic roles in reproduction.

Notes

1. For ease of reading, I am more narrowly using *sibling* to refer only to the relationship between sisters and brothers unless otherwise noted.
2. See n. 27 to the Introduction and also n. 42 to Chapter 2 *in* Weiner 1992.
3. The debates have never ceased on the issues of sibling incest. See discussions of these debates and various conclusions in, Arens 1986; Goody 1956; Schneider 1976; also see de Heusch (1958) on the significance of sibling incest in African monarchies.
4. I recognize that Samoa and Hawaii each represent a different Polynesian cultural division, and I am not suggesting any particular point of contact in the rise of political stratification.

Samoa is part of Western Polynesia that includes other islands such as Pukapuka, Tonga, and the Tokelaus. Hawaii, in Eastern Polynesia, is culturally related to Tahiti, New Zealand, Easter Island, and the Marquesas. Burrows (1940) wrote a classic paper on these cultural and geographical divisions. See also Oliver 1989; Shore 1989.

5. Discriminations are made by elaborate physical and social taboos: Weiner 1976: 49–50, 237–8.
6. Thomas (1989) also points out that the Melanesia–Polynesia division has been overdrawn. This dichotomy and the corresponding diagnostic features of 'equality' and 'hierarchy' have thereby inhibited a more comprehensive understanding of Pacific Island societies.
7. I thank Gyorgy Feher for directing me to this quotation as cited in Shell 1988: 17.
8. Freud 1968 [1908]: 177.
9. Malinowski 1987 [1929]: 416.
10. Fortes 1953, 1958; but see Barnes 1973; and especially Schneider 1968.
11. Lévi-Strauss 1969 [1949]: 25.
12. Fortes 1957; Leach 1957; Schneider 1968; Spiro 1982.
13. Malinowski 1927: 80–1. Melford Spiro (1982) argues that not only was Malinowski mistaken in his ethnographic interpretations but that the Trobrianders have a more severe Oedipal complex than is found in Western societies. See Weiner (1985) for a different point of view.
14. Jones (1925) further showed that Trobriand conceptions of procreation in which the father was denied any role were unconscious expressions of the child's hostility toward his father, a view expanded by Robin Fox (1980) and Spiro (1982).
15. Parsons 1964; see Spiro 1982 for a traditional Freudian reinterpretation of Malinowski's assumptions about the Trobriand Oedipal complex.
16. Beidelman 1971: 181–201. Ultimately he suggests that these incidents may be 'a highly condensed way of describing the insoluble paradoxes or tensions centering upon the conflict between authority, age, and sexuality' (p. 196).
17. See Hopkins 1980 for many instances of brother–sister marriages in Roman Egypt.
18. In the Buganda monarchy of East Africa, a woman and her brother ruled together. Each had a separate palace, army, and

retainers (Ray 1991).

19. Lévi-Strauss 1969 [1949]; Schneider 1961.

20. Groves 1963: 15–30.

21. All chiefly matrilineages are ranked *vis-à-vis* each other, and only the chiefs from the highest-ranking ones are polygynous. But even these chiefs will not find wives unless they can demonstrate their political power (see Weiner 1976: 44–50).

22. Malinowski also reports this: 'The waiwaia [spirit child] is conveyed by a baloma [an ancestor] belonging to the same subclan as the woman, . . . the carrier is even as a rule some near veiola [matrilineal kin]' (1954: 220). Some Trobrianders say a female relative brought the child, but others insist it must be a male relative, emphasizing the ambiguity. In the specific examples Malinowski gives, it is most often a man (ibid.: 219). Even today, when most villagers are aware of Western biological explanations, many still point out how pregnancy began with dreams of male ancestors bringing the spirit child (see Weiner 1976: 121–2, 1988: 53–5 for other examples).

23. Malinowski 1922: 177–80. Men also give their children food and other things. When children become adults they, in turn, support their fathers in economic ways that directly benefit their father and the members of his matrilineage. See Weiner 1976: 121–67 for an in-depth discussion of the exchange relations that involve a man as father.

24. This controversy has had a long-standing history in anthropology (Delaney 1986; Franklin 1988; Leach 1966; D. Schneider 1968b; Spiro 1968, 1982; Weiner 1976, 1988).

25. Malinowski 1987 [1929]: 440.

26. Lévi-Strauss 1969 [1949]: 496. Lévi-Strauss goes on to show that the authority figures are men, who reverse the disequilibrium created by giving a woman to another group of men, whereas their children only serve to validate the perpetuation of these alliances through time.

27. See Weiner 1976, 1988 for details of these exchanges, which differ somewhat from Malinowski's descriptions.

28. Although this kind of marriage rarely occurs, most marriages are with a father's sister's daughter three generations removed (also called *tabu*), so that the rule of marriage given by Trobrianders is accurate in the majority

of cases (Weiner 1979). Also see Fortes 1957; E. Leach 1958; Malinowski 1987 [1929] for earlier arguments about Trobriand kinship terms and father's sister's daughter's marriage.

29. See the same themes in Malinowski 1987 [1929]: 429, 113 and Weiner 1987.

30. Feher (1990) points out these differences. The original text recorded and transcribed by Malinowski reads: *Gala ikamkwamsi, gala imomomsi, u'ula ikarigasi* (1987 [1929]: 465), which means, 'They do not eat, they do not drink, this is the reason they die.' Malinowski's informant's commentary reads: *Gala sitana ikamkwamsi, imomomsi, pela gala magisi, boge ivagi simwalisila, pela luleta ikaytasi* (p. 472). This translation is: 'They do not eat even a bit or drink, they have no desire because of their shame, because they slept together' [translations mine].

31. The exact words of powerful magic spells state that the affected one will refuse all food and all drink. See an example of such magic in Weiner 1983: 704.

32. It is as if all the elaborately ritualized intense sexuality that pervades so much of Trobriand adolescent life is another attempt, unsuccessful at the extreme, to disguise the power of sibling sexuality.

33. For ease of reading, I translate *'àiga* as 'descent group', but, in actuality, the group at any one time or event may only be represented by certain branches rather than the entire unit. See Shore 1982 for an excellent discussion of Samoan kinship.

34. At its core, the members of this descent group trace their ancestry either to a founding woman whose descendants, both male and female, comprise the kin category known as *tamafafine*, or to a founding man, usually thought to be the brother of the female founder, whose descendants comprise the category, *tamatane*: Shore 1982: 236.

35. The term *feagaiga* means 'perpetual kinship' between the two; also 'covenant' or 'agreement'; as a verb, it means 'to stand opposite' or 'to face each other' (Milner 1966: 8). A woman's sacred relationship to her brother and his children extends to the sacredness of her son, called *tamasà*, the sacred child, and to all those who stand as *tamafafine* to her brother.

36. Shore 1982:58. Also see pp. 58–97 and 221–83 for more extensive data on the complexity of Samoan chiefly

organization.
37. See Shore 1982: 91–5 for examples. See also Kramer (1958 [1923]) on the histories of high titles before Samoa was colonized.
38. Titleholders, both women and men, are selected by members of a descent group with the sacred sister's agreement. The highest titles usually are traced specifically to the founders of the original title. Titles of lower rank can be created at any time; one title can be split among several holders; some titles are even destroyed.
39. Kramer 1930 [1902], 1: 54. Kramer gives an example on p. 20 of how a title became so powerful that the holder threatened to become dangerous even to his own descent group, because the title was thought to have increased in power though the efforts of Nafannu, the goddess of war. Huntsman and Hooper (1975: 424) point out that anthropologists emphasize the cursing power of the sacred sister, whereas the other more beneficial powers in which sisters act as 'spiritual' mothers to their brothers' children are ignored. Sacred power, as Beidelman (1986) has shown for ancient Greece and East Africa, is by its very nature ambiguous – at one turn subversive, evil, even mischievous, and at another turn, productive, generative, and imaginative.
40. Schoeffel (1981, 1987) shows that the cosmological justification for rank associated with mana depended upon mana being passed down through women; see also Kramer 1930 [1902]. The sacred sister also receives the high-ranking *tapou* title at an early age. Similarly, her brother, who is destined to become a chief, was given the high-ranking *manaia* title, so that prior to their marriages, brother and sister together officially represented the status, prestige, and potential of the descent group's main branches. Traditionally, they were the leaders, respectively, of the village organization of men and the village organization of women. See Shore 1982: 101–5 on the men's *'aumàga* organization and the women's *aualuma* organization and the contemporary changes. See also Schoeffel 1977 on the origin and organization of women's community associations that replaced the *aualuma* when the missionaries reduced its importance.
41. Of course, the power of individual women varies; if a

woman does not care to enforce and realize her rights, the rights disappear. See also Schoeffel 1981 for contemporary examples of women's decision-making authority.

42. Shore 1982: 235. Only when a young woman is discovered sleeping with someone before marriage does her brother forget his proper role and become angry and often violent with her (ibid.). Further, although a girl and her brother should remain isolated from each other within the household, a man is expected to provide his sister with anything that she needs. Following her marriage, he also accords her husband the highest respect. See also Stuebel, cited in Kramer (1930 [1902], 2: 98).

43. Shore 1982: 235.

44. Shore's informants told him that when 'you think of their brothers, then you have love and pity for the girls, and you know that sex with them is bad' (1982: 229).

45. In the literature this marriage ritual is spoken of as 'defloweration', a highly sexist word that comes from stripping flowers off a plant, or the act of a flower shedding its pollen, and then was applied to the loss of virginity through ravishing. Despite the emphasis placed on virginity for high-ranking women at marriage, marriages of women who were not sacred sisters often took place by elopement, thereby avoiding the ritual.

46. Before the changes missionaries inflicted on these practices, élite women also practised serial monogamy, securing the possibility of rights to various titles in more than one affinal descent group for their own natal kin groups.

47. Schoeffel 1987: 188.

48. Cain 1971: 174.

49. Schoeffel explains that such incestuous marriages produce a heightening and potentially dangerous concentration of *mana*, and therefore incest is deemed the origin of the highest-ranking titles. See especially the discussion of Malietoa La'auli, the son of a brother and sister union (Schoeffel 1987: 186).

50. Beckwith 1932: 195–8.

51. Valeri 1990.

52. Sahlins 1985: 20.

53. Linnekin 1990: 66–8. Reading chiefly genealogies in terms of the direction of marriage exchanges, Linnekin points out that

a pattern emerges in which 'lines of women [from brother–sister sibling sets], three to five generations long, give wives to lines of men' (p. 64).

54. Linnekin 1990: 137–52.
55. Ibid.:154. Kamakau (1961: 315) notes: 'Women in those days were especially devoted to their brothers, and brothers to their sisters. It was common to see younger sisters sitting in their brothers' laps. Brothers chanted verses composed in honour of their sisters, and sisters of their brothers as a sign of devotion.'
56. Malo 1951: 54–5; Kamakau 1964: 9.
57. Elbert 1956/1957: 342. Further, Elbert (p. 346) states that Kenneth Emory in his lectures traced the record of marriages of close relatives from unpublished sources. He listed nine such marriages in the eighteenth and nineteenth centuries, beginning five generations before Kamehameha I. Since marriage and other claims could alter genealogical legitimacy of the most senior lines, in cases where marriage did not occur between true brothers and sisters, marriages between the children from two husbands of a high-ranking woman chief had the second priority, with marriages of classificatory brothers and sisters of high-ranking women deemed the third most sacred (Goldman 1970: 214). Even in those cases where outstanding abilities qualified a person for rulership, a noble had to trace a genealogical connection to at least one ancestor in the senior line within a ten-generation limit (Malo 1951: 192).
58. Sinclair 1971: 3–4.
59. Valeri 1985.
60. Tihi, a female god, was held in such great veneration by the people of Maui that she received the same veneration as the male god, Keoroeva (Ellis 1833, 4: 72); further, both men and women priests officiated at certain temples. See n. 76 and examples from Ellis 1917 [1827]: 67; Kamakau 1964: 20, 28, 67; Malo 1951: 82, 178, n. 7. Compare Valeri (1985), who argues that only Hawaiian men stood in direct descent with gods (see Chapter 2, nn.42 and 43).
61. Sinclair 1971: 6. Kamakau (1964: 20, 28) shows that women had their own temples with their special gods and goddesses.
62. Malo 1951: 191.

63. Hawaiian fine mat and tapa production reached an unparalleled development equalled in this part of the world only by the barkcloth made in Indonesia by the Toradja of central Celebes (Kooijman 1972: 99). Unfortunately, descriptions of Hawaiian barkcloths and fine mats and the exact details of their circulation remain fragmentary because production and use of traditional cloth was discontinued by the mid-nineteenth century. At death, barkcloth was used for wrapping and burying the body, especially of those of high rank (Green and Beckwith 1926: 177–80; Malo 1951: 97; Kamakau 1964: 12). See also Linnekin 1990 for other examples of household use of barkcloth and mats.

64. Donald Rubenstein (1986: 60) writes that in Micronesia, ritual fabrics 'symbolically transform the wearer, tangibly imbuing him or her with spiritual force'. Further, the art of weaving is highly esteemed because it is thought to be 'a gift from the gods'.

65. These skirts were called *pa'u* (Kooijman 1972: 167) and this is also the word used for certain feather cloaks (see Brigham 1899: 59). See Buck 1957:181. Linguistically, the connections between rank and biological reproduction extended to cloth. In Hawaii as well as Tahiti the word matahiapo is often used honorifically to refer to a distinguished chiefly title (Koskinen 1972: 16). *Mata* means first, whereas *hiapo* refers to barkcloth, and according to Handy (1927: 47), the term *makahiapo* was derived from the banyan tree, which provided the special barkcloths worn by the highest-ranking nobles. Further, when a woman died during the birth of her first child, it was said that the *hiapo* closed, the word referring to the woman's loincloth and to her womb (Koskinen 1972: 17).

66. See Kaeppler 1985.

67. Buck 1957; Linnekin 1990: 47. Malo reports that a cloak made only of *mamo* bird feathers 'was reserved exclusively for the king of a whole island, . . . it was his . . . battle cloak'. Also, fine cloaks were used as the regalia of great chiefs and those of high rank, and could not be worn by men of lesser rank (1951: 77). Although Hawaiian women also ruled over entire islands, their possessions are rarely discussed.

68. See also Linnekin 1990: 47–55.

69. Freycinet 1978 [1827–1839]: 85; Kamakau 1961: 183. Brigham (1899) refers to the feather cloak worn by Princess

Nak'ena'ena and knew about the cloaks owned by Liliuokalani and Kapi'olani; see Kent 1965: 210 on Bishop's correspondence with Brigham.

70. Samwell 1967 Vol. 3, Part. 2, p. 1,160. Malo notes that the carved whale tooth and the fly flap were both the 'emblem and embellishment of royalty' (1951: 77), but he only mentions kings.

71. Clerke 1967, 3, pt. 1: 576–7.

72. Linnekin 1990: 52–4.

73. Kaeppler 1985: 111–16.

74. Ibid.: 107. Malo states that the ancestry of high-ranking Hawaiians was recorded for each individual in long chants that, not surprisingly, were literally called 'to weave a song' (1951: 139, n. 5).

75. See Malo 1951: 148; Kooijman 1972: 165 for examples. The idea that cloth itself attracted and contained the gods and their powers is found elsewhere in Polynesia (see the Maori examples in Chapter 2). Among the ancient Tahitians, when the finest barkcloths made by women were spread out, the spirits of the deceased ancestors and gods would enter the cloth and join in ritual events (Henry 1928: 177). Further, special undecorated cloths made by women were wrapped in bales and hung from the ridgepoles and side beams of the sacred houses where the treasures and figures of the gods were kept (p. 153). See Rubenstein (1986) for Micronesian examples. In many other parts of the world, cloth is used in similar ways. See Feeley-Harnik's essay (1989) on Madagascar, where, among the Saklava, cloth was the agent for inducing spirit possession of former rulers; Gittinger 1979 on similar examples from Indonesia; and Renne 1990 on the sacred properties of special kinds of Yoruba cloth.

76. The term *malo kea* referred to a white loincloth and also was used as an epithet for a woman who enjoyed men's privileges. She was exempt from female taboos and could enter the temple sites at any time (Pukui and Elbert 1965: 215).

77. Kamakau 1964: 12. Many other details of this temple ritual demonstrate how closely it follows the rituals observed for the birth of a high-ranking child, such as when braided coconut leaves were wrapped around the belly of the wooden god figure and were called the 'navel cord of its

mother' (Malo 1951: 173). When this was cut, the idol was then girded with fine cloth (Malo 1951: 173–4; see also Valeri 1985: 289–300).

78. In ancient Tahiti, when cloth was wound around a priest's arm, it indicated that a god had entered into the individual's body. See also E. S. C. Handy's (1927: 149) similar accounts. See Mayer (1988) on the use of cloth on Hindu goddess figures which empowers male rulers. Shore (1989) presents a compelling discussion about the way tapu states were associated with protection and binding, so that 'to be tapu was to be empowered, but it was also to be immobilized. . . . to be bound to divine potency and was therefore a considerable burden' (p. 154). See Cook's journals (Beaglehole 1967, 1: 207–8), in which he describes how Tahitian men and women were wrapped in great quantities of barkcloth before the cloth's presentation (see also Ellis 1917 [1827]: 361). Compare the view of Valeri, who, citing the instances when Hawaiian women also rolled themselves in masses of barkcloth, argues that the woman 'represents a wild potentiality that has been tamed and made productive by her husband' (1985: 301).

79. See Gunson 1987: 171 for a list of Hawaiian women rulers.

80. See W. Ellis 1782: 87; Revd. W. Ellis [1827] 1917: 89, 312; 1833, 4: 299; Fornander 1969 [1878–1885], 2: 128, 130, 210, 269; and Kamakau 1964: 10, 20 for specific references to women rulers in earlier centuries. Even after intensive Western contact enabled Kamehameha I to unify his dominance over all the islands, several of his wives and sisters became powerful regents and came to rule for many years (Kamakau 1961; Linnekin 1990).

81. See Allen 1982: 162 on Liliuokalani's banking venture and Hammond 1986 on Hawaiian quilt-making.

82. Mauss 1954 [1925]: 7. Margaret Mead (1930: 73–5) briefly noted the economic importance of fine mats and how they gain value through the expertise of the women who make them.

83. Traditionally fine mats were also used as payments for all services. Today they are still essential, added to money, for certain services, and huge amounts of fine mats are amassed for the opening of churches, schools, or government buildings. A new fine mat, never as valuable as an old one, sells for two hundred dollars or more in the Apia local

market. Large sales of fine mats for American dollars are made to Samoans living in American Samoa because, although production had fallen off there, fine mats exchanges are still essential.

84. See Weiner 1989 for examples of these distributions. In Western Samoa, even though the fine mats sold in Apia's main market are extremely expensive, a new fine mat, regardless of the price paid, cannot replace the value of an old one, even if it is patched and faded brown with age. But in the hundreds of fine mats that circulate for an event, only those presented in certain categories, such as the fine mat of 'farewell' when someone dies, are extremely valuable. Samoans deliberately hoard high-ranking fine mats for important occasions, and the most ancient and valued ones remain stored away for generations, making them inalienable. So important are the strategies in keeping and giving that, at times, a person decides to hold his own funeral distributions of fine mats before he dies, thereby ensuring that the valuable ones are given to the appropriate people. When he dies, even though it may be years later, he is buried without further exchanges.

85. At an event for a chief, each fine mat presented is a political message about the chief 's support. See the examples of actual cases in Kramer (1930 [1902], 2: 50–7, 386–8). These distributions also demonstrate how kin relationships overlap and show the fluidity and boundaries of kin alliances.

86. Shore (1981) presents a different view of Samoan gender relations based on a structural analysis of dual oppositions in which he ranks women secondary to men. But he does not discuss the historical, economic, and political importance of women and fine mat production.

87. Just as chiefs select an orator to talk for them in political debates, so women also select an orator who will pronounce the name and giver of each presentation. At every major exchange event, a woman's brother first makes a formal presentation to her. Called a *sua*, it includes one of a kind of all major foods, such as a coconut, a small pig, and a yam, plus an exceptionally valuable fine mat.

88. Stuebel, as quoted in Kramer (1930 [1902], 1: 100), notes that a chief tells his sons: 'If one of our children takes a wife, the titi ... [fine mat] of the bride is to be brought to my sister and her son. ... Barkcloths and whatever you obtain you are

to take first to my sister and her son!'

89. These exchanges from a man to his sister, like the *sua*, mark the care and dignity given to those who stand as *tamafafine* to those in the *tamatane* category. Similar associations of sisters with sexuality and reproduction are also expressed in the category names of other fine mat distributions. For example, *àfuafu* means to become pregnant and *'afu;* is the name for fine mats presented from the groom's kin to the bride (Milner 1966: 6). *Fa'atupu'* means the breaking of the hymen; the fine mat given as *fa'atupu'* also refers to the impending pregnancy of the women. This is also the name for the highest-ranking fine mat presented at a marriage, and, in cases of elopement, this fine mat is presented at the birth of the first child. See also Koskinen 1972: 17.

90. Kramer 1930 [1902], 1: 54. Ella writes that fine mats were 'often retained in families as heirlooms, and many old *'ie* [fine mats] are well-known and more highly valued as having belonged to some celebrated family. On this account an old and ragged *'ie-toga* would be more prized than a new and clean mat' (1899: 169).

91. Ella notes that 'the manufacturé of the *'ie* [fine mats] is the work of women and confined to ladies of distinction, and common people dare not infringe the monopoly, which is *sà* (*tabu*, or sacred)' (1899: 169).

92. In Samoa, the severing of the umbilicus was performed in a ritualized manner, so that, for example, a Samoan girl's umbilical cord was cut on the board women used to make barkcloth, whereas for a male infant, the umbilical cord was cut on a club, so that he would become strong in warfare (Ella 1892: 621; Turner 1884: 175).

93. See Weiner 1989: 53–4 for details of these exchanges and a discussion of the way exchanges of fine mats and *oloa* have been described in Shore 1982 as reciprocal exchange.

94. See Shore 1982: 19–20 for a contemporary example; also see Mead 1930: 43. Rubenstein (1986: 62–3) notes that on Truk Island a man guilty of adultery or even of proposing adultery to another man's wife had to repay the crime with 'a gift of loincloths', whereas on Faris Island, contemporary divorce payments to the dishonoured spouse still include vast quantities of traditional fabric goods as well as store-bought blankets and cotton cloth.

95. See Kramer 1958 [1923]. The bestowal of high-ranking titles necessitates approval from major branches of the descent group, measured in fine mats. In the last century, a contender for one of the highest titles defeated another 'lawful antagonist' because he had the support of two strong branches, 'owing to their wealth in fine mats' (Kramer 1930 [1902], 1: 26). Another account described how succession to one of the four highest titles only occurred when eight branches of the descent group came forward with huge piles of fine mats (ibid.: 387). When the histories of these special ine mats are read, it becomes clear why certain descent groups and specific titles became so powerful over the last two hundred years (ibid.: 57).

96. Gunson 1987; Schoeffel 1987.

97. Kramer 1930 [1902], 1: 68–69. Ella notes that 'failing a male heir, a daughter may be appointed to, or she may assume, the prerogative of chieftainship' (1892: 631).

98. Untitled Samoan men and women are forbidden participation in village political events, just as they are unable to accumulate fine mats of distinction. As of 1981, untitled men were not even permitted to vote in the national elections.

99. Schoeffel 1977, 1981.

100. The Catholic Church's insistence on serial monogamy also lessened the political advantages of women. Schoeffel claims that female statuses were redefined, and although today many more women hold titles than they did historically, the ritual authority of sisters is limited and a greater degree of patriarchal authority exists (1987: 192). Elsewhere, Schoeffel (1981) makes a convincing case for the political importance of Samoan women before missionary influences. Also see Schoeffel 1987 and Gunson 1987 on the matrilineal transmission of rank.

101. See Linnekin 1991 for additional data on how Western administrators tried to make Samoans convert fine mats into monetary equivalences. Since even then there was much transporting of fine mats between Samoans living in American Samoa and Western Samoa, one administrative issue raised was whether the importing and exporting of fine mats should be subject to duty.

102. This support also includes those who are identified as *tamafafine*. Further, those who trace their genealogical connections through *tamafafine* links are still treated with the utmost respect by those who identify themselves as *tamatane*. Unless an individual holding a title, even one of the highest rank, receives the support of the members of his or her descent group, the title is 'empty' and the chief has no power at all.

103. Since the introduction of cash and Western goods in the latter half of the nineteenth century, inflation has grown in the numbers of bundles and skirts women need. Today, this is even more intensified with the use of cloth and cash.

104. Weiner 1988: 134–6.

105. These contemporary issues are explored in the film *The Trobriand Islanders of Papua New Guinea* (Wason 1990).

106. My argument differs somewhat from the case Irene Silverblatt (1987) describes. Whereas she argues that the establishment of the state transformed gender equality into gender hierarchy, I show that in Samoa, for example, gender hierarchy did not depend upon the emergence of the state.

References

Allen, Helena G. (1982). *The Betrayal of Liliuokalani: The Last Queen of Hawaii 1838–1917*. Arthur H. Clark, Glendale, CA.

Arens, William (1986). *The Original Sin*. Oxford University Press, New York.

Barnes, John A. (1973). Genetrix: Genitor: Nature: Culture. In: *The Character of Kinship*, ed. J. Goody, pp. 61–74. Cambridge University Press, Cambridge.

Beaglehole, John C. (ed.) (1967).*The Journals of Captain James Cook on His Voyage of Discovery. Vol. 3, The Voyage of the* Resolution *and* Discovery *1776–1780, Parts 1 and 2*. Cambridge University Press (for the Hakluyt Society), Cambridge.

Beckwith, Martha W. (1932). Kepelino's Traditions of Hawaii. *Bernice P. Bishop Museum Bulletin*, 95. Bernice P. Bishop Museum, Honolulu.

Beidelman, Thomas O. (1986). *The Moral Imagination in Kaguru Modes of Thought*. Indiana University Press, Bloomington.

—— (1971). Some Kaguru Notions about Incest and Other Sexual Prohibitions. In: *Rethinking Kinship and Marriage*, Rodney Needham, (ed.), pp. 181–202. Tavistock Publications, London.

Brigham, William T. (1899). Hawaiian Feather Work. *Memoirs of the Bernice P. Bishop Museum*, 1(1), 1–86. The Museum, Honolulu.

Buck, Peter (Te Rangi Hiroa) (1957). Arts and Crafts of Hawaii. *Bernice Bishop Museum Bulletin*, 45. Bishop Museum Press, Honolulu.

Burrows, Edwin G. (1940). Culture Areas in Polynesia. *Journal of the Polynesian Society*, 49, 349–63.

Cain, Horst (1971). The Sacred Child and the Origins of Spirit in Samoa. *Anthropos*, 66, 173–81.

Clerke, Charles (1967). *Journal*. See Beaglehole (1967).

Delaney, Carol (1986). The Meaning of Paternity and the Virgin Birth Debate. *Man* (NS), 21, 494–513.

Elbert, Samuel H. (1956/1957). The Chief in Hawaiian Mythology. *Journal of American Folklore*, 64, 99–113, 341–55 and 70, 264–76, 306–22.

Ella, Samuel, Revd. (1899). Polynesian Native Clothing. *Journal of the Polynesian Society*, 8, 165–70.

—— (1892) Samoa. *Report of the Fourth Meeting of the Australian Association for the Advancement of Science*, pp. 620–44. Australian Association for the Advancement of Science, Sydney.

Ellis, William, Revd. (1782). *An Authentic Narrative of a Voyage Performed by Captain Cook*, 2 vols. Goulding, London.

—— (1917 [1827]). *A Narrative of a Tour Through Hawaii, or Owhyhee; with Remarks on the History, Traditions, Manners, Customs, and Language of the Inhabitants of the Sandwich Islands*. Hawaiian Gazette, Honolulu.

—— (1833). *Polynesian Researches During a Residence of Nearly Eight Years in the Society and Sandwich Islands*, 4 vols. J. & J. Harper, New York.

Feeley-Harnik, Gillian (1989). Cloth and the Creation of Ancestors. In: *Cloth and Human Experience*, ed. Annette B. Weiner and Jane Schneider, pp. 73–116. Smithsonian Institution Press, Washington, DC.

Feher, Gyorgy (1990). A Cultural Interpretation of the Trobriand Sibling Incest Taboo, MA thesis, New York University.

Fornander, Abraham (1969 [1878–1885]). *An Account of the Polynesian Race*, 3 vols. Charles E. Tuttle, Rutland, VT.

Fortes, Meyer (1957). Malinowski and the Study of Kinship. In: *Man and Culture: An Evaluation of the Work of Bronislaw Malinowski*, ed. Raymond Firth, pp. 157–188. Routledge and Kegan Paul, London.

—— (1953). The Structure of Unilineal Descent Groups. *American Anthropologist*, 55, 17–41.

Fox, Robin (1980). *The Red Lamp of Incest*. E. P. Dutton, New York.

Franklin, Sarah B. (1988). The Virgin Birth Debates: Biology and Culture Revisited. MA thesis, New York University.

Freud, Sigmund (1968 [1908]). Family Romances. In: *The Standard Edition of the Complete Pychological Works of Sigmund Freud*, ed. James

Strachey, Vol. 9. Hogarth Press, London.

Freycinet, Louis Claude de Saulses de (1978 [1827–1839]). Hawaii in 1819: A Narrative Account by Louis Claude de Saulses de Freycinet, trans. Ella W. Wiswell, ed. Marion Kelly. *Pacific Anthropological Records*, 26. Bishop Museum Press, Honolulu.

Gittinger, M. (1979). *Splendid Symbols: Textiles and Tradition in Indonesia.* Textile Museum, Washington, DC.

Goldman, Irving (1970). *Ancient Polynesian Society.* University of Chicago Press, Chicago.

Goody, Jack (1956). A Comparative Approach to Incest and Adultery. *British Journal of Sociology*, 7, 286–305.

Green, Laura C. and Beckwith, Martha W. (1926). Hawaiian Customs and Beliefs Relating to Sickness and Death. *American Anthropologist*, 28, 176–208.

Groves, Murray (1963). Western Motu Descent Groups. *Ethnology*, 2, 15–30.

Gunson, Neil (1987). Sacred Women Chiefs and Female 'Headmen' in Polynesian History. *Journal of Pacific History*, 22, 139–71.

Hammond, Joyce C. (1986). *Tifaifai and Quilts of Polynesia.* University of Hawaii Press, Honolulu.

Handy, E. S. C. (1927). Polynesian Religion. *Bernice P. Bishop Museum Bulletin*, 34. Bishop Museum Press, Honolulu.

Henry, Teuira (1928). Ancient Tahiti. *Bernice P. Bishop Museum Bulletin*, 48. Bishop Museum Press, Honolulu.

Heusch, Luc de (1958). *Essais sur le symbolisme de l'inceste royal en Afrique.* Université Libre de Bruxelles, Brussels.

Hopkins, Keith (1980). Brother–Sister Marriage in Roman Egypt. *Comparative Studies in Society and History*, 22, 303–54.

Huntsman, Judith and Hooper, Antony (1975). Male and Female in Tokelau Culture. *Journal of the Polynesian Society*, 84, 415–30.

Jones, E. (1925). Mother-Right and the Sexual Ignorance of Savages. *International Journal of Psychoanalysis*, 6, 109–30.

Kaeppler, Adrienne L. (1985). Hawaiian Art and Society: Traditions and Transformations. In: *Transformations of Polynesian Culture*, ed. Anthony Hooper and Judith Huntsman, pp. 105–31.The Polynesian Society, Auckland.

Kamakau, Samuel Manaiakalani (1964). *Ka Poe Kahiko: The People of Old*, ed. Dorothy Barrere. Bernice P. Bishop Museum, Honolulu.

—— (1961). *Ruling Chiefs of Hawaii.* Kamehameha Schools Press, Honolulu.

Kent, Harold Winfield (1965). *Charles Reed Bishop: Man of Hawaii.* Pacific Books, Palo Alto, CA.

Kooijman, Simon (1972). Tapa in Polynesia. *Bernice P. Bishop Museum Bulletin*, 234. Bishop Museum Press, Honolulu.

Koskinen, Aarne A. (1972). *Ariki the First Born: An Analysis of a Polynesian Chieftain Title*. Academia Scientiarum Fennica, Helsinki.

Krämer, Augustin (1958 [1923]). Salamasina, trans. the Association of Marist Brothers. E. Schweizerbart, Stuttgart.

—— (1930 [1902]). *The Samoan Islands*, 2 vols., trans. D. H. and M. DeBeer. E. Schweizerbart, Stuttgart.

Leach, Edmund R. (1958). Concerning Trobriand Clans and the Kinship Category Tabu. In: *The Developmental Cycle in Domestic Groups*, Jack Goody (ed.), pp. 120–45. Cambridge University Press, London.

—— (1957). The Epistemological Background to Malinowski's Empiricism. In: *Man and Culture: An Evaluation of the Work of Bronislaw Malinowski*, R. Firth (ed.), pp. 119–38. Routledge and Kegan Paul, London.

—— (1966). Virgin Birth. *Proceedings of the Royal Anthropological Institute*, 1966, 39–49.

Lévi-Strauss, Claude (1969) [1949]). *The Elementary Structures of Kinship*. Beacon Press, Boston.

Linnekin, Jocelyn (1990). *Sacred Queens and Women of Consequence: Rank, Gender, and Colonialism in the Hawaiian Islands*. University of Michigan Press, Ann Arbor.

—— (1991). Fine Mats and Money: Contending Exchange Paradigms in Colonial Samoa. *Anthropological Qxarterly*, 64 (1), 1–13.

Malinowski, Bronislaw (1922). *Argonauts of the Western Pacific*. Routledge and Kegan Paul, London.

—— (1954). *Magic, Science, and Religion and Other Essays*. Doubleday, New York.

—— (1927). *Sex and Repression in Savage Society*. Harcourt Brace and World, New York.

—— (1987 [1929]). *The Sexual Life of Savages*. Beacon Press, Boston.

Malo, David (1951). *Hawaiian Antiquities (Moolelo Hawaii)*, trans. Nathaniel Emerson. Bernice P. Bishop Museum, Honolulu.

Mauss, Marcel (1954 [1925]). *The Gift*, trans. Ian Cunnison. Free Press, Glencoe.

Mayer, Adrian (1988). Rulership and Divinity: The Case of the Modern Indian Prince and Beyond. Paper presented at the Conference on Divine Rule, New York University.

Mead, Margaret (1930). The Social Organization of Manu'a. *Bernice P. Bishop Museum Bulletin*, 76. Bishop Museum Press, Honolulu.

Milner, George Bertram (1966). *Samoan Dictionary*. Oxford University Press, London.

Oliver, Douglas L. (1989). *The Pacific Islands*, 3rd edn. University of Hawaii Press, Honolulu.

Parsons, Anne (1964). Is the Oedipus Complex Universal: The Jones–Malinowski Debate Revisited and a South Italian 'Nuclear

Complex'. *The Psychoanalytic Study of Society*, 3, pp. 278–328.

Pukui, Mary Kawena, and Elbert, Samuel H. (1965). *Hawaiian Dictionary*. University of Hawaii Press, Honolulu.

Ray, Benjamin C. (1991). *Myth, Ritual, and Kingship in Buganda*. Oxford University Press, Oxford.

Renne, Elishe (1990). Wives, Chiefs, and Weavers: Gender Relations in Bunu Yoruba Society. Ph.D. diss., New York University.

Rubenstein, Donald H. (1986). Fabric Arts and Traditions. In: *The Art of Micronesia*, ed. Jerome Feldman and Donald H. Rubenstein, pp. 45–69. University of Hawaii Press, Honolulu.

Sahlins, Marshall D. (1985). *Islands of History*. University of Chicago Press, Chicago.

Samwell, David (1967). *Journal*. See Beaglehole (1967).

Schneider, David (1961). Introduction: The Distinctive Features of Matrilineal Descent Groups. In: *Matrilineal Kinship*, ed. David Schneider and Kathleen Gough, pp. 1–29. University of California Press, Berkeley and Los Angeles.

—— (1976). The Meaning of Incest. *The Journal of the Polynesian Society*, 85, 149–69.

—— (1968b). Virgin Birth. (correspondence) *Man* (NS) 3, 126–9.

—— (1968a). What Is Kinship All About? In: *Kinship Studies in the Morgan Centennial Year*, ed. Priscilla Reining, pp. 32–63. Anthropological Society of Washington, Washington, D.C.

Schoeffel, Penelope (1981). Daughters of Sina, A Study of Gender, Status, and Power in Western Samoa. Ph.D. diss., Australian National University, Canberra.

—— (1987). Rank, Gender, and Politics in Ancient Samoa. *The Journal of Pacific History*, 23 (3–4), 175–93.

—— (1977). The Origin and Development of Women's Associations in Western Samoa, 1830–1977. *Journal of Pacific Studies*, 3, 1–21.

Shell, Marc (1988). *'Measure for Measure,' Incest, and the Ideal of Universal Siblinghood*. Stanford University Press, Stanford, CA.

Shore, Bradd (1989). Mana and Tapu. In: *Developments in Polynesian Ethnology*, ed. Alan Howard and Robert Borofsky, pp. 137–73. University of Hawaii Press, Honolulu.

—— (1982). *Sala'ilua: A Samoan Mystery*. Columbia University Press, New York.

—— (1981). Sexuality and Gender in Samoa: Conceptions and Missed Conceptions. In: *Sexual Meanings*, ed. Sherry B. Ortner and Harriet Whitehead, pp. 192–215. Cambridge University Press, Cambridge.

Silverblatt, Irene (1987). *Moon, Sun, and Witches: Gender Ideologies and Class in Inca and Colonial Peru*. Princeton University Press, Princeton, NJ.

Sinclair, Marjorie (1971). The Sacred Wife of Kamehameha I:

Keopuolani. *The Hawaiian Journal of History*, 5, 3–23.

Spiro, Melford E. (1982). *Oedipus in the Trobriands*. University of Chicago Press, Chicago.

—— (1968). Virgin Birth, Parthenogenesis, and Physiological Paternity: An Essay in Cultural Interpretation. *Man* (NS), 3, 242–61.

Thomas, Nicholas (1989). The Force of Ethnology: Origins and Significance of the Melanesia/Polynesia Division. *Current Anthropology*, 30, 27–41.

Turner, G. A., Revd (1884). *Samoa, A Hundred Years Ago and Long Before*. Macmillan, London.

Valeri, Valerio (1990). Constitutive History: Genealogy and Narrative in the Legitimation of Hawaiian Kingship. In: *Culture Through Time: Anthropological Approaches*, ed. Emiko Ohnuki-Tierney, pp. 154–92. Stanford University Press, Stanford.

—— (1985). *Kingship and Sacrifice: Ritual and Society in Ancient Hawaii*. University of Chicago Press, Chicago.

Weiner, Annette B. (1983). From Words to Objects to Magic: Hard Words and the Boundaries of Social Interaction. *Man*, 18, 690–709.

—— (1992) *Inalienable Possessions – The Paradox of Keeping-While-Giving*. University of California Press, Berkeley.

—— (1987). Introduction. In: *The Sexual Life of Savages in North-Western Melanesia*, by Bronislaw K. Malinowski [1929], xiii–xlix. Beacon Press, Boston.

—— (1985). Oedipus and Ancestors. *American Ethnologist*, 12, 758–62.

—— (1988). *The Trobrianders of Papua New Guinea*. Holt, Rinehart & Winston, New York.

—— (1979). Trobriand Kinship from Another View: The Reproductive Power of Women and Men. *Man* (NS), 14, 328–48.

—— (1989). Why Cloth? Wealth, Gender, and Power in Oceania. In: *Cloth and Human Experience*, ed. Annette B. Weiner and Jane Schneider, pp. 33–72. Smithsonian Institution Press, Washington, DC.

—— (1976). *Women of Value, Men of Renown: New Perspectives in Trobriand Exchange*. University of Texas Press, Austin.

Index